ASSESSMENT IN YOU

Kerry Baker, Gill Kelly and Bernadette

D1385896

LEEDS BECKETT UNIVERSITY
LIBRARY
DISCARDED

Leeds Metropolitan University

17 0561147 4

First published in Great Britain in 2011 by

The Policy Press
University of Bristol
Fourth Floor
Beacon House
Queen's Road
Bristol BS8 1QU
UK

Tel +44 (0)117 331 4054
Fax +44 (0)117 331 4093
e-mail tpp-info@bristol.ac.uk
www.policypress.co.uk

LEEDS METROPOLITAN
UNIVERSITY
LIBRARY
1705611474
RG-B
CC-125296
15.2.1?
364.360942 BAK

North American office:
The Policy Press
c/o International Specialized Books Services (ISBS)
920 NE 58th Avenue, Suite 300
Portland, OR 97213-3786, USA
Tel +1 503 287 3093
Fax +1 503 280 8832
e-mail info@isbs.com

© The Policy Press 2011

British Library Cataloguing in Publication Data
A catalogue record for this book is available from the British Library.

Library of Congress Cataloging-in-Publication Data
A catalog record for this book has been requested.

ISBN 978 1 84742 636 9 paperback
ISBN 978 1 84742 637 6 hardcover

The right of Kerry Baker, Gill Kelly and Bernadette Wilkinson to be identified as authors
of this work has been asserted by them in accordance with the 1988 Copyright, Designs
and Patents Act.

All rights reserved: no part of this publication may be reproduced, stored in a retrieval
system, or transmitted in any form or by any means, electronic, mechanical, photocopying,
recording, or otherwise without the prior permission of The Policy Press.

The statements and opinions contained within this publication are solely those of the
authors and not of The University of Bristol or The Policy Press. The University of Bristol
and The Policy Press disclaim responsibility for any injury to persons or property resulting
from any material published in this publication.

The Policy Press works to counter discrimination on grounds of
gender, race, disability, age and sexuality.

Cover design by Janna Broadfoot
Front cover: image kindly supplied by Tom Appshaw
Printed and bound in Great Britain by Hobbs, Southampton
The Policy Press use environmentally responsible print partners

FSC
www.fsc.org
MIX
Paper from
responsible sources
FSC® C020438

Contents

List of figures, tables and examples

Figures

Tables

Examples

Acknowledgements

The authors have been fortunate to work with many others in the field of youth justice and we are particularly grateful to the practitioners and managers who have helped to develop our understanding of practice and of young people. They are too many to name but we would like to specifically acknowledge the support, encouragement and inspiration that Colin Roberts and Professor Hazel Kemshall have generously provided. Thanks are also due to colleagues at the Youth Justice Board, including David Monk, Trisha Boyce and Bhavi Teli, for their interest and support.

In addition, we would like to thank the following friends and colleagues who read and commented on earlier drafts – their ideas have been invaluable in helping us bring the book to completion: Mike Goldman and staff from Neath Port Talbot Youth Offending Team, David Goode, Fiona Mackenzie, Alex Sutherland and Jeanette Williams.

Abbreviations

5WH	who, why, what, when, where, how
AIM	Assessment, Intervention and Moving On
BME	black and minority ethnic
CAF	Common Assessment Framework
CSP	Community Safety Partnership
EBPP	Evidence-Based Policy and Practice
GLM	Good Lives Model
HMIP	Her Majesty's Inspectorate of Probation
LSCB	Local Safeguarding Children Board
MAPPA	Multi-Agency Public Protection Arrangements
OASys	Offender Assessment System
OED	*Oxford English Dictionary*
PSR	pre-sentence report
RNR	Risk Need Responsivity
RoSH	risk of serious harm
SAVRY	Structured Assessment of Violence Risk in Youth
SIFA	Mental Health Screening Interview for Adolescents
SQIFA	Mental Health Screening Questionnaire Interview for Adolescents
YJAA	Youth Justice Agency Assessment
YJB	Youth Justice Board
YLS/CMI	Youth Level of Service/Case Management Inventory
YOT	Youth Offending Team
YRO	Youth Rehabilitation Order

Introduction

Assessment matters. It matters because of the impact it can have on the lives of young people who offend. It matters because of the consequences for victims and communities of the decisions that are made by youth justice practitioners. It matters for organisations that have a responsibility for reducing offending, promoting rehabilitation and protecting the public.

Assessment is important because it occurs at all stages of a young person's contact with youth justice services: it affects decisions about bail and remand, about sentencing, about interventions, about custodial placements, about release, resettlement and reintegration into the community. It is important because of the value placed on the issues being considered, namely the needs of young people who offend and the potential harm that their behaviour might cause to others. And it is important because of the serial nature of decision making (Hawkins, 1992); that is to say, the way each assessment influences subsequent decisions. Judgements formed at an initial assessment may be carried over into future assessments and continue to have an impact long after they were first made.

This book is written for people who care about practice. It aims to equip staff in youth justice services with the core knowledge and skills required to understand young people's offending behaviour, explain it, make well-founded judgements, plan appropriate interventions and communicate their knowledge and decisions to others clearly. Some readers will be training to work in youth justice or at the early stages of their careers. Others will be more experienced practitioners or managers with responsibility for supervising and developing assessment practice in their team or organisation. Some may be specialists in other fields who, in a context of increased inter-agency working, find themselves in contact with youth justice teams. Much of the material will also be relevant for those who teach or provide training for the youth justice workforce. In all cases, the authors start from the assumption that people reading this book want to improve assessment practice and want to see better outcomes for young people who offend.

About the book

The book focuses primarily on England and Wales, although references are included to practice in Scotland and Northern Ireland and many of the discussions will be equally relevant to a range of contexts. Much has been written about the reforms of youth justice in England and Wales (Goldson, 2000; Morgan and Newburn, 2007; Smith, 2007; Solomon and Garside, 2008) and these debates will not be repeated here, but it is clear that recent developments (especially since 1997) have significantly affected the way that practitioners go about doing assessment and intervention planning.

These changes include the creation of multi-disciplinary Youth Offending Teams (YOTs) which have brought together practitioners with a range of knowledge and expertise. In terms of the focus of assessments, there has been a greater emphasis on risk and public protection. The process of assessment has also been reshaped through the introduction of structured assessment tools (such as *Asset*) and the increasing reliance on IT case management systems for recording information.

Similar developments in relation to assessment with adult offenders have caused concern among some commentators. Writing in the context of probation practice, for example, Bhui noted an anxiety 'that we may be moving towards *trained* rather than properly *educated* practitioners; technicians, encouraged to do as they are told, rather than professionals who might think independently, question orthodoxy and produce creative and inspired work' (Bhui, 2001, p 638). The authors strongly believe, however, that this need not be the case and one of the aims of this book is to help enable practitioners to work in the professional way that Bhui describes.

Core practice principles

The book is underpinned by the following key principles:

- Practitioners need to understand young people's diverse journeys through childhood and adolescence *and* need to understand offending behaviour when making assessments and plans.
- Assessment and intervention planning are not 'tick box' or technical activities but require professional skill and expertise.
- Young people need to be able to participate fully in assessments and feel some sense of ownership of the plans and decisions that follow.
- Assessments need to be rigorous and undertaken in line with relevant policy requirements, but practitioners also need to be creative in using approaches that are appropriate and relevant for each individual young person.
- Responsibility for the quality of assessment and planning practice is shared between practitioners and organisations.

Inquisitiveness and critical reflection

A recurring theme throughout the book is the importance of *knowing* and *doing*. Being a skilled assessor requires theoretical and empirical knowledge, combined with experience and practical wisdom that can only come from doing the work. In a book of this size it is not possible to discuss every relevant issue in depth, but readers interested in knowing more about specific topics can follow up the references for further information. However, the book aims to do something more than just provide pointers to relevant material (useful though that can be); beyond that, it is intended to encourage inquisitiveness and curiosity. In that sense the authors hope that it will be a jumping-off point for exploring new ideas that will help to improve practice.

Part of this spirit of inquisitiveness involves digging beneath the surface of what we think we know. Assessment and planning may seem like very routine activities – particularly to practitioners who have worked in this or similar fields for a while – and yet there is real value to be gained from looking at the familiar in new ways. Our ways of looking at the world can be shaped by metaphors that we may not realise we are using (Armstrong, 2009). Lakoff and Johnson suggest that the 'essence of metaphor is understanding and experiencing one kind of thing in terms of another' (Lakoff and Johnson, 1980, p 5) and give some illustrations of this. For example, our talk about arguments is often shaped by the metaphor that sees 'argument as war', and this can be seen in the way we refer to 'attacking' and 'defending' positions. Or the metaphor 'time is money' is evident in the way people talk about spending time, although we may not consciously recognise that we are thinking in these terms. Similarly, approaches to working with young people or to assessment can be shaped by ideas that we may not always be aware of.

Metaphors affect our patterns of thinking because they 'create meaning, move minds, motivate people' (Coe, 1996, p 438) and, because of this, they can be relevant to understanding assessment practice (Baker and Wilkinson, 2011). Examples are dotted throughout the book; for example, Chapter One looks at some metaphors for the assessment process and Chapter Four considers some possible metaphors for assessment tools. Using these – and other ways of challenging our perspectives – helps to promote a fresh understanding of what happens now in practice (and why). This in turn can provide a useful guide for deciding what needs to be changed and how things can be improved.

This deliberate stepping back to view practice from new and different angles can help to translate knowledge into action, and exploring metaphor is just one example of the process of reflecting critically and innovatively on practice. The application of the principles outlined in the book will vary, depending on the context in which you work, and so the text is not overly specific about particular policies or procedures which may only apply to some readers. Rather, the aim is to outline core aspects of good practice that apply across all contexts and then allow readers to think through the implications for their own particular working environment.

In each chapter there are a number of reflective questions and activities. These are not essential for understanding the ideas presented, but are designed to help make the link between the discussions and real-life practice. They can be used either individually or in discussion with others. In some cases the reader would, realistically, need to be working in a youth justice context in order to find the questions meaningful, but there are other activities which have wider applicability. It is for readers to decide what is most relevant for them and how best to make use of the material presented.

Reflection

It might be useful to think about how you are likely to read this book and what will help you get the most out of it. Will you read the chapters in sequence or dip into relevant sections, for example?

Outline of the book

The core principles of assessment and planning practice apply across the range of services that youth justice practitioners are involved in, including prevention, pre-court, community and custodial settings. There are some chapters where the focus is more specifically on young people who have been convicted by the courts (such as Chapter Six, which deals with reports), but the majority of the book will be relevant to work with all young people involved in the youth justice system. In addition, where there are issues relating to specific sentences (such as Referral Orders) or particular settings (such as the secure estate) these are highlighted in the discussion, but overall the aim has been to present material in a way that applies to a range of cases (definitions and explanations of terminology are provided in the Glossary at the end of the book).

There are three sections to the book. Part One covers the theoretical basis for assessments in youth justice. Chapter One looks at the foundations for assessment and considers topics such as the processes involved, roles and relationships. Chapter Two focuses on the challenges involved in making judgements and decisions, while Chapter Three reviews the type and range of knowledge required for professional, well-grounded assessments.

Part Two looks at some of the specific practicalities of assessment and planning with young people who offend. Chapter Four considers the use of structured assessment tools and argues that if their capacities and limitations are properly understood, and they are used by practitioners with appropriate knowledge, they can be a useful aid to practice and should support (but not replace) professional skills. Chapter Five covers intervention planning and looks at how to balance the need to produce plans that may cover a range of interlinking factors contributing to a young person's behaviour while, at the same time, ensuring that a young person understands it, has been involved in setting the goals and feels a sense of commitment to the plan. Chapter Six deals with written reports and the challenge of communicating assessment conclusions to sentencers or other key decision makers, and argues that practitioners need to engage persuasively with the decision-making process. Chapter Seven reviews the issues involved in communicating and working with staff from other agencies, concluding that youth justice practitioners need to be both clear about their own expertise and open to ideas and contributions from others.

The focus of Part Three is on developing and improving practice. Chapter Eight investigates the skills practitioners need for assessment and planning, which range from being organised to managing power imbalances, from gathering information to engaging young people. Chapter Nine looks at how individuals and organisations can improve assessment practice, emphasising the value of using questions to identify areas for development and the importance of a learning culture.

Assessment is inevitably 'a human process' (Hawkins, 1992, p 1). Both the practitioner and young person are individuals whose behaviour, attitudes and perceptions will be influenced by numerous factors in a way that is complex and not entirely predictable. As such, assessment and planning should never be a dull process but an interesting, challenging professional activity. Writing books is a human process too. You may disagree with some of our conclusions, and that process of challenging and thinking issues through is itself important. Developing critical thinking skills is important for ensuring that judgements are as good as they can be, within the inevitable limitations presented by the complexities of practice in the real world. The aim of this book is to help equip those working in youth justice to deal with those complexities more effectively, because assessments – or, more importantly, the outcomes of assessments – matter.

Part One
Professional practice in assessment and intervention planning

ONE

Essential foundations of assessment practice

The assessment must be a dynamic interactive process ... within which opportunities for change are created. (Adcock, 2001, p 79)

Introduction

Assessment and planning are core activities that practitioners undertake in some form or other with every young person involved in the youth justice system. The focus and complexity of the process will vary, depending on the type of offences committed, the young person's circumstances or the stage in the criminal justice process at which decisions are being made, but there are common principles that apply in all cases.

A useful starting point is to think about the rationale for assessment and the different activities which it involves. Knowing the purpose – or often purposes – of assessment is important because 'this will influence the content, the emphasis given to various factors, the subsequent analysis of the information gathered and the action planned and taken' (Whyte, 2009, p 73). Assessors also need an understanding of the different stages involved in the process (from information gathering through to decision making) and a willingness to see it as a dynamic activity into which new information can be absorbed at any time.

The context in which assessments occur is constantly evolving. This includes, for example, changes in legislation or policy, changes in patterns of offending behaviour by young people, or changes to assessment tools and frameworks.[1] All of these can affect the scope and content of assessments and the knowledge required to undertake them. For practitioners in England and Wales, the decision to transfer the core functions of the Youth Justice Board into the Ministry of Justice is likely to lead to further policy changes in the future. The core principles of practice, however, will still apply, and the aim of this chapter is to set out the foundations for effective work, in any setting or context, with young people who offend.

The current assessment landscape

Assessment has long been seen as central to social work and criminal justice practice (Davies, 1985; Burnett et al, 2007). In youth justice in England and Wales, this emphasis on the importance of assessment is seen, for example, in the APIS (Assessment, Planning Interventions and Supervision) model promoted by the Youth Justice Board (YJB, 2008a). The need for good quality assessments has also been emphasised as essential for the successful introduction of the new Youth Rehabilitation Order (YRO), in which practitioners are expected to advise courts on which of a 'menu' of interventions would be appropriate for an individual young person (YJB, 2010a).

Youth justice services currently undertake assessment for a range of purposes (Whyte, 2009). These include (not listed in any order of priority):

- to determine suitability for particular sentences, interventions or services
- to ascertain the likelihood of a young person reoffending
- to consider whether a young person is likely to commit offences that would cause serious harm to others
- to identify needs and aspects of a young person's life where s/he requires assistance
- to ascertain whether the young person is likely to be harmed (either through her/his own behaviour or that of others).

This range of purposes reflects, in part, the fact that youth justice straddles the divide between children's services, which focus on 'welfare', and criminal justice services, which place greater emphasis on 'risk' and offending (Hill et al, 2007). This means that assessments in youth justice have to take account of both young people's needs and the potential for their behaviour to cause harm to others.

Assessments are often now made using structured assessment tools and, at the time of writing, all YOTs in England and Wales use the *Asset* framework (YJB, 2006).[2] There are also a number of other specialist tools used across youth justice services in the UK, such as AIM (Assessment, Intervention and Moving On) for young people who sexually abuse (Griffin and Beech, 2004), SQIFA and SIFA for young people with mental health problems (YJB, 2003) and SAVRY (Structured Assessment of Violence Risk in Youth) for young people committing offences of violence (Borum et al, 2003). Another significant change in recent years has been the expansion in the use of IT case management systems. For many practitioners, assessments and intervention plans are completed on-screen and information has to be recorded in ways that comply with IT structures and requirements (the implications of these developments for practice are explored further in later chapters).

Overall, the current picture is quite complex, with assessments being undertaken for a range of purposes by practitioners from different professional backgrounds and with diverse types of knowledge and expertise. The quality of assessments and plans appears to be very variable, with reports from inspections showing examples of good practice but also identifying areas (such as report writing) where significant improvements are still required (HMIP, 2010).

Thinking about assessment and planning

Before getting into the detail of the chapter, this section provides an opportunity for readers to reflect on their own views about assessment and planning.

Initial thoughts

The following questions can be applied to your own practice or to that of those you manage, supervise or teach.

1   What outcomes do you want to see achieved through the assessments and intervention plans undertaken with young people?
2   What do you think the following people would like to see achieved through assessments and plans in youth justice:
   a   Young people?
   b   Victims?
   c   Communities?

Within any team or organisation there will be different perceptions of the assessment process. Some people will regard it as central to practice, while others may see it as taking away from valuable time that could be spent with a young person. Some will see it as a task that can be done instinctively, while others may think of it as something which requires careful planning and preparation. An individual's views may also change in different situations: for example, regarding assessment as being very important at the start of contact with a young person but then giving it less attention as an order progresses. Or seeing it as being more important for some types of cases (or certain offences) than others. In considering these different aspects of practice, it is important for practitioners to identify not just what they think about assessment and planning but also *why* they think that. What have been the factors and influences that have shaped perceptions?

Defining assessment in youth justice

Definitions of assessment can be found in practice literature across health, social care and criminal justice settings. For example, Parker and Bradley suggest that 'the purpose of assessment in social work is to acquire and study information about people in their environment to decide upon an identified problem and to plan effective options to resolve that problem' (Parker and Bradley, 2007, p 17). This highlights three key components of assessment practice that can equally well be applied to youth justice: the acquisition and analysis of information; the need to take account of context and environment; and planning action to address the problems identified.

Moving on to consider definitions more specifically focused on offending, assessment in adult criminal justice services has been described as '[t]he process of determining or estimating the risks posed by an offender as the basis for providing advice to courts or others. Assessment also seeks to identify the causes of offending, and whether anything can be done to reduce the likelihood of repetition. It is the starting point for working out sentence plans' (Hancock, 2007, p 16). Although this helpfully makes clear the integral link between assessment and planning, the authors take the view that this definition would be problematic if applied to young people because it overemphasises the prediction (or estimation) of risk, while other important aspects of assessment, such as *understanding* the complex interaction of factors that lie behind an individual's offending behaviour, take second place.

In the youth justice context, there is thus a need for a definition that both draws on the insights from other fields of practice but also reflects the particular focus of work with young people who offend. This should take account of both adolescent development and wider social contexts when trying to understand offending behaviour. It should also recognise that the actions taken as a result of assessment should have benefit for both young people and society, since 'the objective of meeting the best interests of the young person and the community, in most instances, should not be incompatible' (Whyte, 2009, p 71).

The definition used throughout this book is as follows:

> Assessment is a dynamic, multi-faceted process of information gathering and analysis that leads to in-depth understanding of a young person's offending behaviour. It provides the basis for the planning of interventions in order to:
>
> - help a young person avoid reoffending
> - assist a young person to achieve their potential
> - help to protect victims and communities.

In a busy working environment, there is a danger of forgetting about the overall aims of assessment and seeing it instead as just a procedure, a task that has to be done because a court report is required or because a young person has arrived in custody. Having a clear definition such as this in mind is therefore useful because it provides a reminder of why the work is being done and can help to ensure that assessment and planning activity remains focused on improving outcomes for young people and communities.

Dynamic, multi-faceted assessment practice

By delving into the definition in more detail, we can now look at the different aspects of this complex process.

Essential stages

One helpful way of exploring the process of assessment and planning is to divide it into five steps or stages (Milner and O'Byrne, 2009; Whyte, 2009):

1. Preparation
2. Gathering and recording information
3. Developing understanding
4. Making judgements
5. Making decisions.

In practice, these different stages will overlap and interlink, but it is helpful to first look at them separately to see the key features of each one. More detail will be provided in later chapters, but here the aim is to understand the essentials of these core activities that apply to any type of assessment, at any stage of the system (prevention, bail, pre-court, community sentence, custody, parole/release) and with any (or no) assessment tool.

Preparation

It may seem obvious, but the need to prepare before starting to collect and analyse information is an aspect of assessment and planning that can easily be overlooked. Preparation requires thinking, firstly, about the purpose of the assessment. Secondly, in order to achieve this purpose, what information is required? For example, is there any information which is essential and without which the assessment cannot be done? What information is available from previous assessments and how relevant is it now? Who or what are the key sources of information?

In addition to identifying information needs, McNeill argues that practitioners should also try to 'anticipate the types of aspirations and concerns that the offender may bring to the supervision process' (McNeill, 2009a, p 31). A young person in contact with the youth justice system for the first time may have very different hopes, fears, knowledge of and expectations about the assessment process than a young person with a history of prolific offending. Thinking about the young person's perspective will be an important part of the preparation needed *before* meeting with them and can help to lay the groundwork for a relationship through which personal, and sometimes difficult, issues can be discussed. Chapter Eight looks in more detail at the practicalities of preparing for assessments.

Gathering and recording information

A thorough assessment requires a range of sources and types of information. With regard to *sources of information* it is important to seek out alternative points of view or information. This means not just accepting the young person's account, or perhaps the views of a colleague who has previously supervised the young person, but deliberately looking out for different opinions. Where possible, it should involve seeing a young person in a range of contexts, for example, doing a home visit as well as an office-based interview in order to gain a better appreciation of their living environment or family dynamics. An assessment will also draw on a variety of *types of information*, for example, facts, observations and opinions. It is important to understand the differences between them in order to decide how much weight to attach to a particular piece of information (Chapters Six and Seven look at the implications of this for report writing and working with others).

Assessments will also need to use varied *approaches to information gathering*, for example, different types of questions, visual/diagrammatic tools or self-assessments for young people (and parents/carers). It will be a matter for professional judgement to select approaches which are appropriate for each young person, given their age, maturity, ability and experience of the youth justice system (see the discussion in Chapter Eight).

Recording information clearly provides a means for the assessor to look back on the information gathered but also helps colleagues and young people to see the basis for any decisions. Records need to be clear about where information has come from, and this can help to reveal biases in practice, for example, a greater reliance on certain types or sources of information than on others. Chapter Four looks more specifically at how assessment tools can be used to help with this process of information recording.

Developing understanding

Having gathered a range of information, the next stage is to develop an understanding of a young person's behaviour and situation. This could be expressed in terms of finding meaning, making sense of events (Davies, 1985) and being able to explain why behaviours or situations have occurred. A summary of steps to achieving understanding would include:

- identifying and describing key factors
- considering the meaning of these factors, given the young person's specific situation
- weighing the significance of the different factors affecting a young person's behaviour
- combining these different elements together into a coherent whole that tells a meaningful story (Baker and Kelly, 2011).

Chapter Two looks at analysis and decision making in more detail, but the key point for this chapter is that assessors should aim for depth of understanding. This does not mean knowing everything about a situation or a person, rather, 'depth' means 'reaching helpful explanations or analyses of what is happening and how things could be improved – being more rigorous and systematic' (Milner and O'Byrne, 2009, p 59).

Making judgements

Assessments typically involve two main types of judgement. Firstly, judgements about *what has happened*. What harm was caused? How serious was it? What have been the implications for the victim(s), the young person, his/her family, the community?

Secondly, there will be judgements about *what might happen*. These relate to:

1. *Future offending.* What might the young person do? When and in what circumstances? How likely is this? What harm might be caused? What impact would this have?
2. *The young person's own well-being.* What harm might s/he experience? When and in what circumstances? How serious would this be?
3. *Positive change.* What opportunities or turning points are likely to occur? How will the young person respond to these? What might be the benefits?

Making decisions

The explanations and judgements then have to lead to decisions, because 'judgements about issues are not intended to be an end in themselves, but to inform strategies for managing and reducing risk' (Hollows, 2008, p 57). Assessments can lead to different types of decisions, for example:

- a trigger for additional assessment or referral to specialist services
- a decision about whether a young person meets the eligibility criteria for particular interventions or programmes
- a classification (for example, low, medium, high)
- a recommendation to a court or panel about the types of interventions that could help a young person to avoid involvement in offending behaviour.

Scores and predictions produced by assessment tools will often be factors that influence decisions, but these will need to be applied and interpreted in the context of all the information that you have about a young person. Professional judgement will always be needed when turning judgements into decisions (see Chapters Two and Four for further discussion of these points). Communicating the recommendations and outcomes of assessments is an aspect of practice that can often be overlooked (Carson and Bain, 2008) but is critically important (Part Two will look at this in more detail).

Reflection

Think about each of the five stages. In your experience, which do you or others you work with:

- prefer/spend most time on?
- find more difficult?
- ignore or try to skip over?

A flexible and dynamic approach

The amount of time spent on each stage may vary, depending on factors such as:

- the purpose of the assessment
- the complexity of the case
- the amount of time available.

Some of this will be determined by procedures (for example, there will be less time available and less information required for an assessment of bail suitability than for an assessment leading to a court or parole report). In other cases, the amount of time spent on each stage needs to be determined by the assessor. For example, two cases might seem similar on the surface, but it may become apparent that for one of the young people there are additional complexities which mean that more time should be spent on information gathering. The core steps remain the same – the need to prepare, collect, analyse and make decisions applies in all cases – but professional judgement needs to be used to see the stages as being flexible and to adapt them as appropriate in each case.

Using the stages flexibly is important but, even if this is done, there is still a potential danger of getting stuck with a linear perspective. An example of this would be if information gathering and analysis were seen as being totally separate stages. To avoid this it is necessary to ensure that ongoing review is built into the model. For example, while you are developing an explanation to include in a court report you see some gaps in the information, so you go about doing some more data collection. This process could happen several times for that piece of work. Similarly, it is not always possible to say that analysis only occurs at particular stages: 'when a practitioner is gathering information, reviewing what they know and making a decision, it is difficult for them to identify what part of the process constitutes "analysis" because it can be argued that "analysis occurs throughout the whole assessment process"' (Dalzell and Sawyer, 2007, p 4). The different stages should therefore be seen as overlapping rather than as a one-directional process.

The idea of assessment being a 'cyclical process' (Hancock, 2007, p 16) also applies to the need for ongoing assessment and planning throughout an intervention or order. During the course of a young person's contact with youth justice services there will be a continual need to review and update assessments and plans, which may require new information gathering and analysis. This is why assessment and planning must be seen as dynamic processes, constantly developing and adapting as new information comes to light or previously known information becomes better understood.

Reflection

- What helps assessors keep their assessments up to date?
- What gets in the way?
- How might these difficulties be overcome?

Focus and content of assessments

As the definition makes clear, the different stages of the assessment should lead to an understanding of a young person's behaviour in context which can then form the basis for plans and interventions. This brings us on to the question of what should be considered during an assessment. There are many aspects of this which cannot all be covered here, so the discussion will focus on two key topics in current debates, namely the role of risk and protective factors in assessments and, secondly, the increasing interest in the concept of promoting 'good lives'.

Risk and protective factors

The risk-factor prevention paradigm has sought to identify key factors that impact on the likelihood of a young person committing offences. These risk factors are defined as 'prior factors that increase the risk of occurrence of events such as the onset, frequency, persistence or duration of offending' (Farrington, 2002, p 664). Evidence suggests that an accumulation of risk factors in a young person's life is associated with a higher likelihood of involvement in offending behaviour (Farrington, 2007). Protective factors, on the other hand, are described as factors which reduce, prevent or mediate risks for the onset and persistence of offending behaviour (Lösel and Bender, 2007).

This approach has been influential in youth justice, although it has also been criticised on a number of grounds (O'Mahony, 2009). One objection has been that identifying clusters of risk and protective factors in a young person's life does not equate to providing an explanation of his/her behaviour (Wikström and Treiber, 2008). Other commentators have emphasised the need to take more account of young people's views about what they define as risk or protective factors in their lives (Case, 2007; Ward and Bayley, 2007) and the need to understand the contextual and structural issues which affect the decisions made by young people (Boeck et al, 2006; Kemshall et al, 2006).

Young people will react differently to similar factors (for example, young people living in the same neighbourhood can respond differently to their surroundings) and this illustrates that '[a] risk factor may increase the probability of offending, but does not make offending a certainty' (Shader, 2003, p 2). It is important therefore for assessors not just to identify relevant risk or protective factors but also to consider what significance they have in the life of a particular young person (YJB, 2008a), and subsequent chapters provide examples of how to do this in practice (for example, Chapter Four looks at ways of individualising assessments undertaken using structured tools).

RNR and 'good lives'

The impact of the Risk Need Responsivity (RNR) model on criminal justice services in the UK is one example of the way in which risk has become a central feature of practice. The model is based on three key principles (Andrews et al, 1990; Borum, 2003).

- More intensive interventions are required for those with a higher likelihood of reoffending, while those at lower risk of recidivism should receive less intensive interventions.
- Interventions should be focused on factors closely associated with offending which, if changed, can reduce the likelihood of reoffending.
- The delivery and style of interventions need to take account of factors which affect a young person's ability to respond, for example, age, motivation, maturity, communication skills and learning styles.

Some of the criticisms of RNR are that: it places too much emphasis on risk as located within individuals and fails to take sufficient account of wider social contexts/circumstances; it does not give enough emphasis to motivation and an offender's sense of self-identity; not enough attention has been given to identifying relevant responsivity factors (Ward and Maruna, 2007). It is also suggested that, while addressing factors most closely associated with offending will of course be important, it might also be the case that dealing with other factors first is sometimes required: 'offenders need to be receptive and attentive to interventions and may not be so if basic needs are not being effectively addressed' (McNeill, 2009b, p 84).

The Good Lives Model (GLM) provides an alternative perspective. This approach assumes that people inevitably seek certain goals or primary human goods such as knowledge, autonomy, friendship or happiness. Secondary goods, such as work or relationships, provide different ways of obtaining these primary goods. The GLM suggests that, in addition to managing or reducing risk, interventions should aim to help an individual to find ways of securing primary human goods without causing harm to others (Ward and Brown, 2004; Ward and Maruna, 2007). What might be the implications of this for assessment practice? McNeill (2009a) suggests that as well as addressing risk, needs and responsivity, practitioners should explore factors such as whether there is restricted scope for acquiring some primary goods, whether some goods are being pursued through inappropriate means and whether the person has the capacity or capabilities to achieve their goals. Chapter Five explores the relevance of the GLM for planning interventions in more detail.

As the GLM is a relatively recent model there are still many questions to consider, such as how well it applies to young people who may not have a clear idea of their goals. Further research also needs to be undertaken to ascertain its impact in practice. Nevertheless, it is useful in highlighting the need to take account of factors other than risk and can provide a positive, forward-looking framework for practice. The principles underpinning the model suggest, for example, that practitioners should aim to 'balance the promotion of personal goods (for the offender) with the reduction of risk (for society). Too strong a focus on personal goods may produce a happy but dangerous offender; but equally too strong a focus on risk may produce a dangerously defiant or disengaged offender' (McNeill, 2009b, p 85).

Working with risk in practice

These debates will continue and the models will be further refined; but how do we apply all this to current practice? In the current political and social climate, risk is likely to continue to be a feature of youth justice practice, and hence of assessments. What matters therefore is how it is conceptualised and understood in practice. This brief overview of the risk factor paradigm and RNR has highlighted some important practical applications.

Firstly, assessments need to ensure that risk and protective factors are always considered in the light of each young person's personal situation and social context. This means working out how all the different factors interact and how together they contribute to offending behaviour – or indeed how, in some cases, they can help a young person to avoid offending. Secondly, dealing with risk is important but may not, on its own, be sufficient. Other factors – such as a young person's goals or priorities – need to be taken into account, not least because they will shape his/her motivation to avoid further offending.

This is relevant for planning interventions (see Chapter Five) because 'there are other factors, aside from risk level, that impact a program's effectiveness' (Lowenkamp and Latessa, 2004, p 248). There will be differences between young people assessed as having similar risk levels which mean they may require varied interventions. An example of this can be seen in the evaluation of the Intensive Supervision and Surveillance Programme, where there were clear differences among the group assessed as 'medium risk', which suggested the need for tailored interventions (Moore et al, 2004). In any system of classification, including the Scaled Approach (YJB, 2010b), there will be differences between young people within the same category. Practitioners need to be alert to this and ensure that individual differences are not lost in the delivery of interventions based on risk levels.

Roles and relationships

The quality of the relationship between practitioner and offender is once again being acknowledged as having a significant impact on outcomes, with both adults and young people (Burnett and McNeill, 2005). Having good knowledge of factors contributing to offending will not necessarily lead to effective assessments if inadequate attention has been given to the relationship. Smale and Tuson (1993) provide a helpful summary of several approaches to assessment which illustrate different assumptions about roles, relationships and expertise. These are described here not as definitive examples, but because they can help to reveal assumptions and values about the respective roles of the assessor and young person. They also begin to explore the way in which power is exercised by practitioners during assessments (see also Chapter Eight).

The first of these approaches is termed the 'questioning model' and is based on the assumption that the professional making the assessment is an expert at identifying need. The worker asks questions which will inevitably include 'implicit or explicit criteria or perceptions of the problems that people ... have, and a view of the resources available to meet them' (Smale and Tuson, 1993, p 8). Professional knowledge and expertise are used to interpret the information provided and to produce a 'solution' that is then presented to the client. By contrast, the 'exchange model' is built around the principle that 'all people are expert in their own problems and there is no reason to assume that the worker will or should ever know more about people and their problems than they do themselves' (Smale and Tuson, 1993, p 16). This model emphasises the mutual exchange of information and a process of negotiation through which the worker and the service user agree on the action to be taken. It tries to eliminate the power imbalance implicit in the 'questioning model'. The third approach described by Smale and Tuson is the 'procedural model', which is similar to the questioning model but in which managers or organisations determine the questions that workers should use.

There are strengths and weaknesses in each approach. For example, applying the exchange model to youth justice would imply that expertise is shared between the worker and young person such that 'assessment becomes a process of dialogue rather than fact finding' (Parker and Bradley, 2007, p 6). The advantages of this can be that the lessening of power imbalances and a collaborative approach help to ensure that the young person's views are heard, but the disadvantage could be the potential for collusion and an inability to challenge, for fear of disrupting the relationship. The questioning model assumes that the worker has the expertise required to identify and resolve problems and this type of approach lends itself to a more forensic approach to gathering information about offending behaviour. The danger here, however, might be that useful perspectives and contributions from young people or parents/carers are overlooked.

A pure 'exchange' approach is unlikely to occur where young people are subject to statutory procedures, but this does not imply that a technocratic application of the 'questioning model' is the only option. There will usually be elements of a questioning approach when working with young people involved in offending or anti-social behaviour; but this need not be viewed negatively, as the approach can be used in a way that both produces the desired result of a thorough assessment and encourages participation. Writing in the context of probation practice, for example, Chapman and Hough begin by emphasising the importance of assessing risk in order to meet the needs of public protection but then go on to advocate 'an inclusive approach which respects difference, avoids labels, encourages the active participation of the individual in all processes, is based upon the belief in the capacity of the individual to make changes in behaviour and offers equal and appropriate access to services and programmes' (Chapman and Hough, 1998, p 26).

Typically, approaches to assessment in youth justice are likely to include elements of each model, with some procedures being more towards the 'exchange' end of the continuum and others closer to the 'questioning' end. The choice of approach will depend partly on organisational priorities and policies but also on the type of assessment being undertaken. In cases where time is very limited (perhaps a bail assessment), or where the focus is primarily on obtaining factual information about accommodation or ETE (education, training and employment) status, then one might expect to see more of the questioning/procedural approach. For assessments that are ongoing over a period of time or which involve exploring complex personal issues with a young person, the exchange approach might be more in evidence. There is no single right or wrong approach but it is important to be aware of the assumptions behind these different ways of working and the impact these can have on how practitioners go about core assessment tasks. In particular they will have an effect on how information is *obtained* and how it is *interpreted*. These skills are explored further in Chapter Eight.

Reflection

Think about typical assessment interviews in your working context.

- What is the balance between questioning, engagement and procedural approaches?
- What causes the balance to shift? (For example, the professional background of the interviewer or the amount of time available for assessments.)
- How does the balance affect the questions asked and the weight given to the young person's views?

Thinking again about assessment and planning

The chapter began by asking you to reflect on your views about assessment and planning and this section asks you to continue that reflection in order to think again about ways of developing practice. Although there are stages to be completed (as above) this does not mean that assessment should be seen in narrow, process-driven terms, because there is still scope to be creative about the way in which it is conceptualised and carried out. The Introduction began to explore the value of metaphor as a way of helping to understand practice and this can be a useful way of getting some fresh perspectives on familiar tasks. Consider, for example, the following possible ways of thinking about assessment.

Assessment as research

Thinking about assessment as doing research may prompt these considerations:

- The research question: what are we trying to find out?
- The research hypotheses: what possible explanations are there?
- Testing hypotheses: what information would make us change these explanations?

The parallels between practice and research have been explored by Sheppard et al (2001), who suggest that adopting such a perspective could lead to greater rigour and depth in assessments.

Assessment as biography

Thinking about assessment as a process of finding out about a young person so as to write a biography might make us consider:

- the questions we want to ask in order to elicit the most interesting and illuminating information about a person
- the need to take account of chronology, context and personal characteristics
- the tension between getting close enough to a person to understand them yet also needing distance in order to maintain some objectivity.

An effective biography enables you to understand a person's individual strengths and weaknesses while also seeing how they were influenced by the place and situation in which they lived (Baker and Kelly, 2011) – a goal which also applies to assessment.

Assessment as a journey

A metaphor of assessment that understands it as a process of travelling to a destination raises questions about:

- where we are trying to get to
- what our plan is for getting there
- adapting to changing circumstances, coping with unexpected twists, turns and diversions before reaching the destination.

Thinking about travelling raises questions not only about how to respond to new information (the 'diversion') but also about power and control. Who is navigating or driving? If there are different routes to reach the same destination, who chooses?

Assessment as construction

If we use a metaphor of assessment as a process of building and construction we may think in terms of:

- having good foundations
- the importance of rigour, formal procedures and safety
- the application of creativity and design.

Just as a building will be designed for a specific purpose, so assessments should have clear goals. They should be based on the foundations of theory and knowledge, be undertaken with skill and attention to detail, and also adapted to suit individual and local circumstances.

Any one metaphor or way of understanding will be limited because it highlights particular aspects of practice and conceals others (Lakoff and Johnson, 1980). If we only thought in terms of building or construction there would be a danger of becoming too static and missing out on the more dynamic aspects of assessment and planning – whereas the idea of a journey would take more account of such changing circumstances but might not give as much emphasis to searching for alternative explanations as the 'assessment as research' angle would do. A range of perspectives will therefore be needed to capture the complexity of practice.

The value of these ideas lies in making us think again about things with which we thought we were familiar (Baker and Wilkinson, 2011). One of the challenges for practitioners and managers, therefore, is to be aware of your own conceptualisations of assessment and how they may fit with or contradict those of colleagues. When thinking about which approaches to adopt and promote, the aim should be to choose ones which help in achieving the kind of practice set out in the definition of assessment given earlier, that is, perspectives which encourage the search for understanding, explanation and informed action.

Processes *and* products

So far, the focus of the chapter has been on the process of assessment – the stages and the dynamics of the relationship, for example – but the term 'assessment' is also used to refer to 'products' (such as a completed *Asset*, an intervention plan or risk management plan). This can sometimes lead to confusion and it can be easy to slip into the mistake of seeing these products as being 'the assessment'. To avoid this error we need to be careful about how we talk about practice, for example 'doing an *Asset*' should not be shorthand for 'doing an assessment'. Focusing too narrowly on products can create a situation in which assessment is seen as a tick-box activity centred on form filling. It may also hinder the process of engaging with a young person and prevent them from feeling that they can contribute to the assessment. On the other hand, products are important because they provide records of the assessment and of the reasons for the judgements made. Without them, much of the assessment would remain invisible, hidden in a practitioner's mind. Processes and products are equally necessary therefore: 'a "good" assessment is both a good quality process and a good quality product' (DCSF, 2009, p 23).

Figure 1.1 shows the key elements of both process and product for a critical aspect of assessment with young people who offend, namely offence analysis. The diagram is based on the 'bubble' model that will be familiar to some readers from assessment training (YJB, 2004; see also Chapter Five). It has been adapted here to show the difference between the process and the product and to illustrate how all the different aspects of the process contribute to producing a full analysis which describes what happened and why; outlines the impact of the offence(s); distinguishes between fact and conjecture; and shows the reasoning behind decisions.

Further examples of products and the processes which underpin them are given in later chapters (particularly Part Two, which looks at products such as reports and plans). In each case, the processes need to be right if the products are also to be of value.

Figure 1.1: Offence analysis – process and product

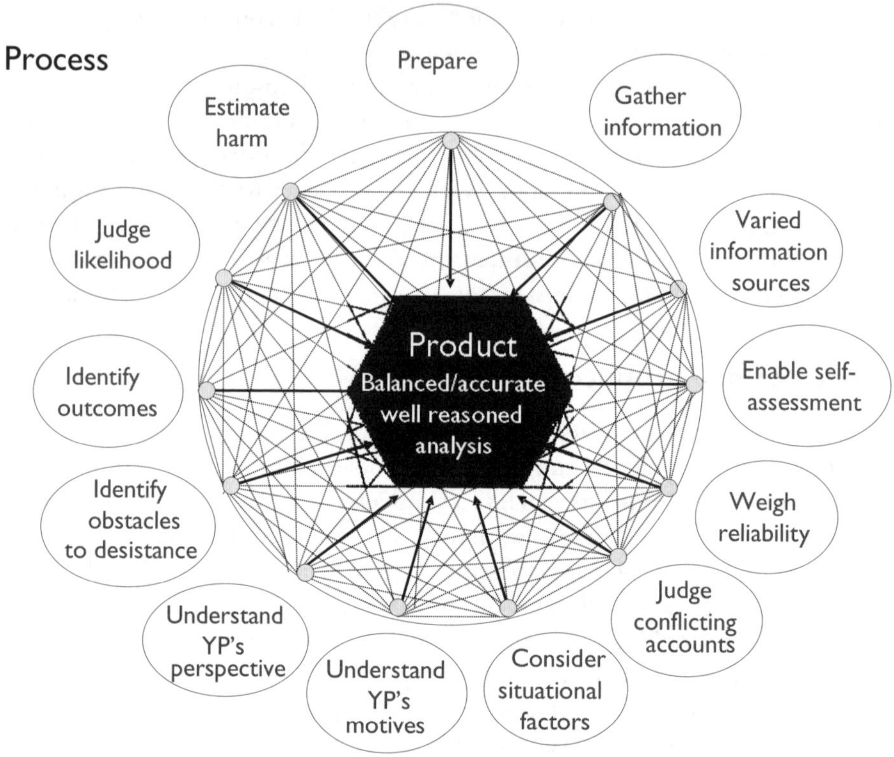

Effective assessment and planning

How would you know if you have achieved the outcomes you identified as being important in the 'initial thoughts' activity at the start of the chapter? Evaluating the quality and impact of assessments requires taking account of a range of information and evidence.

Returning to the definition of assessment given earlier, we can see that an effective assessment would be one where the process leads to an 'understanding in context' of a young person's behaviour and where there are then plans, reports, recommendations and actions which can be linked to achieving the goals of reducing offending and promoting community safety. It will not always be possible to satisfy all parties with the decisions made; for example, where the victim and young person have very different attitudes towards reparation, or where a young person resents the controls that have been put in place to reduce the risk they may present to others. Effectiveness does not necessarily mean that everyone will be pleased with all of the consequences, but rather, that the decisions taken are clearly linked to the desired outcomes and the reasons for action are clearly recorded. Table 1.1 summarises some examples of what to look for.

Table 1.1: Examples of effectiveness

Aspects of assessment	Examples/signs of effectiveness
Processes	Clear purpose, wide range of information collected, appropriate relationship and use of power, information analysed in a way that takes account of a young person's behaviour in context.
Products	Clear and full recording of information, appropriate language, fit for purpose.
Actions taken	Based on clearly reasoned decisions, relevant to achieving specified outcomes, rooted in evidence.

The next question is to think about what information could be used to help judge effectiveness. This could include a varied range of information, such as:

- the views expressed by young people about their understanding of, and ability to participate in, the process
- the amount and balance of time spent on the various stages
- feedback from courts, children's panels or youth offender panels about reports
- quality assurance (QA) tools
- feedback from the secure estate or other agencies about how well they are able to use the assessments they receive.

The activity below provides a basic framework that can be used when evaluating assessments. Future chapters will build on this by providing more detail of what good quality practice looks like. This additional knowledge can then be built into the basic framework provided here and used as a basis for identifying areas for improvement.

Activity

Use the table below to review assessments that you have been involved in. This could be:

- the most recent one
- an assessment you were particularly pleased with
- one that you were dissatisfied with
- any combination of these.

	Strengths and weaknesses	Information used to evaluate
Processes		
Products		
Actions taken		

Conclusion

This chapter has explored some of the foundational aspects of assessment and intervention planning. It has deliberately been quite general and wide ranging in order to avoid being preoccupied with particular tools or procedures. Instead, the aim has been to show that these specific processes (such as *Asset*) or preoccupations (such as risk) need to be located within a broader understanding of the nature of the assessment process. Chapters Two and Three add to this foundation by exploring the process of decision making and the knowledge base required for assessments, while Parts Two and Three will add much more of the detail of practice.

Notes

[1] At the time of writing, the YJB is reviewing the framework for assessment and intervention planning, which could lead to significant revisions in the processes and tools for youth justice assessment in England and Wales (see www.yjb.gov.uk/en–gb/practitioners/Assessment/Assessmentandinterventionstrategy/).

[2] In Scotland, some youth justice services use the Youth Level of Service/Case Management Inventory (Hoge and Andrews, 2002), while others use a Scottish version of *Asset*. In Northern Ireland, the Youth Justice Agency Assessment tool is an adaptation of *Asset*.

TWO

Judgements and decision making

It is what is done with information, rather than its simple accumulation, that leads to more analytic assessments and safer practice. (Brandon et al, 2008a, p 3)

Introduction

Assessment requires the practitioner to exercise a series of judgements about what information to seek and about its meaning and significance; those judgements will influence decision making. In youth justice, judgements are made about the risks posed by young people and these judgements inform decisions about proposals to courts and others. Those proposals and subsequent case management decisions should address the level and content of interventions required, and be aimed at reducing perceived risks, so as to prevent negative outcomes occurring. The tough political rhetoric about crime in recent years has created an atmosphere in which risk has increasingly become an 'organising principle' across many services (Kemshall et al, 1997, p 213). It is important, however, to remember that other judgements are being made, for example about the level of need or about a young person's motivation, which should also inform decisions about the content of interventions and, crucially, how they are delivered.

Judgements, decision making and taking action

Goldstein and Hogarth differentiate between judgements and decision making. They describe judgements as 'the ways in which people integrate multiple, probabilistic, potentially conflicting cues to arrive at an understanding of the situation', whereas decision making can be viewed as the way in which 'people choose what to do next in the face of uncertain consequences and conflicting goals' (Goldstein and Hogarth, 1997, p 4). The place of judgements and decisions and the links between them were also raised in Chapter One. Judgements should inform decisions, which then lead to actions intended both to reduce the likelihood of reoffending and to bring about positive changes in young people's lives.

Decisions have to be put into practice. Munro (2008a) suggests that people are often reluctant to make decisions and take action, are anxious about the burden of responsibility and use procrastination – the avoidance of action – to manage that anxiety. Practitioners may continue assessing, rather than reach a conclusion, or may make routine responses, containing anxiety by minimising the thought given to an individual case. In youth justice practice there is a tendency to concentrate on the initial assessment and making decisions about the levels of risk young people pose, but not as much focus on decisions about what is actually going to be done to deliver interventions. The Audit Commission, for example, suggests that 'some YOTs appear to provide a standard programme for all those on their caseload, rather than tailoring interventions to particular needs' (2004, p 75). Even less attention is paid to reviewing and re-evaluating the decisions that are made (YJB, 2009a).

The context for decision making

Currently youth justice practice in England and Wales is guided by the Scaled Approach (YJB, 2010b) which requires judgements about:

- the likelihood of further offences happening and
- the outcome, should further offences occur, specifically the impact or degree of harm to others that may result.

These judgements, which need to include a consideration of both persistence and whether offending is escalating in frequency and seriousness, are used as the basis for allocating young people to differential levels of intervention. Risk, assessed using the standard tool (*Asset*), has become the basis for significant decisions about the services young people receive, reflecting the wider social climate in which there is increasing concern about the identification and control of risk (Kemshall, 2009).

As risk has increasingly been seen both as synonymous with an often serious negative outcome and as amenable to calculation, the expectation that it can be controlled has grown. Risk decision making is never just a technical activity, however, but is a value-laden process characterised by uncertainty and anxiety (Kemshall, 2003). In reality, determining, for example, who, in a group of young people under supervision, is the one who will go on to commit a serious further offence is not possible to achieve with anything like complete accuracy. But for practitioners, the combined impact of legislation, policy developments, inspections and serious further offence reviews (which are often critical of practice) may be that they feel under pressure to predict, and thereby control, risk. They can be fearful of blame if the outcomes of their decisions are negative, in particular if a young person under supervision commits a serious further offence, or if they are seriously harmed or die, for example in custody (Keith, 2006). Even where there are prescribed tools and structures, practitioners retain considerable discretion in practice and their exercise of that discretion can be influenced by cultures of blame (Baker, 2005; Kemshall, 2010). The complexity of young people's lives means that no policy or framework can ever account for every situation (Eadie and Canton, 2002; Robinson, 2003a).

Although decision-making practice has been heavily influenced by the dominance of risk, it is also important to pay attention to other judgements and decisions that help to guide assessment and planning. The belief in rehabilitation persists in youth justice services (Burnett and Appleton, 2004; Field, 2007), and strengths–based approaches, which place a focus on helping young people make positive changes instead of predominantly being concerned with the removal of risk factors, are gaining prominence (Burnett and Maruna, 2006; McNeill, 2006). There is increasing emphasis on the need to develop approaches which actively engage parents and young people (France et al, 2010) and on children's rights (Whitty, 2009), alongside a growing awareness that positive risk taking is also necessary in order to enable change to occur (Jones and Baker, 2009; Titterton, 2011). One example of a positive risk is given in Chapter Five, which describes a contract designed to help a young person who had sexually offended to attend college safely. Practitioners therefore need to be able to make judgements and decisions operating within policy frameworks, while taking account of a range of perspectives and applying professional discretion wisely (Tuddenham, 2000).

Reflection

In your experience are decisions more influenced by:

■　concerns about minimising risk
■　concerns about helping to develop the strengths of a young person?

Decisions are recorded in assessments, plans and reports, as well as in the notes from meetings, for example. How easy is it in your experience to find recorded decisions about:

■　developing strengths in young people
■　positive risk taking?

Defensible decision making

Practitioners in youth justice are faced with making difficult judgements and decisions in a range of situations, for example, in relation to pre-court interventions, bail, proposals for court reports and breach proceedings. In recognition of the impossibility of always being right, and in the face of concern about a 'blame culture', consideration has been given to the idea of defensible decision making (Carson, 1996; Tuddenham, 2000). Defensible decisions are judged not on the basis of uncertain outcomes, but on the quality of the processes that underpinned the decision at the time it was made and the appropriateness of subsequent actions. Taking the necessary steps to 'get it right' is the focus of defensibility, based on the belief that this will make a favourable outcome more likely, and also on a recognition that risk can be minimised but not completely eliminated (Kemshall, 2008a).

Defensibility is important because of the prevalence of the 'hindsight fallacy', i.e. the belief that 'if a risk assessment concludes that the probability of an undesirable event is low, and if that event does in fact happen, then the risk assessment must have been incompetent' (Beckett, 2008, p 40). An unlikely event occurring does not of itself indicate that the original assessment was at fault, but hindsight can influence inquiries into serious incidents and can leave practitioners blaming themselves for outcomes, rather than adopting the more helpful course of openly reflecting on what they can learn. The importance of organisations taking the latter approach to incidents is discussed further in Chapter Nine.

Defensibility should, in contrast, provide practitioners with security that, if their practice is of a good standard, they will not be unfairly held to blame if there is a serious negative outcome following one of their decisions. Clarity is needed, therefore, about what constitutes good practice standards. In other words, what are the components of a defensible decision? They should, for example, be:

- grounded in evidence
- made using reliable assessment tools
- based on the collection, verification and thorough evaluation of information
- recorded and accounted for
- based on communication with relevant others, and an active search for missing information
- made within agency policies and procedures
- based on the assessment of risk with risk management plans in place (if required), leading to the taking of all reasonable steps
- ongoing, and capable of responding to changes in risk over time. (Adapted from Kemshall, Mackenzie, Miller, and Wilkinson, 2007)

Those statements hide complexities and potential conflicts, however. Practitioners in England and Wales, for example, may be aware of conflicting advice from HMIP and the YJB with regard to different definitions and thresholds of 'harm' and 'serious harm' (Baker, 2010). They may also struggle to balance the requirements of defensible decision making with other demands, for example, the timescales for the production of reports. Defensible decision making therefore must be a joint responsibility between practitioners, managers and policy makers.

The components of defensible decision making require knowledge and skills, but are also about compliance with procedures (Baker and Wilkinson, 2011). How an organisation views its responsibilities and the role of staff will influence the nature of procedures which, in turn, may make a difference to how individual practitioners think about the assessment task. A focus on achieving the compliance of staff with agreed processes may create the impression that defensible decision making is just about 'back covering' rather than good practice. Even robust policies and processes won't be effective if practitioners are half-hearted about their use (Munro, 2008a), and organisations therefore need to consider how practitioners interpret and implement policies on the ground (Gillingham and Humphreys, 2009; Kemshall, 2010).

Activity

Use the defensible decision making checklist to review a real and difficult decision about a specific young person. Think about:

- how defensible the decision was
- how many of the above criteria were met (thinking about the skills used as well as the procedures followed)
- how the agency either supported defensible practice or made it more difficult to achieve.

Methods for making judgements and decisions

When undertaking assessments, practitioners need to be aware of the dangers of false positives – for example, when a young person who is not in fact going to seriously reoffend is treated as high risk – and also of false negatives – for example, where a young person who commits a serious further offence has been categorised as low risk. A lot of attention, typically focused around achieving greater accuracy in predicting future outcomes, has been paid to assessment processes that help to avoid these dangers (Howard, 2009). Such solutions are only part of the answer, however, and the assessment process should not be made so technical that it overwhelms professional judgement.

Typically, judgements in criminal justice derive from actuarial and clinical approaches, both of which have strengths and weaknesses. In undertaking actuarial assessment assessors use information drawn from knowledge of groups, based largely on factors not susceptible to change – static factors. Such approaches may take account, for example, of age, gender and criminal history, and calculate what proportion of a group of young people with similar characteristics may go on to offend further. Actuarially based estimations are more accurate than the unstructured judgements of individuals in indicating the likelihood of further offending, partly because they draw on the risk factors with the best 'track record' of predicting offending outcomes (Kemshall et al, 2007). They are important elements of screening processes that attempt to reserve more in-depth assessments for those who pose a higher risk. They also have significant limitations, however. They do not tell the assessor whether any given individual is an exception to the group (Hart, Michie and Cooke, 2007). No actuarial processes are 100% accurate and they are better at predicting common-place events than rarer but graver situations. They also do not give a full picture of the individual and their circumstances and, while useful in guiding the extent of intervention, are of limited value when making decisions about the detail of plans.

Actuarial assessment alone is not enough and is instead used alongside clinical assessments, including information derived from interviews and observation. Clinical assessments use information about a range of potential influences on behaviour and view individuals in the wider context of their lived experiences. They aim to identify those aspects of an individual's life that can be changed for the better and that can form the basis of an individual plan of action. These clinical assessments in youth justice can also be structured, for example by the use of assessment tools, to ensure consistency and comparability, so that every practitioner covers the main personal, situational and environmental factors associated with risk and analyses and records that information in a shared format. Actuarial and clinical approaches are not mutually exclusive and are typically now used alongside each other in a process of structured professional judgement (Kemshall et al, 2007): 'There is no necessity for an either/or choice between actuarial risk assessment on the one hand and the qualitative, appreciative investigation of young people's experiences, aspirations and needs on the other' (Case, 2007, p 102).

The assessment tools now widely used in youth justice (discussed in depth in Chapter Four) support structured professional judgement and have had a positive impact on the range of information routinely gathered by practitioners (YJB, 2008a). Baker recognises this positive impact of assessment tools on the quality of the information collected, but points out that 'further consideration needs to be given to ways of deepening knowledge and improving analysis, rather than just collecting more information' (Baker, 2007, p 25). In a review of serious further offences committed by adult offenders, for example, Craissati and Sindall (2009) conclude that the current assessment tools used with adult offenders in England and Wales (particularly OASys (Offender Assessment System)) need to place more emphasis on helping assessors gather information about situational risk factors. Examples of situational factors would include: who else was involved in an incident; how the victim behaved and the nature of the relationship between the offender and the victim; whether the offence was linked to a particular subculture or to gang-related activity; and how the offender perceived and understood the situation in which the offending occurred (Topalli, 2005).

As discussed in Chapter One, 'risk factors are an aid to thinking not a substitute for or a limit to it' (Carson and Bain, 2008, p 190), and assessments need to include analysis of the significance and interaction of risk factors. This is fundamental to understanding the individual young person in context, which is an essential foundation for planning and delivering interventions (Farrow et al, 2007).

Reflection

Think about your own experiences of assessment. Are you content with the balance struck between gathering information about a range of factors and the analysis of their significance and interaction?

The extent of professional judgement: the potential for bias and error

Even when using actuarial measures, an individual's actions and judgements can lead to error, for example, mistakes in accurately recording information. Bias is most apparent, however, in clinical judgements – creeping into choices about the information gathered, how best to obtain it, the meaning of the information collected, and its implications for the level and nature of risk and need (Strachan and Tallant, 1997). Structured approaches help to guard against such biases, but are no panacea, and errors and misjudgements can still occur.

Making up your mind

Practitioners may ignore information that doesn't fit with an existing view of the world, or that is in conflict with their values and beliefs. Assessors can also be influenced by prejudices and stereotypes and by dominant understandings which prevent them seeing more complex realities. Sale (2006) suggests that, in the context of child protection, practitioners don't always fully understand cultural differences between families and that this can affect decision making, leading to them under- or over-intervening. There can be confusion between the likelihood of an event occurring and the impact that it would have, particularly when fear about the potentially serious outcome of a very rare event leads people to overestimate its likelihood (Carson and Bain, 2008). For example, are people who are scared of flying thinking less about the objective probability of an incident and more about the likely severity of the effects, should an incident occur?

Information overload can limit the ability of individuals to deal with complex detail and reach decisions. Overloads may result from the ease of access to a wider range of information through IT. It may be a reflection of the complexity of some young people's lives, or the extent of demands placed on practitioners. Faced with a lot of information, sometimes contradictory, we find it hard to make sense of it all. Hollows uses the metaphor of the 'busy screen' to explain this, that is, the difficulty of working out what is important in a 'flood of data' (Hollows, 2008, p 56). In a study of the assessment of adult offenders, Ansbro (2010) found evidence of the operation of the 'precautionary principle'. In a context of competing priorities (high through-put of cases, combined with expectations of high levels of accuracy) and in a culture of blame, practitioners were sometimes questionably inflating risk when faced with a conflict between information derived from clinical processes and actuarial predictions.

Changing your mind

Assessors typically like their decisions to be unambiguous and may be reluctant to accept new information that is not directly related to the central problem being considered. Hollows calls this the 'decoy of dual pathology' (2008, p 56). For example, if a young person poses a high risk of serious harm to others it may be more difficult to see evidence that they are also at risk themselves, or vice versa.

When faced with complex ambiguous situations, individuals use cognitive shortcuts to help make sense of the world. The most significant of these shortcuts in this context is confirmatory bias: holding on to an initial judgement even when evidence questioning that judgement becomes available (Strachan and Tallant, 1997; Towl, 2005). Cognitive shortcuts are functional in simplifying everyday life. If I have found someone to be unreliable in the past, for example, it is helpful to make that assumption when I next deal with them and to manage the interaction accordingly. They become unhelpful, however, when they are based on poor information or a limited understanding in the first place and when they are too rigidly applied. If you think about someone you strongly dislike, can you recognise that your dislike will affect how you perceive everything they do, even their potentially positive actions?

Confirmation bias doesn't allow for the process of change and protects against the challenging impact of new information. If an assessor has concluded that a young person is unmotivated, they may find it hard to spot evidence that the level of motivation is changing, either ignoring it or attributing it to an attempt to 'pull the wool over the assessor's eyes'. Conversely, if a young person is compliant and being judged as a success story, information that the young person is behaving less pro-socially elsewhere may be dismissed.

A reluctance to change decisions has also been attributed to 'anchoring and adjustment' bias (Carson and Bain, 2008, p 194). Once a judgement has been made, this acts as an 'anchor' and we are reluctant to make more than small adjustments to that original 'anchoring' point. These common processes may be even more relevant when practitioners are in situations of stress and anxiety, when changing your mind can feel unprofessional and be open to criticism (Smith, McMahon and Nursten, 2003).

Reflection

If you take a shortcut you may get there more quickly, but what have you missed on the journey?

Identify the shortcuts you are most likely to make, perhaps when under pressure. For example:

- Not pursuing lines of questioning or enquiry in case they raise issues that change or complicate an assessment.
- Getting reports gate-kept by someone who is unlikely to question your judgement.
- Assuming you know everything there is to know about a well-known family and young person.

Using structured assessment tools doesn't solve all of these problems, but they can help to combat some of these sources of bias and error. This will be discussed further in Chapter Four.

Styles of decision making: finding the 'right' balance

Throughout this book there is a recognition that youth justice practice is about holding a number of difficult balances, for example between public protection and the welfare of the individual young person. Practitioners also have to balance the demands of workloads, procedures and legal requirements with spending time with young people, increasing their professional knowledge and reflecting on their practice. Good judgements leading to good decisions are needed, exercised by assessors who are able to balance priorities and live with sometimes conflicting understandings and ways of thinking. Broadly speaking, this requires individuals to balance different approaches, from structured and rational on the one hand to analytical and intuitive on the other. Figure 2.1 summarises a continuum of approaches to decision making.

Figure 2.1: Continuum of thinking styles

Rational	Intuitive
Risk factors	Hypothesising

Rational and intuitive decision making

Risk assessment tools are 'procedures for rational decision making given an uncertain future' (Schwalbe, 2004, p 565). Their development has been rooted in an understanding of decision making that stresses rational choice; collecting and weighing up evidence to arrive at an accurate conclusion. Decision theory and research into how decisions are made have, however, distinguished this type of decision making from a contrasting naturalistic or intuitive approach (van de Luitgaarden, 2009). Intuitive judgements have been found to be particularly prevalent in situations where speed is of the essence and in extreme situations, for example those faced by fire-fighters (Klein, 1999). Schwalbe (2004) suggests that in the context of assessment it is helpful to think about both types of decision making as having a place on a continuum, with their use being held in an appropriate balance. Different decisions in different situations require practitioners to operate at different points on the continuum. The question of whether social work is an art or a science is also sometimes used to make a similar point, with a contrast being made between the 'practice wisdom' that experienced practitioners build up over time and more formal rational knowledge (Evans and Hardy, 2010). Individuals may instinctively incline more towards one style than another and these individual preferences don't necessarily support the choice of the most appropriate approach. In order for policies and procedures to be effective in improving practice, managers and policy makers therefore need to consider how they can help practitioners to operate at the most appropriate point of the continuum for the different types of decisions that they have to make.

The precise point that is appropriate for a particular decision or class of decisions will depend a number of variables. A youth justice worker delivering a group-based therapeutic programme will, in order to manage the group successfully, have to make a series of speedy decisions about group process. These cannot always be based on carefully thought through rational choice, but will often be intuitive, based on the worker's past experiences and immediate grasp of the situation. Rational choice will be important, however, in systematically reviewing the impact of those more intuitive decisions, to guard against prejudicial judgements and to inform choices about future content and process.

Risk factors and hypothesising

This second aspect of decision making similarly implies a continuum of approaches. As discussed earlier and in Chapter One, practitioners are asked to gather and record information about a wide range of potential risk factors, to estimate likelihood of offending and begin to identify areas to be addressed in the intervention plan. On its own this is not sufficient to reach a full understanding of the young person, or to make decisions about the details of interventions. For this, assessors need to develop hypotheses rooted in the analysis of information which seek to provide explanations based on causal inferences. Those detailed and more personal understandings should build on the structured information about risk factors to inform decision making.

Returning to the group-work scenario introduced earlier, young people may be selected for a group that aims to address violent behaviour on the basis of specified risk factors, such as: seeing themselves as an offender; seeing themselves as a victim; having poor temper control; and believing that violence 'works'. The group includes activities addressing each of these elements for all the group members. A good group worker, however, will not just understand the links between risk factors in theory but will also develop hypotheses about how they interact for specific young people in the group. The worker will actively help an individual to make connections, for example, to understand how their temper control is, in part, about a tendency to jump to victim mode, which then stops them trying other approaches to dealing with difficulties.

Accountability and discretion: finding an organisational balance

Practitioners have to make judgements because, 'however precise the law, theory or policy might be, there is always a certain flexibility, ambiguity or discretion in how it is applied in practice' (Gelsthorpe and Padfield, 2003, p 3). These judgements occur in the context of particular organisations and they, in turn, need to consider the balances they promote between stressing accountability through technical approaches to decision making and allowing for the exercise of professional freedom. This continuum is illustrated in Figure 2.2.

Figure 2.2: Organisational accountability and professional discretion

Accountability   Discretion

Recent research relating to use of the Common Assessment Framework (CAF) suggests that the balance has perhaps shifted too far towards accountability: 'bland and standardised accounts of children may be seen to be safer because they are less open to challenge' (Thomas and Holland, 2009, p 14). These safer accounts may unnecessarily limit the work done with children. Similar tensions can arise in criminal justice settings, but the suggestion in this chapter is that the place of professional judgement should still be seen as central. Eadie and Canton (2002) believe that what is needed is a mixture of high accountability, to ensure fairness and defensibility, and high discretion, to allow the assessor to work with the individual in context. Again, this suggests that it shouldn't be an either/or choice, but finding a place on a continuum that balances the two and uses each appropriately.

Accountability tends to be supported by structured rational processes, while discretion can allow for a greater use of intuitive styles of decision making. Being able to evidence that you have considered all potential risk factors is important for accountability, but to work well with the individual, developing ideas or hypotheses about their behaviour that you can test out in practice, may need more intuitive approaches and greater discretion. To return to the group work example once again, an ideal balance of accountability and discretion might involve having the flexibility to exercise professional discretion in the day-to-day running of the group, within a structured approach that asks the group to address agreed areas and where there is regular review to ensure that it is delivering what was intended.

Reflection

Look back to the continuum diagrams.

- Where would you place yourself on the first continuum in relation to the different elements and why?
- Where, on the second continuum, would you place youth justice organisations?
- Does this raise any questions for you about your own practice or about a particular agency's expectations?

Decision-making styles in practice

As the discussion so far has shown, rational structured approaches play an essential part in decision making. Individual assessors can't always hold in their heads the wide range of knowledge required and need structures to help ensure the consistency and comprehensiveness of practice. Intuitive approaches are also very important, for example for sustaining relationships (Munro, 2008a). The challenge for practitioners is to combine the two appropriately and the next sections consider some ways of doing this for the key aspects (or stages) of the assessment and planning process.

Gathering information and building the relationship

Ensuring that an assessment covers a wide range of factors does not, of itself, guarantee the *quality* of information generated. Chapters One and Eight consider the nature of the interviewing process and its impact on the young person. Interviews are dynamic processes which develop in the light of the responses received from the interviewee (this two-way process of communication is also considered further in Chapter Seven).

To manage this complex process well, practitioners will need to use a rational, planned approach to guide information gathering. As the interview goes on they will also need to begin to see patterns emerge that inform their understanding of the basic facts; a more immediate, intuitive element of decision making may be helpful here. A young person may respond to a question about their family with minimal verbal replies, but in their body language and emotional response the worker may see clues that more is happening. The sense they make of this, and how that guides the next set of questions, will be informed by previous experience and by what they know about young people and families (see Chapter Three). They may choose to pursue it further, or simply to note their impression. What is important, however, is that this clue is not lost or ignored, and equally that the sensitivity of their response supports the building of an open and trusting relationship with the young person.

Reaching the most accurate understanding

Assessment practice in youth justice should be carried out in a way that helps young people develop their own understandings of their lives and behaviours and how they might begin to make changes. Schwalbe (2004) talks about the 'good story', the human tendency, found in both assessors and young people, to be influenced by narrative and to seek explanations for behaviour. Similarly, Presser (2009) suggests that offenders' own narratives can help to explain their behaviour.

An overemphasis on a highly structured rational approach based on risk factors may make it harder for the assessor to have a sense of connections in the young person's life. A failure to understand connections and engage with narrative may make a significant difference to the accuracy of the conclusions drawn during the risk assessment process. It is important for assessment and planning not just to identify the risk factors, but to contextualise them and to see the young person as a particular individual, operating in a specific context (Baker, 2005; Craissati and Sindall, 2009). The ability and freedom to hypothesise is therefore important (Baker, 2008). Hypotheses are described by Sheppard et al as 'propositions made about the case, or an aspect of it, against which subsequent assessments or investigations could be made' (Sheppard et al, 2000, p 474), and assessment can be described as 'ongoing hypothesis building' (Barry, 2006, p 31). In other words, assessment is, in part, a process of developing and, if necessary, challenging narratives that explain how different elements of a case come together and influence outcomes.

While analysis is built into structured processes and is part of the formal report to court, for example, intuitive processes may also play an important part in seeing connections. Successful intuitive decision making is reliant on the ability of the decision maker to recognise patterns which they have seen before, or which connect with patterns they recognise from research or wider knowledge of young people who offend (Klein, 1999; Munro, 2008a). Pattern recognition is also about the ability to look ahead to the likely effect of actions and take this into account in decision making.

Structured processes can support pattern matching, as they also draw on research, and guide the range of areas covered. Experienced practitioners will also draw on their own knowledge, derived from experience, research and theory, so that their pattern matching is more accurate and rooted in reality. For example, an experienced practitioner might be able to recognise that some of a young person's challenging behaviour, rather than just being about rebellion, is a result of anxiety, rooted in early problems with attachment. This will be more likely to happen if an assessor has a depth of understanding of research, of theory and of young people and their families (see Chapter Three), and the skills and confidence to use that understanding appropriately (see Chapter Eight). They also need a self-aware approach that is sensitive to bias, so as to ensure that their pattern matching is not mere prejudice or lazy thinking. Both Schwalbe (2008b) and Baker (2007) suggest that the assessment process and the tools that are associated with it should be designed to support the pattern-matching process by helping assessors to focus on the most pertinent risk factors and by helping to present the evidence that supports causal hypotheses about the case: in other words, hypotheses that tell a story based on evidence – a story which is coherent, but also open to change and review. Chapter Four will consider in more detail how tools can be used in this way.

Reflection

- Are you aware of pattern matching in assessments?
- If so, what makes it helpful and more likely to be accurate?
- Do you have any concerns about bias influencing your own or others' judgements?

From assessment to planning

Hypothesising needs to relate to more than just one aspect of a young person's situation; it should be a step towards generating a 'whole case hypothesis' (Sheppard et al, 2001, p 863), thinking about the complex interactions that come together in understanding the young person. A young person's substance misuse may make them more likely to engage in acquisitive crime, for example, but their offending may also be tied up in relationships. A balanced approach will help identify the most relevant risk factors, their connections and interactions, so that the plan of action can properly relate to them as an individual.

Parker and Bradley suggest that 'a social work assessment is a focused collation, analysis and synthesis of relevant collected data pertaining to the presenting problems and identified needs' (Parker and Bradley, 2007, p 14). The *Oxford English Dictionary (OED)* defines analysis as 'the resolution or breaking up of anything complex into its various simple elements'. Synthesis, on the other hand, is defined by the *OED* as 'the putting together of parts or elements so as to make up a complex whole'. The implication for assessment practice, therefore, is that once the specific issues and problems have been considered there needs to be a process of recombining them in order to look at the picture as a whole.

Having made an assessment and identified direct and indirect links leading to offending behaviour, interventions should be planned that in some way change or interfere in those links (Wikström and Sampson, 2006; Wikström and Treiber, 2008), thus reducing the likelihood of further offending. This is considered further in Chapter Five. This is complex thinking, and strategies may be needed, particularly for very difficult or contested decisions, to avoid confusion and information overload. The problem-solving model, widely used in cognitive behavioural programmes with young people (Callahan et al, 2009), helps to identify:

1. A range of options.
2. The potential consequences of each option.
3. How likely each consequence is, and its pros and cons.

Such an approach could be used to support decision making in intervention and risk management planning.[1] As the case progresses, of course, plans don't always run as expected, unexpected consequences occur and case managers have to adapt, sometimes with urgency. The evidence is that in these situations professionals will often fall back on intuitive decisions and will act on the first solution with a chance of working that comes to mind (Klein, 1999). This may be a useful and effective ability in dealing with a crisis, but a balance needs to be struck. Structured processes must then support a more considered and rational review of changes over time, to ensure that the consequences of decisions have been fully considered and that ongoing decision making is defensible.

Keeping an open mind

> What separates the creative social worker from the mere technician is the capacity to shift from one perspective to the other. Parton and Marshall put it well when they say this demands that we can make up our minds about what to do but still remain open-minded. (Milner and O'Byrne, 2009, p 71)

Hypotheses need to be reviewed and, if necessary, altered as situations change and new information comes to light. Review is, however, something with which, evidence suggests, many practitioners are failing to engage adequately (HMIP, 2009a).

'ROP.
ERSITY
LIBRARY

As the earlier discussion suggested, it is challenging and time consuming to alter your view of a case. While dramatic changes may force reconsideration, small pieces of information have the potential to change the picture fundamentally, and practitioners may be reluctant to face that kind of rethink (Taylor and White, 2006). A young person may have a poor relationship with a parent, who is uncooperative with the practitioner; poor parenting is part of the hypothesis which informs the intervention. Some comments by the young person and observations during a home visit, however, suggest that in fact the young person may be violent towards the parent. This would indicate the need for a significant rethink, but if the practitioner is overloaded, or uncertain about how to deal with this issue, they may be tempted to minimise the significance of the new information.

Chapter Nine considers how organisations can support open-minded thinking. Discussions and reviews of judgements and decisions between professionals, managers and practitioners are one of the strategies suggested. These interpersonal processes are themselves not unproblematic, however, and may not always have the impact intended. Many practitioners will have the experience of being involved in gate-keeping arrangements that become just another routine process. In conversation they sometimes express dissatisfaction with the supervision they receive, experiencing it as checking on targets, rather than helping to develop thinking. Countersigning may become 'rubber stamping' and make individuals less likely to engage in discussion (Crawford, 2007, p 162). Structural and interpersonal processes between individuals and in groups will affect the usefulness of discussions. Based on a study of cases of fatal child abuse, Reder and Duncan suggest that 'a closed professional system' where a fixed view about a case dominates might militate against the open sharing and discussing of difficult situations (Reder and Duncan, 1999, p 16). This can be made worse by role confusion and difficulties in communication, with professionals sometimes treating new pieces of information in isolation, rather than in the context of the case as a whole.

Formal structured processes for analysis and review may not, therefore, be enough. The intuitive ways in which individuals respond to each other and to the situations in which they find themselves will have an effect. Structures for working together (how meetings are chaired, for example) need to help individuals make the most of these contacts, to develop thinking and not to close it down. Working with others is covered in more depth in Chapter Seven.

Activity

The next time you are in a meeting or discussion with others about a young person, look out for:

- times when the discussion does encourage a reassessment of existing views
- times when it seems to be 'going through the motions'.

Identify what behaviours were helpful in encouraging the first approach.

The impact of information technology

This is one of the influences on human thinking and decision making that we are only just beginning to understand (Zuboff, 1984; Garrett, 2005). The completion of assessments on-screen will be considered again in Chapter Four, but, anecdotally, discussions with practitioners suggest that completing assessments on computer does make a difference, particularly perhaps by making it harder to see the whole picture, but possibly also limiting the ability to respond intuitively. IT systems that 'micro manage' the process may have an unhelpful effect on decision making, with practitioners focusing on getting through the process quickly, rather than on quality (Broadhurst et al, 2010). In this context, it is helpful to be reminded of the need to keep in mind the human dimension: 'since there is considerable emphasis currently on electronic information sharing, it is very important to remember the power of personal contact' (Brandon et al, 2008a, p 5).

Conclusion

Structured, rational decision making and good systems of information gathering and recording are essential if assessments resulting in evidentially based judgements are to inform intervention planning and provide accountability and defensibility in practice. But there is also an element of art in good practice with people (Whyte, 2009). Intuitive thinking, the proper exercise of discretion and a real understanding of narratives are also essential, while carefully avoiding the traps of bias. Practitioners need to balance these different approaches in all aspects of their work, including in their professional working partnerships and relationships with young people.

Chapter Four looks in considerable detail at assessment tools and will help you to think about this some more. The chapters on knowledge and skills are also essential to helping you ensure that you have the right basis for decision making and the skills necessary to put those understandings into practice. Developing practice is the responsibility of agencies as well as of individuals, and Chapter Nine will consider how organisations can strengthen the knowledge and skill base of staff.

Note

[1] A more detailed discussion of skills that encourage the consideration of a range of options and their consequences can be found in Chapter Eight.

THREE

The knowledge base

> Professional bodies of knowledge should aim to assist practitioners to make sense of the world around them, and offer practical support. Knowledge is a means to an end. (Evans and Hardy, 2010, p 11)

Introduction

Having a rationale for work with young people is central to the notion of effective practice. Assessors need to know why they are doing what they are doing, and be able to justify that to themselves and others. *Knowing*, that is, the theory, research and experiential base of work in youth justice, needs to underpin the *doing*, that is, the interventions, methods and skills employed.

What constitutes a relevant knowledge base within social work and criminal justice settings has long been a matter for debate (McWilliams, 1985, 1986; Whitehead and Thompson, 2004; Evans and Hardy, 2010), but one common theme emerging from these discussions is that knowledge is a fluid and evolving 'commodity'. So it is with the body of knowledge relevant to working with young people who offend. It is not static but is increasing all the time through research, evaluation, development of theory and also through reviews of practice (such as inspections). Practitioner knowledge is also dynamic in that it is extended and refined by ongoing professional experiences and through critical reflection on these experiences (see Chapter Two) and support and supervision (see Chapter Nine).

Knowledge comes from a range of sources, both personal and professional: what we bring to the job (our past experiences, values and beliefs) and what we learn via the job (practical, research and theoretical knowledge; professional ethics and standards of practice). This chapter cannot provide a detailed account of all that is known about young people and their offending. Instead, the focus will be on knowledge particularly relevant to the core tasks of assessment, such as understanding an individual's behaviour in context and making appropriate plans to help him or her desist from offending.

The aims of this chapter are therefore:

- to illustrate the range and types of knowledge required for making assessments in youth justice
- to signpost key references and resources for readers to follow up
- to help practitioners to understand the strengths and limitations of different types of knowledge

- to encourage an approach to assessment which is 'youth-aware' (Farrow et al, 2007) as well as offence oriented.

Reflection

Take a moment to think about the idea of *knowing* and *doing*. In the light of your experience in youth justice:

- What knowledge do you or others already have about young people, their lives, and their behaviour?
- What gaps in knowledge need to be filled?

Knowing the framework for assessment practice

The job of youth justice practitioners is defined and shaped by a range of legal requirements, policies, procedures and guidance. These speak to the different tasks of youth justice and the responsibility to address offending behaviour while also paying attention to the welfare of young people. This section sets out the legislative and organisational framework for the assessment and planning process, as these need to be understood before moving on to the later sections, which focus more on the practicalities of assessing young people.

Legislation

This defines the parameters and scope of responsibilities in the youth justice system. Practitioners will need to be familiar with key elements of the legislative framework, in particular those relating to:

- *the justice system*: including (in England and Wales), the Crime and Disorder Act 1998, which defines the purpose of the youth justice system, and the Criminal Justice and Immigration Act 2008, which sets out the current sentencing framework relating to young people;
- *young people's welfare*: for example, the Children Act 2004, which led to the establishment of Local Safeguarding Children Boards (LSCBs);
- *decision making and risk management in relation to serious offending*: particularly in relation to public protection sentences and Multi-Agency Public Protection Arrangements (MAPPA) (the Criminal Justice Act 2003 and the Criminal Justice and Immigration Act 2008);[1]
- *information sharing and the principles of confidentiality* (the Data Protection Act 1998).

National policies, guidance and reports

This knowledge is derived from and shaped by legislation and includes:

- National Standards (YJB, 2010b), practice guidance (especially *Case Management Guidance* for practitioners in England and Wales, YJB, 2010d) and guidance on assessment tools (YJB, 2006; Hoge and Andrews, 2002);
- guidance relating to other agencies with whom youth justice services work, for example, guidelines for courts (Sentencing Guidelines Council, 2009) and guidance about youth justice practitioners' roles in the safeguarding process (HMG, 2010);
- policies which formalise the desired outcomes and/or entitlements for children and young people (HMG, 2003; Scottish Government, 2008; Welsh Assembly Government, 2009);
- significant messages about practice from Inspections, Serious Incident Reports and, in relation to safeguarding, Serious Case Reviews.

Local organisational policies and guidance

Organisational knowledge at the level of local services and agencies consists of procedures and guidance which operationalise national policies within the context of local conditions. Practitioners need to be aware of, and have access to:

- risk management policies clarifying internal decision making and local MAPPA protocols and procedures;
- Local Safeguarding Children Board policies and procedures;
- procedures underpinning practical relationships with other agencies, for example with local schools, children's and specialist services;
- data protection/sharing policies – what sort of information you can share and with whom;
- agreed referral processes, the entitlements of young people and regulations about when and if they are excluded from services.

Local team policies, procedures and practice information

Team knowledge includes all the information that should be routinely available to practitioners, including:

- guidance about local custom and practice: for example, health and safety guidance and expectations relating to home visits or dealing with aggressive young people; how to work well with administrative support staff; arrangements for local team risk-management meetings; gate-keeping procedures and quality assurance monitoring arrangements;
- specific knowledge about local services, what they offer, whether they already have particular relationships with the team or individuals and key contacts;
- knowledge about particular aspects of practice via, for example, the expertise of specialist colleagues within multi-agency teams;

- informal knowledge derived from practitioner experience and encompassing straightforward practical information about communities, local resources or social networks as well as examples of individual good practice.

Reflection

In your experience:

- Are policies and procedures easily accessible and widely referred to?
- Is knowledge about the local area and resources up to date and easily available?
- Is specialist knowledge for particular cases or situations easily accessible?
- How do you learn from the experience of colleagues?

Research, theory and practice knowledge: an overview

Parker and Bradley talk of assessment as involving, among other things, 'systematically applied knowledge in practice' (2007, p 4). Knowledge that actually makes a difference to practice should help assessments to capture the individuality, depth and complexity of each young person's life and inform intervention plans which recognise the uniqueness and diversity of individuals and which tailor services to meet their needs.

Turney suggests that the knowledge required to support an analytical approach to social work assessment includes (2009, p 6):

> a thorough understanding of child development and informed by relevant theory ... knowledge about particular social problems, such as mental ill-health, substance misuse and domestic violence, and ... [their] ... impact on parenting capacity and children's health and well-being ... an understanding of factors such as poverty and racism and ... [their] ... impact on individuals' and families' experiences ... an awareness of risk and of different approaches towards risk management.

The range of knowledge described by Turney combines understanding of wider societal issues as well as the specific implications of these for individuals and includes research data, theoretical perspectives and the practical application of both. Such a multi-dimensional knowledge base is equally relevant to work with young people who offend.

Research and data

Data, both quantitative and qualitative, can be derived from a range of sources, and different types of studies will each have particular strengths and weaknesses.

Large-scale research studies or reviews

Key sources here include longitudinal studies such as:

- the Edinburgh Study on Transitions (www.law.ed.ac.uk/cls/esytc/)
- the Peterborough Adolescent and Young Adult Development Study (www.pads.ac.uk)
- the Offending Crime and Justice Survey (http://rds.homeoffice.gov.uk/rds/offending_survey.html).

Other relevant sources include specific studies (such as Graham and Bowling, 1995) or reviews of research literature (such as Rutter et al, 1998). In addition to these studies which focus on young people's offending, the British Crime Survey now provides data on young people's experiences of victimisation (Millard and Flatley, 2010).

These studies highlight trends and themes, and also provide the data which underpin actuarial approaches to assessment and the design of assessment tools (see Chapters Two and Four). They inform broad theories about young people and crime, offer insights into the wider population and can help practitioners to see things in proportion by setting an individual's offending within this wider perspective. The Edinburgh Study, for example, publishes data around topics such as substance use among 12- to 17-year-olds which can help assessors gain some bench-mark perspectives on the prevalence and patterns of drug use in that age group.

Topic-specific studies

These are often smaller-scale qualitative research projects that investigate the links between particular issues and offending behaviour, generate theories about particular types of behaviour and sometimes suggest suitable ways of intervening. Smaller studies help put flesh on the bones of larger-scale studies. They can help practitioners formulate questions and then analyse information and make professional judgements. In relation to substance use again, for example, Melrose (2004) explores the different reasons why young people, at key transitions in their lives, use substances; others consider the influence of particular social networks on how young people obtain cannabis (Duffy et al, 2008) or how alcohol influences bar-room aggression (Graham and Wells, 2003). Sometimes the value of these limited, smaller-scale studies is open to question because their data are limited in scope and methodologies are less robust. Used mindfully, however, they can stimulate insights and ideas about specific young people and their situations that go beyond the messages emerging from the larger-scale research.

Local knowledge

This includes locally generated data about offending patterns, the needs of young people in the area and characteristics of the local environment. It informs an understanding of the issues for young people in their community, for example, is there an issue locally in relation to the availability of particular substances or young people's preferred patterns of substance use? This local knowledge is also essential to making plans which are realistic and relevant (see Chapter Five).

Theoretical perspectives

As well as this range of research and data, a variety of criminological theories offer explanations of offending, helping us 'understand what the "facts" are saying' (Evans and Hardy, 2010, p 42). Since knowledge is sometimes incomplete and insufficient in specific situations, theories can also 'fill gaps in knowledge' (Evans and Hardy, 2010, p 42) to arrive at provisional explanations which can then be tested out in practice. Theories tend to fall between two perspectives, as represented in the continuum in Figure 3.1.

Figure 3.1: A theoretical continuum

Society   The individual

At one end, some theories explain crime largely as a social phenomenon, with offenders driven more by their environment than by personal characteristics; at the other end, they emphasise individual characteristics and choices. Between these two extremes there are a range of other theoretical standpoints which vary in the emphasis they give to social or individual factors: for a more detailed overview of relevant theories and the different insights they provide see, for example, Muncie (2004), Tierney (2006), Hopkins-Burke (2009), Whyte (2009), McLaughlin and Newburn (2010).

Theoretical perspectives offer conceptual frameworks against which to evaluate and interpret data about offenders and offending. They are open to debate and do not offer hard and fast rules (Muncie, 2004). Individually we tend towards different theoretical standpoints which, in turn, may influence our perception of a problem, and then how to deal with it. If I view youth crime as explained largely by how structures and processes work in society, I may be more likely to regard individual young people as disadvantaged and disempowered and focus my efforts upon increasing their participation in decision making and helping them change their world. Conversely, if I take the view that, irrespective of societal processes, crime is an individual act with individual explanations, I may see my role as predominantly to work with individuals to increase their sense of responsibility and pay less attention to community and family influences. In reality, practitioners will be balancing those extremes, applying understandings about individuals within their social groups and communities. It can, however, be easy to assume that you have that balance right while in fact still overemphasising one kind of explanation in practice.

Reflection

Take a moment to think about different theories and the range of research available to you.

- What theories do you routinely apply to explain offending? Where do these fit on the spectrum?
- How might you be influenced in your use of research/data by your theoretical preferences?
- How will this influence what you might expect to gain from this chapter?

Practice knowledge

In developing a knowledge base it is important not to overlook the 'information generated by practitioners from interactions with clients and client narrative ... [which is] ... equally valid and valuable evidence for practice' (Whyte, 2009, p 48). Evidence-based practice that only relies upon formal research knowledge and theories can become outmoded or inflexible in the face of the ambiguities and complexities of work in the real world (Evans and Hardy, 2010; Porporino, 2010). The challenge for practitioners is to integrate research and theory into their work with young people while, at the same time, not undervaluing their own practice knowledge but rather finding ways of communicating this to others.

The notion of the reflective, research-minded practitioner has long been advocated and critical reflection is central to assessment practice and decision making (see Chapter Two). How practitioners record their reflections on the young people they work with, find ways of describing what they actually *do* with young people that is effective and share their knowledge and good practice remains an issue for those supervising and inspecting practice (see Chapter Nine).

The dynamic and evolving knowledge base

The relationship between research, theory and practice should ideally represent a dynamic process, as illustrated in Figure 3.2 below. Just as practitioners need to draw upon research and theory, so researchers should find ways of tapping into the knowledge held by practitioners, as well as of drawing on formal theories. Equally, theories need to be tested out against the realities of work with young people. This model also suggests that practitioners need to be able to draw upon a range of both theoretical *and* empirical knowledge in order to achieve a balanced understanding of the individual. They need to be aware of their own preferences, taking care not to overlook other helpful sources of knowledge or to over-simplify what can be a complex picture.

Figure 3.2: The knowledge triangle

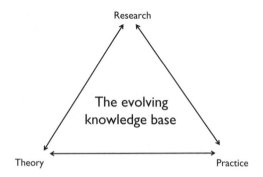

Formal knowledge should not be considered in isolation from the knowledge that comes from young people themselves. An informed assessment process can help them to think about what is important and to make sense of the web of influences upon them. Assessment can be a two-way, mutually educative process which can then inform professional knowledge and theory development.

Activity

Use the triangle to review an assessment of a young person.

- What types of research/data helped make sense of their behaviour in context?
- What theoretical perspectives were drawn on to help explain their behaviour?
- How has practice knowledge (for example, about young people in the area or about the local community) informed the assessment?

Using research and theory thoughtfully

Of itself, knowledge cannot eliminate uncertainty but, rather, professional practice is 'based on ... [the] ... thoughtful use of different bodies of knowledge' (Evans and Hardy, 2010, p 6). That is to say, knowledge has to be applied in ways that are appropriate to the type, amount and sources of data available and which are relevant to the specific context or case at hand.

Evaluating evidence

Faced with a large quantity of evidence of varying types and quality, it can be difficult to know how to make use of it or which research to give credence to. The recent emphasis on Evidence-Based Policy and Practice (EBPP) has been one response to this and has had a significant influence on the world of youth justice (Stephenson, Giller and Brown, 2007). EBPP focuses on using evidence from methodologically robust research to inform the development of policy and guide the selection of interventions. It has particularly been concerned to find evidence about interventions which have a measurable impact on the problem being considered, and in youth justice this usually means an impact in terms of reducing reoffending. Key features of the approach include the idea of a 'hierarchy of evidence', in which randomised control trials are seen as the 'gold standard' of research methods, and the use of systematic reviews and meta-analysis of data (that is, combining the results from a number of studies).

Based on this, some have argued that youth justice services should 'only use programmes and interventions that have proven effective or promising' (Wikström and Treiber, 2008, p 6). However, 'there is still a great deal that we know little about in any systematic way' (Whyte, 2009, p 49) and there are aspects of practice (such as how best to work with communities, for example) where the evidence is very limited. Researchers and those that fund research choose where to focus their efforts, and those choices may be driven by political and practical imperatives. In addition, not all questions can be answered through impact studies, and understanding how or why particular interventions work will require the use of other (more qualitative) types of research methods (Nutley, Walter and Davies, 2007).

This discussion has only been able to briefly summarise a complex topic; however, key implications for practice include:

- Planning for interventions should be informed by the available evidence base wherever possible (see Chapter Five). In the field of social policy, there are now a number of resources designed to make such evidence more accessible, for example:
  - www.campbellcollaboration.org/
  - www.scie.org.uk/
  - www.kcl.ac.uk/schools/sspp/interdisciplinary/evidence/
- Evidence will sometimes be incomplete or conflicting. Practice decisions will need to be informed by the application of theoretical knowledge and practice wisdom as well as by research data.
- Practitioners and managers need to understand the strengths, weaknesses and limitations of different types of data and have some knowledge of how to interpret the results of studies (see for example, Government Social Research Unit, 2007).

Knowledge and diversity

The majority of research into young people, their offending and effective interventions still relates to young white male offenders, not least because they make up the majority of the offending population. Theories about behaviour also tend to have been standardised on the majority group (Robinson, 2001). This does not mean that they have no value for other groups, but highlights the importance of being alert to the individual detail of young people's lives and applying knowledge with these specific contexts in mind.

Evidence suggests that there are similarities in risk factors for offending across ethnic groups and for males/females, but that some risk factors occur more frequently in particular groups than in others (YJB, 2008a). There can also be differences in the significance or impact of risk factors for different groups. For example, Williams, in considering specific risk factors in relation to girls, makes the point that 'although broadly similar for both genders, risk factors are ... likely to be experienced differently and impact differently on boys and girls' (J. Williams, 2009 , p 3; see also Joughin and Morley, 2007; Evans and Jamieson, 2008; Sharpe and Gelsthorpe, 2009). Similarly, there is some agreement that the basic developmental theories about human behaviour, developmental stages and needs are generally applicable, although there will be some differences in the experiences of children from minority groups or those with special needs (Hall, 2000; Robinson, 2001; Bailey, 2003).

The implications for assessors are threefold:

- They need to inform themselves about a range of diverse experiences to complement the core knowledge and theory base.
- They need to recognise that young people are not a homogenous group, that each individual is different, and therefore to take account of the young person's perspective.
- They have a responsibility to ensure that the experiences of young people from minority groups are accurately recorded and shared in order to expand the core knowledge base.

Youth and crime: keeping a balance

There is general agreement that offending by young people peaks in the mid to late teens, as illustrated by the Age–Crime Curve (Home Office, 1998; Ezell and Cohen, 2005; McVie, 2005). Yet offending is not the sole defining feature of young people entering the justice system – many will, with increased maturity and appropriate support, desist from offending (Farrington et al, 2006). One of the potential effects of EBPP so far has been a tendency to be concerned with the evaluation of approaches focused on the individual and on 'deficits' in their social and cognitive functioning. Commentators, however, emphasise the importance of maintaining a balance and keeping a sense of proportion by not focusing solely on problematic behaviour but also recognising young people's strengths and the positive contributions that they can make (see for example, Muncie, 2004; Fionda, 2005; Smith, 2007; Brown, 2009).

Young people also differ in the patterns and extent of their offending (Sampson and Laub, 2003; Farrington, 2007). Some may be prolific and persistent, their behaviour being more entrenched; others may be less experienced and not seriously involved in an offending lifestyle. Working with the first group may require in-depth knowledge about patterns of offending and how these are reinforced by life experiences; for the latter group, it may be enough to understand the 'trials and tribulations' of growing up, how anti-social or risky behaviour can be a response to this (Thom et al, 2007), and then to intervene with a lighter touch, avoiding more intrusive and potentially stigmatising courses of action (McNeill and Weaver, 2010). It is important to use knowledge appropriately, to see young people's behaviour in perspective and to avoid becoming overly negative about their prospects of changing and maturing.

The wider context: childhood and adolescence

Assessors in youth justice require knowledge not just of offending behaviour but also of key elements of child and adolescent development. Rights and responsibilities are gradually given to individuals over an extended period, the bulk coming between 12 and 18 years, reflecting the public journey to adulthood (Muncie, 2004). Alongside formal rights and responsibilities come the reordering of close relationships – reduced dependence upon the family and increased reliance upon friends and other adults. Individual young people will differ in how well they cope with these changes. An individual's capacity to cope can be influenced by how they see themselves, their emotional and cognitive development and how they experience and deal with the risks associated with growing up. Several areas of research and theory in the field of child and adolescent development are particularly relevant here.

How young people's identities are shaped by experience

- Identity formation is central to adolescence (Rogers, 1959; Erikson, 1968; Marcia, 1980) and it is important to recognise the variety of factors (social, cultural, gendered and sexual) which can influence this.
- In relation to young black adolescents, research in the US has begun to develop some alternative models (for example, Cross's model of black identity development (1980)) and there is evidence that attention needs to be given to how their experiences, particularly of discrimination, shape their developing identities (Bowling and Phillips, 2002; Farrow et al, 2007).
- How social identities are influenced by an individual's attachment to friends and different expressions of youth culture is especially relevant to work with young people. Social identities vary depending upon factors such as local context, class, gender and whether young people feel included or excluded (White and Cunneen, 2006). A young person's choice of friends, how friendships evolve and the purpose they serve can act as a window upon the developing sense of self, helping to reveal what the young person regards as important and how confident they are in their relationships (for example Murray, 2009).

Cognitive, emotional and moral development

Adolescence often brings with it some necessary but unsettling transitional moments of separation. A practical understanding of attachment theory (Bowlby, 1988) can be helpful in exploring the quality and security of a young person's close relationships and their capacity to cope with change and separation. These early experiences can influence the development of empathy and moral reasoning (Ansbro, 2008), the absence of which is so closely associated with some offending (Wikström and Treiber, 2008).

The developmental journey involved in the acquisition and development of cognitive skills, especially around making moral judgements, is also important in understanding choices to offend (Wikström and Butterworth, 2006). Kohlberg, building on the work of Piaget, provides a practical schematic description of the six stages of moral development (described in Farrow et al, 2007, p 68). His research has been adapted by programme writers largely in the cognitive–behavioural field (for example Goldstein, 1999). The impact of language development on cognitive development and understanding may also be an issue for some young people in that it affects how well they are able to communicate with adults in interviews and then respond to interventions (Bryan, 2004).

Risk taking and growing up

It has been argued that '[n]owhere is the tension between the need to prevent risk and the necessity of learning to manage and take calculated risks more apparent than in the process of growing up from childhood to adulthood' (Thom et al, 2007, p 1). Risk taking is part of everyday life; coping and problem-solving skills are acquired by having to deal with the unexpected (Boeck and Fleming, 2011).

However, ongoing exposure to problems such as poverty, poor health, difficult family relationships, as well as specific disturbing or disruptive events, can increase the likelihood of some children responding to the pressures of adolescence by taking unacceptable risks and making themselves or others unsafe. Sometimes this is because it is 'the best that can be done in difficult circumstances' (Hine, 2009, p 36), since young people may feel that their 'choice is reduced to fate, and personal agency is restricted' (Boeck, Fleming and Kemshall, 2006); sometimes it makes them feel better (for example through the 'buzz', being part of a group, expressing their feelings).

Risk factors in young people's lives do not, however, necessarily lead to negative outcomes (Kemshall, 2009). Children differ in their exposure and response to risky behaviour: some avoiding it or being protected from it; others being able to negotiate risk effectively and develop resilience; and for yet others, risk and recklessness become problematic and endemic in their lives (Murray, 2009). Assessors therefore need to have an understanding of processes of development as they apply to all young people and to take account of individual differences in the experience of growing up and the ability to navigate the risks encountered in adolescence.

> ## Reflection
>
> Look back over the knowledge that supports a thoughtful and wider perspective on understanding young people.
>
> ■ Are there ideas or elements of knowledge that are new to you?
> ■ What might these new ideas mean for your own or others' assessment practice?

Analysing offending

Analysing offending behaviour is central to assessment. The ABC model is a simple, well-known way of analysing offending, breaking down the events(s) into what happened before (the Antecedents), what the young person did (the Behaviour) and what happened afterwards (the Consequences), as shown in Figure 3.3.

Figure 3.3: The ABC model

A

Antecedents
Long term and
immediate

B

Behaviour
Offence type
Frequency
Meaning

C

Consequences
of offending
Effect of
interventions

In the following sections, this basic model is used as a framework to organise knowledge about young people and offending. For each of the three stages – A, B, C – examples are given of the different types and sources of relevant knowledge.

Antecedents

Studies have identified a wide range of factors associated with offending, anti-social and/or challenging behaviour (YJB, 2005b; 2008a; Joughin and Morley, 2007; Margo, 2008). As discussed in Chapter One, however, it is important not merely to identify risk factors but also to consider their significance in the lives of each young person. Antecedents can usefully be grouped into three categories:[2]

• longer-term (often historical) influences
• current situations, behaviours, attitudes and personal characteristics
• immediate triggers associated directly with offending incidents.

Longer–term influences

Assessors should have knowledge of contextual influences that impinge upon children's development. These influences may not all be directly associated with offending, but may increase a young person's susceptibility to offending choices or lifestyles. They include:

- the circumstances of a child's birth and early care;
- low income, large family size and poor housing, particularly where these combine to produce overcrowding (Farrington, 2007). These types of hardship can make 'other forms of adversity more difficult to cope with' (Hooper et al, 2007, p 2);
- experience of neglect or abuse;
- difficult family relationships, remembering that family patterns and problems will differ across culture and class (Haas et al, 2004) and that judgements about particular families should not start from a stereotypically white perspective (Robinson, 2001);
- experiences of discrimination (Bowling and Phillips, 2002);
- social disadvantage and isolation, resulting in limited horizons and restricted opportunities (Boeck, Fleming and Kemshall, 2006; Barrow Cadbury Trust, 2008).

Individual characteristics will interact with these developmental influences and, while again they do not directly predispose the individual to offending, they can sometimes exacerbate the effects of contextual disadvantage and have an impact on the young person's situation (Dodge, 2006). They can make it more difficult for young people to integrate into wider society (Hall, 2000) and can make family life harder by adding to the pressures faced by already over-stretched parents. Assessors should be aware of the significance of individual characteristics such as health problems, social conduct disorders or learning disabilities. There is also evidence that young people experiencing significant levels of mental health problems during adolescence (Joughin and Morley, 2007) are prominent in the offending population. This group would include some who have also demonstrated signs of conduct disorder (Perry et al, 2008). All of these characteristics can influence the cognitive and adaptive development of children, including the acquisition of language and social skills (Ripley and Yuill, 2005; Snow and Powell, 2008), potentially making it more difficult for them to navigate the risks and problems they encounter.

Current situations, behaviours, attitudes and personal characteristics

Assessors then need to understand how those longer-term influences are translated into current experiences, thus requiring knowledge about issues such as:

- experiences in education, such as low achievement and negative labelling;
- exposure to risk-taking behaviour, being alert to differences between communities, and between rural and urban locations (Duffy et al, 2008);
- the quality and range of friendship groups;
- levels and types of substance use;
- social skills;
- anger and self-control;
- moral beliefs.

This is not an exhaustive list and there are still significant gaps in knowledge, for example about the lifestyles of young people. Although 'spending time with friends is a prime social activity for most young people' (Batchelor, 2009, p 408), the dynamics of exactly how friendship/peer groups operate in relation to problematic behaviour (for example, in co-offending episodes) remain a relatively under-researched area (van Mastrigt and Farrington, 2009). There is a developing body of work around gang culture (Young et al, 2007; Melde, Taylor and Esbensen, 2009), and the place of relationships in girls' offending has long been recognised (Batchelor and Burman, 2004; J. Williams, 2009), but the psychological dimensions of friendship groups have not yet attracted detailed attention (Wood, 2009). The detail of adolescent relationships may be difficult to access because research is often undertaken by adults (Harden et al, 2000). Murray employed a peer-led research method, however, allowing young people 'to speak collectively with no adult present' (Murray, 2009, p 127), and the results provide insight into the influence of social networks and how young people negotiate the tensions within and between them. This also has implications for how practitioners can extend their own knowledge base by using their skills in working with young people (see Chapter Eight) to uncover details of individual lives that might be missed by more formal research methods.

As with the longer-term issues above, these factors do not in themselves make offending behaviour a certainty. But if actions are 'the outcome of the interaction between a person and his and her environment' (Bouhana and Wikström, 2008, p 37), then these issues are important for understanding why the young person's situation might increase the probability of offending. For example, opportunities to offend might regularly arise out of a young person's life in their specific community or social networks (Cohen and Felson, 1979). This highlights the importance of having local knowledge and understanding the detail of neighbourhood life, as experienced by the young person.

Immediate antecedents and triggers

The preceding sections have identified a range of factors that affect young people's development and consequently may affect their perceptions about offending behaviour and responses to offending opportunities. However, even people with extensive criminal histories and lots of these factors evident in their lives don't offend all the time. The same applies to those who commit very serious offences: 'most of the time, the most dangerous, most violent persons are not doing anything violent. Even for these people, the *dynamics of situations* are crucial in explaining what violence they actually do' (Collins, 2008, p 3, emphasis added).

This requires knowledge of how the immediate circumstances surrounding incidents of offending behaviour – such as particular pressures and triggers that a young person is experiencing – can affect behaviour (Dodge, 2006). Craissati and Sindall (2009) show the significance of this for understanding some episodes of violence, illustrating how seemingly small factors, such as looking at someone the wrong way or saying the wrong thing, can quickly escalate into a serious incident in a context where certain groups of young men place immense importance on maintaining status and reputation. When considered alongside theoretical understandings of how young people make choices (for example, Cornish and Clarke, 1986, or Wikström, 2010, forthcoming) such knowledge can help assessors make sense of the web of influences (historical and immediate) that have culminated in the incident, uncovering the '[i]ndividual cognitions and meanings ... [that] ... interact with structural life events' (Savolainen, 2009, p 301).

An understanding of immediate triggers is also important for ongoing assessment and planning. The concept of 'acute' risk factors is useful here (Hanson and Harris, 2000). Intervention plans may be addressing difficulties that have been a feature of a young person's life for some time, for example their emotional and mental health. It is important to be alert to the acute changes that move a relatively stable risk of reoffending to something more urgent. For example, if that same young person stops medication or attending therapy it may be a sign that further offending is likely in the short term.

Behaviour

Having understood the influences leading up to an offending incident, assessors need to understand what happened. What did the young person actually do, where, when, with whom, and how does that fit with the young person's previous behaviour? An understanding of an offending incident should be weighed against knowledge about particular types or patterns of offending by young people, including:

- prevalence
- key features of different types of offending
- what is known about the function and meaning of offending for young people.

Such knowledge can complement the practitioner's own experience to provide the types of research-based patterns which can increase the accuracy of decision making, as described in Chapter Two.

Prevalence

When starting an assessment, it is helpful to get a sense of the incidence of types of behaviour both in the general population (through national crime statistics, academic research reviews and large-scale studies such as those highlighted above) and locally (through the team's own data bank or informal intelligence). Such background knowledge can alert the assessor to useful questions to explore: for example, is this behaviour commonly associated with young people or is it unusual and distinctive? Is this significant for the assessment in this particular case?

Types

Assessors need knowledge about a range of behaviours, particularly since studies suggest that young people (with the possible exception of some posing a high risk to the public) tend not to specialise in particular types of offences (Whyte, 2009). Useful sources of information about particular types of offending include the *Handbook on Crime* (Brookman et al, 2010) and studies such as those looking at offenders who commit serious offences (Powis, 2002), although their focus is generally on adult offenders. In addition, however, there is also literature focusing on specific types of offences committed by young people, for example:

- young people who sexually abuse: Grimshaw et al (2008); Calder (2009);
- serious violent offending: Bailey (1996); Falshaw and Browne (1997); Dent and Jowitt (2003);
- firesetting: Thomas (2009);
- aggression (approaches relevant to different types of violent offending are described in Farrow et al, 2007, drawing upon Bush, 1995; McMurran, 2002; Smith et al, 2002);
- partner abuse/violence in teenage relationships: see, for example, Barter (2009).

When considering particular types of offences – such as property or violent offences – there will be a variety of subgroups to consider. Some types of offences may be associated with particular groups of young people, for example, theft from shops is more frequently seen among girls than boys (IYJS, 2009). In relation to violence, patterns are changing, with evidence showing an increase in girls' violent behaviour, although this still tends to be less serious than that of boys (J. Williams, 2009). Increased alcohol use is also associated with increasing levels of violent behaviour, whereas paying for drugs tends to be more associated with property offending and street crime. Trends like this, identified at a 'macro' level, may be reflected in local data analysis and assessors should use these themes and patterns as a baseline from which to evaluate information and refine their enquiries about individual cases.

Meaning

Another strand of research draws upon the accounts of young people, giving insight into the meaning inherent for them in particular types of offending. A study of 'recreational rioting' in Belfast, for example, revealed that young people have complex and sometimes conflicting views about involvement in such violence, seeing it as both fun and yet also dangerous (Leonard, 2010; see also Lyng, 2005). Another example relates to how a sense of futility about the future – in particular the expectation of an early death – can be a factor in explaining young people's involvement in gang activity (Brezina et al, 2009).

Other examples of studies which give insight into young people's perceptions include: Graham and Wells (2003) on aggression in young men; Batchelor (2005) on young women and violence; O'Connell (2006) on joyriding. With such insight, assessors are less likely to be satisfied with 'easy' answers and more inclined and confident to ask searching and challenging questions (the use of questions is explored further in Chapter Eight).

Consequences

In addition to understanding the meaning of behaviour for a young person, practitioners need an awareness of what have been the immediate and longer-term consequences of offending for them and also of how they perceive those consequences. Assessors should have an understanding of how consequences, both positive and negative, can reinforce or deter future offending. Relevant areas of knowledge include:

* research (as described above) exploring young people's perspectives on why they commit offences and what they think they gain from it;
* how consequences can shape future behaviour. Understanding the power of consequences is central to social learning theory (for example Bandura, 1997) and to cognitive-behavioural methods commonly used with offenders (McGuire, 2000);
* theory and research about motivation (Prochaska and DiClemente, 1983; Miller and Rollnick, 2002; Burrowes and Needs, 2009), for example, understanding the 'pros' and 'cons' of behaviour, what drives it and sustains it;
* problem-solving approaches (Hollin et al, 2002);
* strengths-based perspectives (McNeill et al, 2005) and future-focused approaches such as the Good Lives Model (see Chapters One and Five).

Chapter Five will look in detail at how to select interventions and construct plans that will help young people to understand and address the consequences of their behaviour. The aim should be to draw on the range of knowledge discussed in this chapter – including research, data, theory, practice wisdom – to design interventions which address offending behaviour and which are also 'balanced by a focus on positive strengths and promoting the development of resilience; emphasis ... [is] ... placed ... on the future rather than dwelling on past mistakes ... [and involve] ... fostering a sense that the young person can change, and reinforcing an awareness of what he or she has to offer' (NACRO, 2007, p 5).

Reflection

Look back over the knowledge that can support an 'ABC' analysis of offending.

- Note ideas or pieces of knowledge that are new to you.
- What might these new thoughts mean for your assessment practice?

Conclusion

This chapter has set out key areas of knowledge that assessors need for undertaking assessments. The issues that have been covered are neither exhaustive nor absolute, but the aim has been to provoke an interest that will then prompt readers to a further exploration of the research literature and a willingness to look to others for specialist knowledge and understanding when required. Parts Two and Three of the book now go on to look at how knowledge is applied in practice to the tasks of assessment and planning; a recurring theme throughout all the subsequent chapters, however, will be that knowledge is never static but needs to be continually developed, challenged and refined.

Notes

[1] More detailed consideration is given to the practical implications of multi-agency arrangements such as LSCBs and MAPPA in Chapter Seven.

[2] These categories are not completely separate and there will be overlaps between them, but it is helpful for simplifying the array of possible relevant influences to group them in this way.

Part Two
Tools and processes

FOUR

Using assessment tools

> The designers have always emphasised that such tools can only ever
> be aids to practice and, in effect, are only as good as the practitioner
> completing them. (Whyte, 2009, p 85)

Introduction

As discussed in Chapter One, assessment frameworks and tools are one component
of the assessment and planning process but are not in themselves 'the assessment'.
The aim of this chapter is to suggest ways of understanding and using assessment
tools that can help to improve decision making and therefore, also, outcomes for
young people. The focus will be on tools used in the UK and, specifically, risk
assessments (rather than assessment tools designed to screen for particular needs
such as health or literacy).[1] The chapter will not provide detailed guidance on
particular tools, as this is available in the guidance and manuals attached to each
tool (Hoge and Andrews, 2002; Borum et al, 2003; YJB, 2006), but will instead
look at the wider principles of how to use assessment tools effectively.

Tools are there to help you achieve something: 'tools are not inherently valuable;
their worth lies in their ability to accomplish some other end' (Douglas and
Kropp, 2002, p 623). When using an assessment tool, therefore, you need to keep
in mind the goals that you are working to – reducing offending, for example, or
strengthening the positives in a young person's life – and focus on how the tools
can help to achieve those aims.

There are some general principles that will apply to all tools, for example:

• they help you do a job but don't do it all for you;
• there will be some requirements and procedures for how to use them;
• you may need more than one tool for some tasks.

There will also be additional factors in relation to each individual tool, for example:

• its particular purpose and function;
• its specific capabilities and limitations;
• how its components can be adapted (depending on the nature and complexity
  of the task in hand).

This begins to highlight a number of practice issues, for example: the need to know
which tools to use and when; how to use them; understanding what they can and

cannot do. Using tools inappropriately (for purposes they weren't designed for or without the skills and knowledge required) is likely to lead to problems, but using them judiciously can contribute to more consistent and rigorous practice. This requires (in addition to the range of knowledge outlined in Chapter Three), awareness of the general principles of using assessment tools *and* an understanding of the specific characteristics of each tool being used.

The assessment tools debate

The expansion in the use of assessment tools has not been without controversy. This applies not just to youth justice, but to parallel developments in probation and children's services, where there have also been debates about the value of standardised approaches to assessment (DH, 2000a; Garrett, 2003; Robinson, 2003b; Mair et al, 2006; White et al, 2009). Familiarity with key issues in these debates is useful because it helps to show the strengths and weaknesses of the tools, and this is an important foundation for the more practical discussions about how to use them which follow later in the chapter.

History and development

Chapters One and Two discussed the increasing focus on risk. One of the consequences of this in criminal justice organisations has been the emphasis given to the 'risk principle', that is, that higher-intensity interventions should be reserved for those with the highest risk of recidivism (Andrews and Dowden, 2006). Assessment tools which produce a prediction of likelihood of reoffending have become a core part of the RNR approach (see Chapter One) as a means of identifying who needs the higher-intensity interventions. Some tools have been developed using primarily static factors, that is, those which cannot be changed by intervention (such as previous criminal history). The Offender Group Reconviction Scale is one example of this (Howard et al, 2009). Recent developments have focused on tools which also include a range of dynamic factors, that is, factors associated with offending which can be changed (such as substance misuse or pro-offending attitudes) (Merrington, 2004; Bonta, 1996). *Asset* and YLS/CMI would both be examples of this because they produce scores which can be used to group young people into reoffending categories. However, this is not the only – or necessarily the most important – factor that has influenced the development of tools and there are other issues to consider.

Evidence from social work assessments, for example, suggested that practitioners were regularly missing out or failing to consider key factors for child abuse identified in the literature (Warner, 2003). One of the main arguments for tools has thus been that they can help to promote comprehensive and consistent approaches by setting out research-based frameworks for practice (Hoge, 2002; Whyte, 2009). This is particularly relevant in multi-agency settings such as YOTs, where assessors may come from very different professional backgrounds – tools can provide a common baseline for practice.

Claims and counter-claims

The debates about structured tools are extensive and what follows is therefore necessarily a summary. In relation to the *content* of tools, claims that they assist practitioners by providing a comprehensive framework have been countered with arguments about factors which may be overlooked: for example, tools have been criticised for focusing too much on individual factors and not taking sufficient account of social problems (Webster et al, 2006). A further concern has been that the focus on offending might contribute to the emergence of a practice culture in which the welfare of young people is sidelined (Field, 2007). Others have questioned the applicability of tools to female offenders and ethnic minority groups (Hannah-Moffat, 2006).

In terms of the *process* of assessment, the use of numerical scores as the basis for decisions about intervention levels has been one key area of discussion (Smith, 2006; Case and Haines, 2009). It has also been argued that the use of tools restricts practitioners' ability to use professional judgement. For example, it has been suggested that the introduction of *Asset* means '[t]he core beliefs of those who see a central place for individual decision making in working with young offenders are thus fundamentally challenged' (Smith, 2007, p 114). Others argue that this is not the case because using the tools requires considerable professional skill (Baker, 2005) and Ballucci suggests that 'standardized risk evaluations tools do not stand opposed to professional discretion, but are themselves the conduits and structure through which such discretion is exercised' (Ballucci, 2008, p 192). Another perspective is to see tools as providing an analytical approach to complement the more intuitive reasoning styles that assessors may instinctively prefer (Munro, 2008a; see also the discussion in Chapter Two).

Practitioners' views about assessment tools

Studies of practitioners' views of assessment tools from adult offender services (Aye-Maung and Hammond, 2000; Robinson, 2003a and 2003b; Mair et al, 2006) and youth justice (Roberts et al, 2001; Baker, 2004; Burnett and Appleton, 2004) reveal a range of opinions. For example, practitioners sometimes complain about the length of time required to complete assessment tools or may perceive them as 'de-skilling'. In some cases they are seen as adding little to the decision-making process and are used to record a decision that has already been taken (Gillingham and Humphreys, 2009; Phoenix, 2009). On the other hand, practitioners identify some advantages to using assessment tools, such as greater consistency, quality, credibility and improved defensibility in decision making (Lancaster and Lumb, 2006).

Perceptions of tools are often strongly influenced by the context in which they are used and the surrounding organisational culture (Baker, 2005). Some try to avoid the tools, use them as little as possible, complete them with only minimal information, or ignore the results and conclusions. In contrast, there are others who depend on them too much by, for example, ignoring issues not mentioned in a tool but important to a young person or by placing too much confidence in the numerical scores.

Reflection

Take a few minutes to imagine the impact on assessment and planning practice if, tomorrow, the tools were removed and all practitioners were asked to assess without them.

- What would the impact be?
- What does that tell you about your view of some of the debates around the usefulness or otherwise of formal tools?

No tool will be perfect, but the authors agree with the view that:

> The real strength of standardised approaches is less their predictive validity and reliability and more their transparency in identifying which individual domains practitioners associate strongly with criminality, evidence that can be accepted or challenged, and the degree to which those identified 'needs and risks' can then be incorporated meaningfully into an action plan which is dynamic, open to revision and for which service providers as well as service 'users' are accountable. (Whyte, 2009, p 85)

If viewed in this way, tools can be a useful aid to practice, and this chapter aims to help practitioners use them in constructive ways that will contribute to improved decision making.

Understanding assessment tools

Different assessment tools may look similar on the surface but each one will have distinctive features and components. Understanding what a particular tool or framework does – and therefore how to use it – requires knowledge of the following.

Scope, foundations and purpose

The scope of a tool refers to the range of young people it was designed to be used with. Relevant factors include age, gender, ethnicity, pre- or post-conviction and offence type. 'Foundations' refers to issues such as the theoretical framework that a tool is based on or whether it assumes a particular 'model of change' in relation to young people's lives. With regard to purpose, tools may be intended to: predict specific outcomes such as reconviction; trigger other assessments or referrals; determine the level or intensity of intervention; identify areas for intervention; measure change over time. Some tools will focus on just one or two of these, whereas others cover multiple purposes.

Structure and content

Tools can be structured around different concepts, such as:

- *Time*: for example, looking for trends and patterns in a young person's behaviour over a specified period.
- *Events or incidents*: in this case the unit of analysis may be particular offences or episodes of offending behaviour.
- *Domains or 'needs'*: sections of the tool look at specific issues such as family, education or substance use.

Example 4.1 illustrates this by comparing the structures for different components of the *Asset* framework.

Example 4.1: Understanding tool structures

Tool	Structure
Core Asset Profile	*Based on domains (the 12 'dynamic' sections)*
Risk of Serious Harm Asset (RoSH)	*Time-based:* section A = past behaviour, section B = current risk indicators, section C = future behaviour (YJB, 2006)

In addition to understanding the structure, it is important to know what is included in the content of a tool. This could include: individual and social factors; problems and positives; offending–related factors and wider needs; static and dynamic factors. You need to know which ones are included, where they are in the tool and the balance between them. Another factor to consider is how a tool takes account of the views of young people and parents/carers, that is, how their views are recorded and how much weight is attached to them.

Use and application of professional judgement

Using a tool requires knowledge of:

- *When professional judgement is required*. For example, scoring the criminal history section of *Asset* does not require professional judgement because this is based on factual data about previous offending, but scoring the dynamic sections of *Asset* does require professional judgement (YJB, 2006).

- *How to evidence judgement.* In *Asset* this is done through the 'evidence boxes', which provide an opportunity to demonstrate reasoning. Other tools will provide different ways of doing this.
- *What types of decisions judgements contribute to.* Similar processes can lead to different applications of professional judgement (Example 4.2). For example, bail *Asset*, core *Asset* and the RoSH part of *Asset* all require the use of judgement in analysing the significance of a range of risk and protective factors in a young person's life, and for this to be explained in evidence boxes, but they lead to different types of decisions and results.

Example 4.2: Different applications of professional judgement

Tool	Decision	Results
Bail Asset	Suitability for bail support services	Recommendation
Core Asset Profile	Significance of particular factors for likelihood of reoffending	Numerical scores
RoSH Asset	Estimating the likelihood of a young person committing an offence that will cause serious harm to others	Classification (on a 4-point scale)

Evaluation and evidence

Assessors need to be aware of evidence relating to the effects of tools in practice. This could include research findings concerning the experiences of practitioners, young people, parents/carers and other agencies regarding the use of a tool. It also covers evidence in relation to outcomes, for example, the accuracy of numerical scores in predicting reconviction, or the match between a risk classification and future serious offending. A summary of references and key findings for tools such as *Asset*, SAVRY and AIM2 can be found in the Appendix. Another useful source of information is the Risk Assessment Tools Evaluation Directory (RMA, 2007a), which summarises the evidence underpinning different tools.[2]

Why this matters

Is it really necessary to know all this? It may be tempting to just pick up a tool and use it without considering these issues; but not understanding 'scope' creates problems, for example, where practitioners have mistakenly used the *Asset* RoSH form to assess the potential for harm to a young person. Lack of clarity about whether a tool is structured around domains, time or events may result in not knowing where information should go in a tool, which will then make it more difficult and time-consuming to complete. Not being aware of evaluations means that you may not know how well a tool works for particular groups, such as young people from minority ethnic groups or girls. As discussed earlier, using a tool requires knowledge of its purpose, capabilities and limitations, so understanding these features and components really does matter.

Reflection

This section has shown the range of things you need to know in order to use a tool well. Consider the tool(s) with which you are most familiar.

■   Is information about the intentions, limitations and evidence base for the tool available? If not, do you know where to find it?
■   Is it being used for the people/purposes it was designed for?

Applying tools to practice

Understanding a tool in some depth provides a basis for using it effectively. In addition, several other issues need to be borne in mind. Firstly, although the focus of this chapter is on how individual practitioners use tools in their own work, tools also have a role in making practice more transparent. The value of tools in enabling people to see the reasoning behind decisions has already been noted and this also means they have value for challenging those decisions. Research indicates continuing evidence of bias in assessments of adult offenders from minority ethnic groups (Hudson and Bramhall, 2005), for example, and although tools can't eliminate this completely, they can make it easier to ask challenging questions because of the shared approach and greater transparency which they provide (Schwalbe, 2004; Baker, 2005).

Secondly, the impact of IT on the use of tools needs to be considered. It is not just that IT systems provide a different place to record and store data but that they can also change the way people work (Aas, 2004; Munro, 2008b). For example, where a tool is being used electronically the structure may not be so clear (because you tend to view one screen at a time and may not get the overview of the whole document that you could get from a paper-based version), but it is important to 'look behind the screen' to understand why a tool is designed in a particular way.

Activity

If you are able to do so, compare a hard-copy version of a tool with its on-screen version.

■   List any significant differences you can find, either in the content or in the ways in which the process is laid out and organised.
■   If there are any significant differences, what impact might these have on your own or others' practice?

Using assessment tools: gathering and recording information

Collecting and recording information are the initial tasks of an assessment, but also part of the ongoing dynamic process that occurs all the way through the period of contact with a young person. How can tools assist with these tasks?

Collecting information

As noted in Chapter One, assessments need to be 'prepared for' and an assessment tool can be useful in guiding thinking about the range, content and sources of information required. For example, some practitioners using *Asset* find it helpful to use either a list of different domains or a diagram (such as Figure 5.1 in Chapter Five) as a reminder of key areas that need to be considered. Where a tool has a self-assessment component for young people and/or their parents and carers (such as 'What do YOU think?' in *Asset*), then that should form part of the information-gathering process.

Tools vary in the way that they support the information-collection process. Some provide an interview schedule to follow, for example YLS/CMI includes an interview guide and a list of questions (Hoge and Andrews, 2002). Other tools, such as *Asset* or SAVRY, don't provide a list of questions, but the factors they include can be taken as prompts to shape the content of an interview. In using tools for this purpose, bear the following in mind:

- Don't be limited by the items or questions listed in a tool – there may be other issues in a particular case that need to be considered and the tool should not be used as an excuse to miss those out.
- Adapt the questions to suit the age, maturity and language skills of the young person (see Chapter Eight).

At this stage of the assessment process the type of tool required is one that provides a reminder of key issues to consider – assessment frameworks can fulfil this role if they are seen as useful aides-memoires rather than as inflexible questionnaires.

Recording information

The demands of recording information, particularly if IT systems are rather cumbersome, can sometimes create resentment if it seems that it has to be done just to satisfy bureaucratic requirements. On the other hand, if we return to the idea of tools as being there to help achieve specific goals, the value of assessment frameworks for recording information becomes clearer. Using tools to record information can have benefits for the individual practitioner because it provides evidence of what has been done. It also has benefits for colleagues, who are able to see the reasons for the decisions that have been made.

Tools assist with recording information by providing a structure in which assessors can:

1. Identify information sources and record relevant information either about the strength/reliability of that information or about any concerns regarding inaccuracies or gaps in the information.
2. Distinguish between facts, descriptions and inferences/judgements: for example, the young person's address (fact), a summary of some of the problems with the accommodation/neighbourhood (description) and an explanation of how that might be contributing to the young person's offending behaviour (inference/judgement).
3. Strike a balance between providing comprehensive and detailed information but not filling up the assessment with too much irrelevant material.

The following is the first of a series of activities that can help you to actively review the use of tools in a specific context.

Activity: Reviewing tools 1

For tools that are frequently in use in your work context, list the key information that a particular tool should record and answer the following questions:

- Is it clear where and how to record these different types of information in the tool being considered?
- Are there types of information that are difficult to record/capture? What are they and how might you get around this?

Where you have examples of assessment tools that have been completed:

- How regularly/consistently are views recorded about the strength or reliability of information?
- How useful would colleagues find the recording of information in the tool if they had to pick up a case while the assessor was away?

Information recorded in assessment tools may continue to influence perceptions about a young person way beyond the initial assessment (O'Rourke, 2010). Research in social work, for example, has shown the impact assessment records can have in creating powerful images of young people (Holland, 2004; Thomas and Holland, 2009), and this can apply to any written record, including assessment tools and reports (see also Chapter Six). The way in which information is recorded matters because 'experience is not simply known or conveyed to others, but *takes on its meaning* within descriptive frames or contexts' (Gubrium et al, 1989, p 197, emphasis added). Once meaning has been given within a form or assessment tool, this may persist over quite long periods of time: 'The importance of the written records, reports and files are crucial to the way "cases" are constructed. After a while a file takes on a life of its own, and it can be very difficult to question what it appears to represent' (Teoh et al, 2003, p 157). Interviews with (adult) offenders have also shown that they are often concerned about the possibility that 'inaccurate or out of date information could be held in their files and subsequently used in assessment and decision-making' (Attrill and Liell, 2007, p 196). Appropriate recording of information therefore involves not just practical consideration of issues such as the use of language and the need to avoid stereotypes, but also requires an awareness that the overall 'picture' of a young person presented through a tool can have significant and long-term effects.

Using assessment tools: finding meaning and giving explanations

How can tools help with the next stage of the assessment process, that is, the difficult task of making sense of – and explaining – the information that has been collected and recorded?

Analysis

As explained in Chapter Two, analysis is about breaking down something complex into its constituent parts. The initial stage is the *identification and description* of key factors. Depending on the tool, these may be referred to as risk/protective factors, strengths/needs, problems or positives. Whatever they are called, one of the advantages of assessment tools is that they provide a framework for clearly outlining the range of factors affecting a young person's situation and behaviour. Descriptions of these factors should include not just statements about what they are but some additional explanation, for example, whether a protective factor has developed recently, following professional intervention, or whether it has been an established part of the young person's life for a long time.

Secondly, there is a need for *individualisation and contextualisation* of these factors. As discussed earlier (Chapters One and Three), the presence of risk or protective factors does not automatically increase or decrease the likelihood of offending. The key question to consider should always be: what is the significance of this factor in this particular young person's life at this point in time, given his/her situation? Answering this will require both theoretical knowledge (Chapter Three) and awareness of the need to avoid bias and error (Chapter Two).

Some have tried to argue that tools based on identifying risk and protective factors assume that young people are 'hurtling towards pre-determined outcomes' (Case and Haines, 2009, p 305). This might be a fair comment if tools did not allow for the use of professional judgement, but a careful look at tools such as *Asset* or the Youth Justice Agency Assessment (YJAA) shows that this is not the case. As the scoring systems are based on practitioner judgement and the evidence boxes enable assessors to explain why certain factors do/do not affect a young person's behaviour, there is scope to take full account of social context and individual circumstances and to begin to tease out which factors may be the most significant in influencing anti-social or offending behaviour (YJB, 2008a). The evidence boxes are included in the design precisely to get away from the idea that particular factors predetermine outcomes. By requiring assessors to demonstrate and explain the significance of the range of factors identified, tools can actually help to promote individualisation and contextualisation.

Assessment tools can also help with the third stage of analysis, that is, *weighing the significance* of problems and strengths. You can use the format and questions of the tool to help with this, for example:

- *Asset*: the requirement to give a rating requires consideration of questions such as whether a factor is a direct or indirect contributor to the offending behaviour (YJB, 2006).
- SAVRY: the requirement to rate each item as low/moderate/high/critical requires consideration of the frequency and severity of each factor in a young person's life.

The type and style of questions varies between tools and none of them is perfect. However, they can be useful as prompts for your thinking about the significance of different aspects of a young person's life.

Synthesis

How do tools affect the putting together of discrete parts or elements to make a whole (Chapter Two)? Examples could include:

- the picture of a young person presented in an assessment tool takes account of character *and* context *and* time (Baker and Kelly, 2011);
- the assessment explains the situations that the young person experienced *and* his/her responses to those situations;
- the explanations provided relate to both immediate short-term issues *and* the longer-term perspective (Sheldrick, 1999).

Whereas assessment tools can be quite good at helping with analysis because of the way they break issues down into specific sections or domains, they tend to be weaker when it comes to recombining all the pieces of information to present a rounded picture. One of the limitations of tools which are structured in terms of domains/needs or risks is that '[t]he reduction of the offender's unique human story to a catalogue of components, however, offers little insight into the meaning of offending within the offender's life as a whole or into personal desires, goals and ambitions, strengths and solutions' (Hayles, 2006, p 69). This can be a particular issue with IT systems where information is stored in separate sections and, where this is the case, special effort needs to be made to draw different components and items of information together.

Despite these difficulties there are still ways of synthesising information, within the prescribed structure of tools, to help present a rounded picture. These could include:

- *Cross-referencing between comments/evidence boxes.* This may seem obvious, but research suggests that it doesn't always happen, because of a 'failure to adequately consider the interrelationship between differing identified needs' (Crawford, 2007, p 165). Similarly, in a study of *Asset* RoSH forms, examples were found of related items of information recorded in different sections of *Asset* but with little or no linkage between them (Baker, 2008). Where a tool provides space for free text or explanation, cross-referencing is required if information is to be effectively combined.
- *Cross-referencing between different components of the same tool.* The importance of cross-referencing applies also where a tool has distinct components; for example, information needs to be consistent across core *Asset* and RoSH.
- *Summaries/offence analysis.* There are other places within tools where you have scope to draw disparate items of information together. In *Asset* or the YJAA one place for doing this is the 'offence analysis' section. Although this comes near the beginning of the tool it doesn't necessarily need to be done first but can be done later on, after weighing up the meaning and significance of the full range of behaviours, risks and positive factors.
- *Cross-referencing between different assessment tools.* In some cases several assessment tools may be used, for example, *Asset* and AIM where a young person has committed sexual offences. It is important that relevant information from each tool is recorded in the other (in accordance with local data-sharing protocols).

Using assessment tools: conclusions, judgements and decisions

As noted in earlier chapters, assessors may sometimes be nervous of reaching conclusions, perhaps because of reluctance to summarise complex information into a single 'result' or because of a fear of giving the 'wrong answer' (the false negatives or positives discussed in Chapter Two). This section focuses on two aspects of tools which come into play at the judgement-making stage of the assessment process and which practitioners often find difficult: interpreting numerical scores and making classifications (for example, assigning a risk level). It is helpful to see scores and classifications as:

- *An opportunity to crystallise all the evidence and thinking that has gone into the assessment so far.* Without them, there might be a tendency to drift or to avoid the most difficult questions about what you think the young person might do in future – having to give a classification or rating can prompt sharper thinking.
- *Indicators, but not answers.* They can be useful guides to action but should not be seen as restricting practice.

- *Dynamic and able to be updated as new information comes to light.* This means that you make the judgement on the best available information at the time but know that you can revise it in future, as circumstances or information change (as discussed in Chapter Two).

Interpreting numerical scores

Knowing how to interpret numerical scores and predictions is an important part of using an assessment tool. However, there is sometimes a danger that, because numbers 'have an air of authority and objectivity' (Munro, 2004, p 881), practitioners and sentencers may attach too much certainty to them (Kemshall, 1996, 1998a). In contrast, some people may be tempted to disregard them because of a dislike of using numbers to capture something as complex as offending behaviour. Given that scores are often a feature of tools that practitioners have to work with, however, what might a balanced and defensible approach (avoiding these errors) look like?

Firstly, it is important to understand the distinction between groups of young people and individuals. Predictions from assessment tools relate to aggregated groups and are 'expressed in terms of statistical probability' (Kemshall, 2008, p 10); for example, a score might be said to indicate a 70% likelihood of reoffending within 12 months. What this means is that 70% of young people with a particular set of characteristics will reoffend within this time period, but it does not tell you whether a specific individual will be in the group that reoffends or will be one of the 30% who do not. That remains a question for practitioners to consider on a case-by-case basis.

Secondly, interpreting numerical scores also requires taking account of both a total score and its constituent parts. Two young people with a similar total score may require different types of intervention if different risks and needs have been identified (Schwalbe, 2007). This links back to the discussion in Chapter One about risk level not being the only determinant of interventions and the need to retain a focus on individual differences. A tool which provides ratings for particular sections or factors can assist with this.

Thirdly, there is value in comparing different types of scores, in particular those derived from actuarial methods and those from clinical judgements. This can be especially important in relation to those who might present a risk of serious harm to others. In a review of serious incidents involving adult offenders Ansbro (2010) highlights cases where the actuarial predictor was of less value and the clinical judgements about dynamic factors were of most significance and, vice versa, cases where the actuarial score should have been given more attention. 'Amalgamating the clinical, the actuarial, the static and the dynamic is a tricky business' (Ansbro, 2010, p 258) and there are no easy or neat rules about how to balance conflicting information. One key lesson for practice, however, would be that a comparison of actuarial and clinical indicators can provide a useful 'flag' to identify cases where particular care needs to be taken when making judgements. For staff in YOTs, this could mean comparing the static factors score with the dynamic scores from *Asset*. Where one is high and the other low, for example, this signals a need for further analysis and discussion with colleagues or for greater managerial oversight.

Fourthly, no assessment tool can be accurate in all cases and there will always be some cases that don't fit into the usual pattern. The scores from assessment profiles should be used as an indicator of likely future behaviour; but there will be occasions when professional judgement needs to override the result from an assessment profile, for example, because other information has come to light which was not captured in the initial assessment process. This is generally recognised by tool designers and policy makers (the Scaled Approach model (YJB, 2010b), for example, allows for professional override of the assessment tool scores).

Making classifications

An example of a risk classification can be found in the final section of the *Asset* – RoSH form, which asks for a classification of the risk of a young person causing serious harm to others as either low, medium, high, or very high. The SAVRY tool requires a similar classification in relation to violent offences, of low/moderate/high. These are not based on any numerical score but require the assessor to estimate *outcome* and *likelihood* in relation to future events (see Chapter Two).

In assessing possible harmful outcomes, it is important to be clear about the definitions used by a tool (Baker, 2010). The SAVRY manual provides a detailed definition of what is included in the term 'violence' (Borum et al, 2003), for example, and in RoSH the outcome being considered is serious harm to others, which is defined as: 'death or injury (either physical or psychological) which is life threatening and/or traumatic and from which recovery is expected to be difficult, impossible or incomplete' (YJB, 2006, p 26). Once the definitions have been established, the following need to be considered:

- *What is the timescale under consideration?* The classification cannot capture the risk of a young person committing a murder in 10 years' time, for example, so the timescale will need to be more defined; for example, the period of statutory supervision or the next 12 months.
- *Within this timescale, what could (reasonably) happen?* It is important to think about a range of outcomes or scenarios (although it will not generally be helpful or possible to spend time on considering every remote possibility) (Kemshall et al, 2007; RMA, 2007b).
- *How much harm would be caused by this behaviour/these offences?* For a very informative and more detailed account of all the factors to take into consideration when assessing outcome and likelihood, see Carson and Bain (2008).

In relation to judging likelihood it is again important to be clear about definitions of terms such as low, medium and high (Babchishin and Hanson, 2009). For assessing the likelihood of events occurring, consider:

- What is the evidence from research/actuarial data about the frequency of these events occurring?
- What are the particular factors in this case that might make the behaviour more or less likely to occur?
- What opportunities does s/he have for committing these offences (Kemshall, 1998b; 2003)? For example:
  - Is he/she likely to find him/herself in situations (for example fights) where this could occur?
  - Would he/she commit the behaviour if an opportunity arose?
  - Is he/she actively trying to find/create opportunities for offending (for example grooming or instigating violence)?

The requirement in a tool to provide a risk classification should therefore be an opportunity to consider questions such as these in detail. It is never possible to be totally sure of what a young person will do in future, but a rigorous approach to thinking about outcome and likelihood helps to ensure that decisions taken on the basis of the classification judgement are clearly thought through.

Activity: Reviewing tools 2

It is very important that the distinction between the likelihood of further offending and its potential outcome is clear. This activity suggests that you review completed assessments so as to decide if that distinction has been held to and clearly articulated.

- Has the assessor made clear both how likely the offender is to reoffend and the range of potential outcomes that may follow?
- Has the evidence for both of those judgements been made clear?
- Have any scores been interpreted correctly?

Thinking again about assessment tools

Now that we have looked in some detail at how tools can be used to support the assessment and planning process, the chapter concludes with a wider reconsideration of how tools are perceived and used in practice.

How we perceive tools

How we think about tools will affect how they are used. The value of metaphor in helping to illuminate practice has been noted throughout the book and in Chapter One, for example, we considered some possible metaphors for the assessment process – research, biography, journey and construction. Here we think more specifically about some of the different ways in which practitioners may conceptualise assessment tools. Common perceptions include seeing a tool as (Baker and Wilkinson, 2011):

- *Calculator:* I tick the boxes, add up the numbers and it gives me the 'correct' answer.
- *Safety net:* If things go wrong I will be protected from the 'fall-out' because I used the designated tool.
- *Protective body armour:* For back-covering.

The limitations of these examples are that they focus either on finding a right answer or on protecting the reputation of the practitioner and organisation rather than on understanding a young person's behaviour.

Reflection

Are you aware of sometimes using one or more of the above metaphors?

Can you identify other, more helpful metaphors that might support good practice?

To further illustrate the impact that perceptions can have, think about the assessment tool you use most regularly and consider the difference between seeing it as a map or as a sat-nav. As Baker and Wilkinson explain:

> If it's a map, then it will be seen as providing guidance and important cues, but the responsibility for interpreting it, and for choosing which of the possible routes available to use, rests with the traveller. In the case of a sat-nav, there is typically less use of knowledge and fewer choices to make because it's more a case of following the instructions. You may get to the same destination but may not understand how you got there, may not have developed an awareness of landmarks on the route or know how to do it again if you didn't have the sat-nav. (Baker and Wilkinson, 2011)

Highly structured or prescriptive approaches can still be useful sometimes, of course, but over-reliance on them can result in a failure to develop other skills. In thinking about risk-assessment tools, the authors would want to argue that it is more helpful to see them as maps rather than sat-navs, because this places the emphasis more on applying knowledge, rather than just complying with instructions. As this example illustrates, knowing how you conceptualise the task can help you to understand your use of tools. Ideally, the focus should be on ways of thinking that promote understanding and require the application of skills.

Keeping the focus on decision making

Over time, confusion can sometimes build up regarding the purpose of an assessment tool or there may be competing views within an organisation over what the main priorities should be. The implementation of 'risk technologies', such as assessment tools, is rarely straightforward and what happens in real life may not be quite what policy makers or senior managers expected (Horlick-Jones, 2005; Kemshall, 2010). Tensions can arise, for example, if practitioners feel that the role of tools in providing data for performance monitoring has become more important than the contribution they can make to decision making (Robinson, 2002; Gillingham and Humphreys, 2009). As the discussions in this and earlier chapters have highlighted, tools can have a variety of functions, but the authors hold the view that the main purpose of tools should be to assist with individual case-level decision making and that the other uses (in relation to collating aggregate data, for example) should be secondary. It is important to be aware of the balance of priorities within any team or organisation so that managers and practitioners can take steps to help ensure that the focus remains on decision making.

Activity: Reviewing tools 3

Think about the tool you use most regularly and use the table below to review:

1   How your current approach to using the tool helps/hinders the different aspects of the assessment process.
2   What you/your team can do to use tools more effectively.

Aspects of assessment	Current use of tool	Future/what could change?
Collecting information		
Recording information		
Understanding behaviour		
Explaining behaviour		
Making judgements		
Sharing information		

Professionalism requires taking responsibility for how you use assessment tools and applying them in ways that make the most of their strengths and mitigate their limitations. Chapter Nine will also look at some of the ways in which organisations can support the appropriate implementation and use of tools. There will be some influences on practice that you cannot change directly, for example, the design of the tools or of the IT system. But this need not mean being passive about these issues. There may be opportunities to request changes or to give feedback to tool and system designers, and it is important to be pro-active in seeking out or taking advantage of any such possibilities.

Conclusion

This chapter has emphasised the need to see standardised assessment processes and frameworks as 'tools' to assist practice. All such tools have strengths and limitations and none will be perfect or appropriate for use in all cases. But this does not mean that they have no value:

> Their limitations however, do not provide an excuse for avoiding their use; indeed the opposite is the case. They provide all the reasons why they must be used critically, rigorously and transparently. The case for using them critically is compelling to add to professional competence and innovation but not to detract from or replace practitioner judgement. (Whyte, 2009, p 85)

Chapters Five and Six go on to look at how assessments are used when preparing plans and reports. Chapter Eight looks more at some of the skills that can enable assessors to use assessment frameworks as tools to help in the decision-making process.

Notes
[1] For details of tools used in other jurisdictions, see for example Hoge and Andrews (1996; 2010).

[2] It should be noted, however, that RATED may provide only a partial picture, as it focuses on measures of statistical validity and reliability, but pays less attention to other relevant issues such as practitioners' views about tools.

FIVE

Planning interventions

[T]he aim of assessment is to guide action. (Reder et al, 1993, p 83)

Introduction

Good assessments should be at the heart of achieving positive outcomes in youth justice, by guiding plans and the resulting interventions. Why is it, then, that the contents of intervention plans are so often found to have weak links with the assessments that precede them (Audit Commission, 2004; YJB, 2008a; HMIP, 2009a)?

The reasons are likely to be complex, as the discussion of decision making in Chapter Two suggests. Individual assessors may fall into the trap of 'tunnel vision ... when professionals get into the habit of treating all cases with a fixed pattern of response' (Munro, 2008a, p 103). Working practices and time limits are also likely to make a difference, if they restrict the depth and quality of the initial assessment (Sutherland, 2009a). Limited resources, and the difficulty of influencing some of the circumstances of young people's lives, will also impact on the choices made. Plans made in the secure estate may focus too much on what is available in the institution and not enough on planning for the young person's return to the community. All of these influences may foster an approach to planning based on pragmatic choices that suit the worker, or the organisation, rather than planning based on understanding of an individual young person.

Such influences may also make it less likely that the young person will be at the heart of the planning process: it is all too easy to plan *for* a young person, rather than *with* them. The chaotic and quickly changing nature of some young people's lives will make any structured approach more difficult. Involving young people in a planned way is important, however, for delivering clear and specific interventions that they can 'buy into'.

Reflection

Compare the amount of time and effort that you, your team or organisation give to:

- assessment
- planning interventions.

Is the young person involved equally in both?

Are these the right balances? Why/why not?

Planning for positive outcomes

In a nutshell, the planning process has to draw on assessments to decide upon:

- the intensity of interventions
- their content
- how those interventions should be delivered.

The planning process has to take into account the legal basis for action, reflecting the fact that young people will be subject to a variety of (sometimes statutory) requirements. There will be significant differences between planning for prevention or pre-court interventions as compared to interventions for young people subject to community penalties, for example, as the latter involve a greater degree of compulsion. Others will be subject to specific requirements, such as bail supervision and support. Some will receive custodial penalties and plans will have to be made to deliver services in custody, as well as on release (YJB, 2010d). The length of time the young person will be involved with youth justice will vary, as will the extent to which other organisations are involved in a young person's life. Whatever the case type, stage or context, however, plans should all be geared towards achieving the core purposes of assessment in youth justice (see Chapter One), as explored in the following sections.

Preventing offending

The principles of RNR (as outlined in Chapter One) have led to a focus in youth justice on evidence-based risk factors, used to help target interventions at young people presenting the highest likelihood of reoffending (Andrews et al, 1990; YJB, 2008a). The risk principle means that plans for young people with a higher likelihood of reoffending should include more contact time, and potentially a greater range of interventions, than plans for young people with a lower likelihood of recidivism (Andrews and Dowden, 2006). The RNR model also suggests that the content of plans should address those factors most strongly linked to offending behaviour and interventions should reflect the specific ways in which different factors affect a particular young person (Wikström and Treiber, 2008). In addition, there should be a consideration of responsivity and *how* interventions should best be delivered. In recent years practice development has tended to pay insufficient attention to this (Farrall and Maruna, 2004; McGuire, 2004; McNeill et al, 2005; Bonta et al, 2008), but the more recent and developing focus on this aspect of service delivery has, however, recognised the importance of staff skills and interpersonal relationships for supporting change (Raynor, 2004; Burnett, 2004; Mason and Prior, 2008).

It also matters that we understand how young people move out of an involvement with offending. This process of desistance is more than simply the removal of risk factors, as the RNR approach might suggest. Instead, 'current research suggests that the initiation into crime and the conversion out of crime are dissimilar experiences' (Serin and Lloyd, 2009, p 355). Increasingly, for example, there is support for the importance of developing resilience and protective factors, as well as addressing risk (Maruna, 2000; Burnett, 2000; Farrall, 2004; McNeill, 2006, 2009a). Strengths-based approaches that support the development of pro-social self-concepts and community investment in rehabilitation should be built into the range of services on offer (Burnett and Maruna, 2006).

Supporting well-being and positive development

Although reducing reoffending is a priority for youth justice, criminal justice agencies also have a responsibility for safeguarding and promoting the well-being of the young people with whom they work (Whyte, 2004; YJB, 2010d). Many young people will be at risk, as well as likely to reoffend (Boswell, 1996). Writing in the Scottish context, McGhee and Waterhouse suggest that children categorised as 'welfare' or 'justice' have 'many similarities in their underlying circumstances' (2007, p 108). Many (as noted in Chapter Three) will experience obstacles to healthy development from their own families, because of structural disadvantages or from experiences of racism. Young women who offend may be subject to a gendered experience of disadvantage; gendered and racialised experiences may also then be mirrored in young people's experiences as they encounter criminal justice agencies (Bowling and Phillips, 2002; Burman and Batchelor, 2009; Sharpe and Gelsthorpe, 2009; J. Williams, 2009).

Workers in criminal justice have a responsibility for 'taking all reasonable action to keep to a minimum the risk of a child or a young person coming to harm' (HMIP, 2009b) and should be clear about roles and responsibilities between agencies and the procedures that must be followed, for example in relation to safeguarding (DCSF, 2010b). If a specific risk to a young person, for example a serious substance misuse problem, is also related to offending, then it should be part of the intervention plan. This does not mean that all such risks to young people should be directly addressed in a criminal justice context, however, as young people should also receive services from other agencies (children's services and health services, for example).

Protecting young people at risk is important on ethical grounds. All young people experiencing significant need should feel confident that agencies involved with them take those needs seriously and, if not able to intervene themselves, will help them to access provision from others. Young people's welfare is also important for successful criminal justice interventions, as a young person facing personal difficulties is likely to find it harder to engage successfully with change programmes. The process of helping young people meet wider needs is not easy, with resource limitations and inter-agency relationships sometimes meaning that services are not readily available (Fielder et al, 2008), and these issues are considered further in Chapter Seven.

There are particular considerations in relation to young people in the secure estate. They have to be protected from bullying or abusive behaviour and, given the impact of the experience of custody, they have to be protected from self-harm and suicide. Planning for children in the secure estate will explicitly address vulnerabilities, but this is an issue beyond just individual plans, as it affects practice more generally, for example influencing policy about the use of physical restraint (YJB, 2008b). While young people are in establishments, planning should also take into account difficulties they may face on their return to communities and how they might best be helped to prepare.

Planning for young people who are experiencing, and presenting, a range of challenges is complex partly because '[t]he relationship between risk, resilience and vulnerability needs to be better explicated and developed into more effective models' (Titterton, 2011). Boeck and Fleming also remind us that

> many young people seen as 'at risk' quite often tend to be 'risk averse', in the sense they can be unwilling or unable to take the risk of leaving their present situation, their immediate networks of family and friends and the locale where they live. Being able to take actions to loosen such ties can be crucial for 'pathways out of crime'. (Boeck and Fleming, 2011)

This suggests a need to sometimes take positive risks in order to achieve better outcomes for young people and reductions in offending.

Reflection

In your experience of youth justice, to what extent do the plans made for young people:

- adjust the intensity of interventions to match the likelihood of reoffending?
- protect young people who are 'at risk'?
- take appropriate positive risks to help young people develop resilience?

Planning for the delivery of interventions

> [T]he causes of a young person's criminal activity are a complex network of interacting variables of the young person's characteristics and circumstances. (Hoge and Andrews, 2002, p 1)

Many young people will be assessed as having risk factors in a number of areas, some individual, for example thinking skills and impulsivity, and others contextual, for example family and peers. McGuire (2002) points out that, given the complexity of factors influencing offending, multi-modal plans containing a number of different components will be needed. It will not be possible to address all the potential risk factors for many young people and attempts to do so might overwhelm and confuse, so plans have to be based on a selection of those areas most likely to bring about the desired reduction in offending.

In selecting areas for intervention, Wikström (2007) draws our attention to the importance not just of identifying risk factors, but of developing hypotheses about which of them are directly, or indirectly, influencing offending behaviour and the causal processes that mediate that influence. The importance of an assessment that goes beyond simply noting the existence of relevant factors, and that develops working hypotheses about how they make a difference to offending, has already been fully acknowledged in this book (for example in Chapters One and Two). Plans therefore need to address not just the factors themselves but the ways in which they impact on the offending.

While there may be a wide range of factors associated with offending (both immediate and longer term) there may be smaller numbers of causal processes. These processes lie in the interactions between individual characteristics and experiences, the context in which the offending behaviour takes place, and the nature of that offending. The model illustrated in Figure 5.1 summarises the clusters of risk factors included in the *Asset* assessment tool. It is included here not to represent that particular tool, but to illustrate that risk factors don't operate alone, or in any straightforward linear way. All of the risk factors in the model have a potential impact on offending behaviour – sometimes direct, as suggested by

Figure 5.1: Direct and indirect influences of behaviour

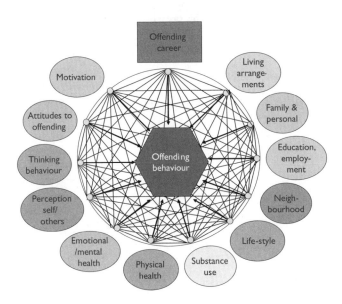

Source: Adapted with permission from original material produced by Colin Roberts

the bold arrows. However, risk factors also influence offending indirectly, through their relationships with each other, as suggested by the network of connections running between them.

The following examples illustrate this.

> **Michael**: Relationships with pro-offending peers have developed slowly, largely because of the area in which he lives, but now provide offending opportunities and social pressure to offend and are having a growing influence on his pro-offending attitudes and beliefs. Michael's family is not supportive of offending behaviour.
>
> **Carl**: For Carl, family life and values have influenced pro-offending beliefs and attitudes from an early age and these have encouraged him to seek out pro-offending peers. His attitudes to offending, which have their roots in his family situation, are now reinforced by those peers. As well as offending with peers, he also offends alone and with family members.

In Figure 5.2 lines have been drawn for Carl to suggest connections between risk factors and between those factors and offending behaviour. A similar diagram completed for Michael would show a somewhat different pattern of connections.

Figure 5.2: From assessment to planning

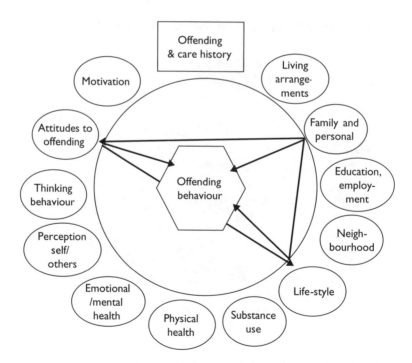

Source: Adapted with permission from original material produced by Colin Roberts

Both young people would have their peer relationships (life-style) as a risk factor and both view offending differently from young people who don't offend (attitudes to offending). The different patterns of interactions suggest different interventions, however. Michael may be best helped by positive approaches that move him away from those peers to form more pro-social relationships, and will have family support to draw on. He may need help with attitudes, but this might be, at least partly, achieved through those positive contacts. Carl is likely to need a more intensive change programme in order to work through more entrenched attitudes to offending and, given the family influence, significant family-based interventions may also be required. Positive supports for building pro-social relationships could still be given, but would require a lot more support and help if they were to succeed.

An understanding of risk factors and causal processes helps to select targets but, as the above example suggests, should also help to decide on how those targets are addressed. Wherever possible, selected change programmes should be evidence based, adopting methods found to be effective, which currently include cognitive behavioural and multi-systemic interventions (Goldstein, 1999; Utting and Vennard, 2000; Graham, 2004; Wikström and Treiber, 2008). Programmes should draw on evidence about pro-social modelling and developing resilience (Trotter, 2006; NCH, 2007). The evidence base is, however, partial and incomplete. Where evidence exists it should be used, but an overly narrow focus on only those interventions that have the highest level of validation could artificially restrict service provision (see Chapter Three). It is also important, therefore, to base choices of intervention in well-founded theory, on an understanding of the reasons for the offending behaviour and on an appreciation of the young person's situation. Two of the authors have experience of design and delivery of cognitive behavioural interventions with individual young people. It is our experience that one of the most helpful approaches is to link this work to the realities of the young person's circumstances. Cognitive behavioural work with Michael, for example, might be best targeted towards helping him identify and strengthen his positive beliefs, rather than focusing on cognitive deficits. He could also be helped to strengthen social skills, so as to support making good relationships with others.

Activity

It is important that interventions address not just risk factors, but how they interact with each other and influence offending. Draw out a rough copy of the diagram above and use it to track some key influences for a specific young person. Then think about the intervention plan in place for that young person.

- How well does that plan match the connections on your diagram?
- Is the plan evidence based and/or based on a clear theory of change?

Building in pathways out of offending

If offending is understood through the metaphor of a journey, then, as well as understanding the route into offending, the pathway out is also central (France and Homel, 2006; France et al, 2010). Mapping out and navigating such pathways requires the involvement of the young person (and their parents/carers where appropriate) and a focus on positive future goals. Plans will also need to take into account both individual and situational risk factors; the social context is part of the explanation for offending, but also the setting within which any change will have to occur (McNeill, 2006; 2009c).

The active engagement of the young person

Guidance on planning and writing intervention plans usually includes the SMART acronym, and goals set with young people do need to be Specific, Measurable, Achievable, Realistic and Time bound (YJB, 2010c). Even SMART targets that have considered links with offending and developed plans accordingly will not, however, achieve their aims if the young person is not motivated to engage. Active engagement means that young people are helped to make changes for themselves, to discover and develop their own abilities. At a very basic level they have to be able to understand the language of the plan and what it is seeking to achieve. They should also be encouraged to play an active part in agreeing the content.

Chambers et al (2008) point out that problematic patterns of thinking linked to offending may also have an impact on the individual's readiness to change. For example, violent offenders tend to think that others are hostile in their intentions towards them. Such thinking will make a difference to how young people engage, as they are more likely to be suspicious of others' motives, including those of practitioners. As already discussed, young people involved with youth justice will also often be experiencing a range of other difficulties, which will take up their energy and that of the worker and make engagement more difficult (Mason and Prior, 2008).

Plans have to match the reality of the young person's life and experiences. Levels of literacy and numeracy need to be taken into account (The Communication Trust, 2009). Plans for young women should be both gender specific and gender sensitive (Williams, 2009). While girls and boys who offend may have similar risk factors, the ways in which they impact on offending may be different and their pathways out of offending may also be different (McIvor et al, 2004). A gender-specific plan will have taken account of those different processes, for example the impact of family difficulties on young women's early assumption of parental responsibilities, or engagement in sexual activity as a means of survival. Styles of delivery should also differ. There is, for example, some evidence that young women respond better to processes that acknowledge relationships; gender-sensitive programmes will build those differences in (Burman and Batchelor, 2009).

'Young people *and their families/carers* contribute to the assessment process' (Scottish Government, 2008, p 26, emphasis added). The young person's family, if able to do so, should also be involved with interventions; sometimes, as subjects of orders themselves, through parenting interventions, but more usually as active participants in supporting the young person to change (YJB, 2008a).

The following activity is the first of a series of boxes reviewing intervention plans, based on the issues raised in this chapter.

Activity: Reviewing an intervention plan I

- Is the plan relevant to that young person, the particular risks they pose and their circumstances? Or is it an 'off the peg' plan, just like many others produced?
- Has the young person been asked to sign up to a plan already written, or have they genuinely been helped to make suggestions about and develop the content?
- Is the language in this plan appropriate to the age and abilities of the young person and will they be able to understand it?
- Has professional terminology been translated? For example, has 'developing victim empathy' become 'understanding how my offences hurt other people'?

Good lives, desistance and building strengths

The 'Good Lives Model' (GLM) was introduced in Chapter One, and this section now builds on that discussion to consider the implications of the model for intervention planning in more detail. The model is useful in asking the assessor to consider a young person's values and strengths, as well as risk factors. It suggests that people who offend are, like all of us, seeking to achieve primary human goods (Ward, 2002; Ward and Stewart, 2003; Ward and Maruna, 2007). Examples of such goods would include:

- seeking a sense of belonging
- creativity
- gaining knowledge and skills
- achieving physical and mental health
- a secure environment in which you can exercise control.

We pursue secondary goals – academic achievements, friendships, for example – as means to achieving these primary goods. Individuals who offend, however, find it hard to achieve some or all of these goods through pro-social means because of individual characteristics and/or because of the nature of their environment. They may therefore pursue secondary goals that are problematic. For example, a young person may want to feel that they belong and have good relationships, but family and school-based experiences have made it difficult for them to do so. They may instead choose to achieve a sense of relatedness through involvement in groups of offenders, including gang-related activity (Smith and Bradshaw,

2005). Similarly, rather than developing skills through education and training, they may feel competent in terms of offending-related skills, such as being able to win a fight or fence stolen goods. The GLM suggests that they should be helped instead to achieve primary goods through pro-social secondary goals, for example, achieving skills and physical health through involvement in a sports team. It suggests a future-oriented approach with a focus on building strengths and capabilities and is supportive of motivation to change in that the offender is working towards goals relevant and rewarding to them.

The RNR approach remains important; it is developed rather than replaced through Good Lives and other strength-based approaches, which have their own limitations (Kemshall, 2008a). However, in contrast to a more deficit-focused approach implied by an exclusively risk factor focus, the implications of the GLM would be that intervention planning therefore needs to draw on the young person's hopes and to help them move towards realising desired goals pro-socially (McNeill and Weaver, 2010). Risk factors still have to be the targets for change, but how change is pursued may be different. Educational problems linked to offending should be the target for intervention as a significant risk factor, but Good Lives would emphasise finding out from the young person what they wanted to achieve in education and agreeing routes that help them.

Like the work around desistance, this focus on achieving desired goods suggests positive changes, not just in young people but also in their environment (McNeill, 2009b). Positive pro-social environments and the development of social capital are necessary to engage motivation and to support young people in changing (Boeck, 2009). Burrowes and Needs identify a range of psychological factors that might affect motivation, but conclude by recognising the impact of the 'realities of change', that is, the situational constraints on those personal processes (Burrowes and Needs, 2009, p 46). Plans should therefore concentrate on developing both human and social capital. In other words, young people need human capital, such as pro-social skills, beliefs and capacities, and they also need the opportunities to enable them to make the best use of those capacities. These opportunities constitute social capital, and might include the chance to engage in work or training, to develop leisure activities and to have access to a set of pro-social relationships (McNeill, 2004; Barry, 2006; Boeck, Fleming and Kemshall, 2006). The need for both of these was illustrated in the discussions of Michael and Carl earlier in the chapter.

Setting approach goals

Changing to a non-offending way of achieving goals in life, particularly for persistent offenders, entails a significant effort. Plans have to maximise the supports for young people in making those efforts. The characteristics and skills of workers more likely to achieve engagement and a positive focus are relevant throughout assessment and planning and include reinforcement, problem solving and being interested in the young person's well-being (discussed further in Chapter Eight).

Plans need to build in attention to developing the young person's self-belief and sense of agency, that is, the sense that they are able to take action to make changes in their lives.

The kinds of goals young people work towards are important, with 'approach' rather than 'avoidance' goals being most appropriate (Beech and Mann, 2002; Barnett and Mann, 2010). An approach goal is positive and active and involves working towards something, whereas an avoidance goal is about stopping or avoiding, which is more negative and passive in focus. For example:

- An avoidance goal is 'I am not going to eat chocolate biscuits when I get in from work'.
- An approach goal would be 'I am going to eat at least two pieces of fruit when I get home, before I eat anything else'.

The avoidance goal means that even if you eat no biscuits for a week, the day you have a single biscuit you have failed and you haven't learned anything as a result of your efforts. The approach goal means that, even if sometimes you still have a biscuit, you are likely to eat fewer than previously and you have acquired a new and positive behaviour as a fruit eater. Far more opportunities for success are built in and you have learned something as a result of your efforts.

Activity: Reviewing an intervention plan 2

- ■ Does the plan include the development of both human and social capital?
- ■ Do interactions with the young person during the assessment and planning process model an optimistic, problem-solving approach?
- ■ Does the plan focus on positive-approach goals that actively involve the young person and focus on what they want to achieve in life?

Practical, relevant, attainable plans

Having analysed the different factors influencing behaviour and worked with a young person to establish relevant pathways out of offending, the next challenge is to produce a plan that adopts appropriate methods for delivering the required interventions. Plans have to be manageable and contain within them opportunities for the young person to experience success and to make progress. Practitioners should be realistic about the obstacles some young people face, and be alert to even small opportunities that might support desistance (Farrow et al, 2007).

Choosing methods of delivery

From the outset, the planning process should keep a focus on how interventions should be delivered. For example, is a group-work programme the most appropriate method for a particular young person? A danger is that choices about methods are pragmatic decisions about the availability of groups, or the need to make full use of a particular resource. A decision about group-work provision should instead take into account a range of considerations, such as the composition of the group and the potential for more experienced offenders to adversely influence others. Practicalities of attendance are important, for example gang-related 'postcode' issues that make some young people reluctant to enter certain neighbourhoods. In rural areas practical difficulties around travel may be significant. Some young people may 'hide' in the group from the personal implications of the work done. On the other hand, the group experience may offer richer opportunities for learning and deliver a more planned and focused approach. Work on a one-to-one basis may be less likely to be planned and can more easily fall into the trap of always responding reactively to what the young person brings with them. So in an ideal world one-to-one provision should also not necessarily be a default choice, but should equally be weighed up for its advantages and disadvantages.

Writing an achievable plan

The intervention plan also has to be realistic and achievable. Of course the content of the plan will have been influenced by the decisions of others, the courts, the children's hearings and youth offender panels. In the context of the YRO there are a number of possible requirements (YJB, 2010a) and those requirements may be court ordered, rather than arising from the content of the assessment. A worker might be in the position of having to include activities not of their choice (Jones and Roberts, 2006). Perhaps equally likely, as the experience of similar orders with adult offenders suggests, some of the possibilities will be under-used, as workers over-rely on easily available and familiar resources (Mair et al, 2007).

Another key challenge of a multi-modal approach is that, for some young people, the range of interventions may involve them in relationships with several service providers. Agencies may share responsibility for a young person, for example looked-after children placed in the secure estate. Young people posing a high risk of harm to others will be subject to particular requirements, including MAPPA (Baker and Sutherland, 2009b), which will require the involvement of other services in the planning processes (see Chapter Seven).

Taking account of all of the above, the intervention plan therefore has to take into account what is realistic for a young person to manage:

- Interventions don't always stand alone and may be in a dependent relationship to each other: there can be causes of causes, or indirect patterns of effect on offending behaviour (Wikström and Sampson, 2006). If, for example, a young person's lack of social skills and aggressive beliefs are fundamental to other difficulties, there is little point in getting them a training place without either first, or alongside, also addressing these skills and beliefs.
- The sequencing of interventions should be considered, so as to ensure that young people are not overloaded or confused, or that demands aren't being made of them which they are not in a position to meet.

- Other plans may be in place – such as a plan for a looked–after child, plans within education, or MAPPA risk management plans, and care will have to be taken to ensure that those plans don't contradict each other.
- For young people in custody, plans for work to be done during the sentence should be developed with attention to their eventual return to the community. For some young people the intensity of attention and support provided in a secure children's home or secure training centre contrasts sharply with their lives outside and this undermines attempts to continue progress. Links between community and custody are therefore vital from the outset.

Structural inequalities and patterns of disadvantage are important (Webster et al, 2006). They are beyond the scope of this book, just as they are beyond the scope of an individual plan, but addressing those wider issues should not be forgotten. Policy has tended to place the responsibility for change on the individual young person, paying less attention to structural influences, but these influences can have a powerful effect on young people's behaviour: 'it is difficult for young people to exercise responsibility as "active citizens" if they are fatalistic about their future' (Kemshall, 2008b, p 30). Plans have to take into account the structural and societal obstacles young people may encounter in seeking to make changes. Planning for reintegration into the community following a custodial sentence (YJB, 2010d), for example, will involve work with the individual young person, but also attention to the circumstances to which they will return.

Coordinating and sequencing interventions appropriately may be quite demanding in terms of systems and processes. There is a danger of a complex case management process 'devaluing face-to-face contact with the individual' (Farrow et al, 2007, p 211). The role of the case manager can help to ensure that the young person can make their way successfully through the complexities of the order (Holt, 2000 and 2002). Plans that support this will: be clear about what they and the young person are seeking to achieve; identify priorities; and build in time with a consistent figure or figures who can develop working alliances with a young person (Bordin, 1979; McNeill et al, 2005).

Activity: Reviewing an intervention plan 3

- Does this plan set out a reasonable set of demands? Has time been spent to establish with the young person any obstacles that might get in the way of their compliance, and have strategies to help overcome these barriers been identified?
- Do the planned interventions build on each other and avoid clashes and confusion?
- Has time been taken to find out from the young person what they like and dislike and what methods of work are more likely to engage them?
- Have the individual characteristics of the young person been taken into account? Is the plan culturally sensitive and aware of the influence of gender?

Looking back at all of the activity boxes, a plan that follows these principles is more likely to achieve compliance and hoped-for outcomes.

Involuntary clients

Young people involved with the criminal justice system are 'involuntary clients' (Trotter, 2006), and this affects their relationship with service providers and the nature of the planning that has to take place. It is very important that young people are clear about expectations and boundaries and the penalties for non-compliance, and that practitioners help them to distinguish between what is negotiable and what is laid down by legal requirements (Mason and Prior, 2008). Part of the challenge in effective planning with young people is achieving all of this while at the same time encouraging an active, engaged relationship. It brings home, perhaps more than any other aspect of this discussion, that planning is not a just a paper (or computer-based) exercise, but an interaction between worker and young person that needs to be skilfully managed. Practice needs to engage and motivate reluctant young people and 'the qualities and skills of workers remain vital in developing the relationships within which such magical processes occur' (McNeill and Batchelor, 2002, p 40).

The needs of individuals should be met, while delivering services that are realistic in their resource requirements and experienced as consistent by young people. This is not just an individual responsibility, but requires a 'whole system' approach (Hobbs and Hook, 2001). The principles of pro-social modelling (Cherry, 2006; Trotter, 2006) emphasise the importance of communicating consistent messages. For example, if practitioners in a youth justice team take very different attitudes to breach decisions, it will be harder to help young people to develop trust in the fairness of the system. If young people in secure settings see staff behaving inconsistently in implementing rules, it will make them more likely to learn lessons in 'playing the system', rather than learn that living within fair rules can be a good thing. It is important to recognise therefore that inconsistency can undermine the effectiveness of individual plans (Raynor and Vanstone, 1996).

Risk of serious harm to others

Some young people will have been assessed as posing a risk of serious harm to others, and in such cases greater attention needs to be paid to measures to control their behaviour and to victim protection. For practitioners using the *Asset* assessment tool, there is a requirement to complete a risk management plan for these young people which focuses on 'internal' and 'external' controls of risk (Wilkinson and Baker, 2005; YJB, 2006). Others sometimes refer to the alternative terms of 'constructive' and 'restrictive' measures (HMIP, 2009b). What both mean is that, when addressing risk of serious harm to others, it will be important to consider measures such as monitoring the young person's behaviour and progress, tagging, curfew conditions in licences, and orders that restrict freedom of movement (Kemshall et al, 2007). These external controls help to manage risk and to protect potential victims, but on their own they are unlikely to help the young person make the changes needed to reduce risk. They need to be supplemented by the constructive approaches discussed throughout this chapter and will include, for example, change programmes designed to address attitudes and beliefs supportive of harmful behaviour.

When working with young people who pose a high risk of harm to others, public protection has to be balanced with work helping the young person to change. The Good Lives Model, for example, has been used in work with high-risk-of-harm offenders, including adult sex offenders (Barnett and Mann, 2010). However, it is important that this does not 'obscure attention to risks' and that it is 'combined with a risk management approach' (Kemshall, 2008a, p 96). One practical approach to achieving a balance and to allowing strengths-based approaches to be used with high-risk-of-harm offenders was identified by Wood and Kemshall (2007). Behavioural contracts allowed offenders to take up opportunities in the community and to take responsibility for self-risk management. An example of a contract used for a young person convicted of a sexual offence is as follows:

- I will ensure I attend college only on the specific days stated on my timetable.
- If I am unable to attend college for any reason I will contact the college to inform them of this.
- I will ensure that I am never alone with young people under the age of 16 years; this includes breaks and lunch times.
- I will ensure I do not access the internet using a college computer or a fellow student's computer.
- I accept that certain people within the college will need to be aware of this contract and this will be on a 'need to know basis'. I understand that I will be aware of the people who are given this information and the reason why they need to know this information.
- I understand that if these conditions are broken the college will have no alternative but to prohibit me from attending and will have the responsibility to report this to my probation officer.

Source: This example was provided by Durham and Teesside Probation Trust for training and teaching purposes and reproduced from MAPPA training material provided to the authors by Kemshall.

Change efforts should, of course, still be directed towards those aspects of the young person's situation that have an effect on the harmful behaviour. The above contract would not stand alone; the young person would also be engaged in therapeutic approaches and additional monitoring might be taking place. However, it would allow positive, strengths-based goals to be included in the intervention plan, while retaining a clear focus on public protection.

Activity

Look at the plans in place for a young person assessed as posing a risk of serious harm to others.

■ List, in the table below, constructive and restrictive measures in the plan.
■ Then write down how each of those measures is intended to address risk of serious harm to others.
■ Consider the overall balance of the plan and whether the two kinds of measure are used effectively to manage risk.

Internal/constructive measures		External/restrictive measures	
Measure in plan	How does it addresses risk?	Measure in plan	How does it address risk?

Review and reflection

Planned approaches also support evaluation and the gathering of more information about what makes a difference in young people's lives, both individually and on a larger scale. A first step in an evaluative approach, discussed in more detail in Chapter Three, is the regularity of review, informed by national standards, but also decided upon on a case-by-case basis. Some cases will need more frequent updating, if for example the young person's life is very unstable, or if significant change occurs. Review is essential, as departures from the plan need to be monitored and understood so that it can be brought back on track, or if necessary a new plan agreed (McGuire, 2004). This makes a difference to compliance and enabling ongoing attention to barriers for change; it allows for necessary enforcement; and it is essential for risk management, where issues of harm to others are concerned.

Review is also important for the young person and their family. Bottoms et al point out that often 'progression is faltering, hesitant and oscillating' (2004, p 383). If the plan is seeking positive change and using approach goals to help a young person acquire different understandings and learn new skills, then it is important to create opportunities for them to reflect on their progress, consolidate their learning and receive praise for positive changes they have made (Callahan et al, 2009). Review also assists practitioners and agencies to evidence work that has taken place and to learn from successes and failures. This process is considered in more depth in Chapter Nine. It is important that the review focuses not just on the young person's behaviour and learning but on the services that have been delivered and the agency's success, or otherwise, in supporting change. This is particularly relevant for those young people whose offending is prolific and who have a lengthy involvement with criminal justice. Persistence and 'stickability' are likely to be key characteristics of an effective practitioner, that is to say, not giving up hope and continuing to seek avenues that might produce change. Such a practitioner will take every chance to help the young person and to support them in discovering their own ability to bring about change.

Reflection

- How do you (or others that you supervise or teach) actively involve young people in reviewing their experiences and achievements in working with youth justice staff?
- How might this aspect of practice be further developed?

Conclusion

It is important that there is a clear relationship between assessments, goals set and the methods used to deliver those goals; any plan should be, as far as possible, delivered as planned (McGuire, 2002). Every stage should be supported by clear theory and, where available, an explicit evidence base (Wikström and Treiber, 2008). This chapter is suggesting that plans should be rooted in a structured assessment of risk factors, both individual and situational, with explicit hypotheses about their influence on offending. It should also draw on theories of desistance and of supporting 'good lives' with a positive, future-oriented approach, addressing barriers to change and building human and social capital. Public protection should be balanced with engaging with and meeting the needs of young people. Plans should be reviewed and evaluated, further informing the assessment and future planning and delivery. This chapter has built on the thinking in Chapters One and Four about assessment and using tools. Working with others to assess, plan and deliver services is considered further in Chapter Seven.

SIX

Reports

The capacity to elucidate theories – frameworks of understanding, ways of making meaning – is what essentially separates the report of a person having some expertise, whose opinion should be taken seriously, from the lay person in the street. (Swain, 2005, p 46)

Introduction

Reports are frequently the main formal vehicle for conveying what is known and understood about a young person when critical decisions are being made. This chapter will be concerned with reports for audiences who have responsibility, shared or otherwise, for determining what should happen to reduce the likelihood of reoffending, protect the public and promote the best interests of children and young people. These reports are often read in the absence of the writer (in courts or community panel meetings, for example). They need therefore to communicate information with a degree of clarity that isn't always necessary in verbal exchanges. Colleagues representing the organisation in courts or other meetings may also need to be able to answer to the content of reports they didn't write.

The formal nature of these written documents means that any discussion about practice needs to take account of factors such as:

- reliability (the evidence a report is based upon)
- professionalism, 'the application of professional frameworks of understanding to what is known by a ... (skilled) practitioner' (Swain, 2005, p 46)
- tone and presentation (Hill, 2010)
- the longevity of records and the continuing impact of professional judgements about young people over time (as discussed in Chapter Four with regard to assessment tools).

Reports are open to a range of audiences – professional and non-professional – and can be an explicit element of a judicial decision-making process, itself open to scrutiny. The quality of formal written reports can thus determine how effectively information is received by the reader(s) and, consequently, how far it influences decision making. This chapter focuses on reports which take the practitioner's core assessment into the public arena, inform decisions and help determine the foundations of future work. It will describe common characteristics of good practice as well as highlight differences of emphasis that apply to reports prepared for particular contexts or decisions.

The purpose of reports in youth justice settings

Youth justice practitioners prepare reports for a variety of decision-making processes, notably in relation to court sentencing, Referral Orders, the Children's Reporter and Children's Hearings in Scotland, parole hearings and breach proceedings. Those working in early intervention teams also present written reports to multi-agency decision-making bodies such as Youth Inclusion Support Panels. In all cases, an understanding of the young person's behaviour in context is central and the report-writing process similar. What distinguishes these reports from each other, however, is the audience that will read them, the types of decisions that they make and the role of the practitioner in each case.[1]

A report is 'an evaluative account or summary of the results of an investigation, or of any matter on which information is required (typically in the form of an official or formal document), given or prepared by a person or body appointed or required to do so' (OED). Reports are not the same as the assessment but are a product of an assessment process (see Chapter One). An important distinction between reports and assessment in a justice setting is that assessment, though structured and formally staged, is an ongoing process, while reports are documents associated with decisions fixed in time and context. They condense information into a digestible form and are organised so as to lend a purposeful narrative to that information. This may be why readers (and even sometimes assessors) have preferred the narrative style of reports to the segmented format of assessment forms, even though the stories that reports tell may be selective summaries of a more substantial assessment (White et al, 2009).

Reports communicate the most relevant information to the reader, but not necessarily everything that has been considered during the assessment. This implies the need for a distinctive writing process to identify, organise and edit pertinent information. In addition, reports usually have a specific intention or purpose. For example, they can be:

- descriptive: providing a detailed picture of people, events or situations, acting as the audience's 'eyes and ears';
- summative: 'boiling down' information for the reader, highlighting key points;
- narrative: giving shape and meaning to information and speculating about what might happen next;
- prescriptive: telling the audience what course of action should be taken;
- persuasive: putting an alternative case or justifying a particular position.

Core assessments in youth justice, upon which reports are based, are comprehensive and holistic, covering offending, risk to the public and the welfare of the young person; they include a wide range of information relevant to practitioners planning interventions. The readers of reports, however, do not always need to know all there is to know. Their interests and remit may be more specific (as determined by their roles and responsibilities) and they will require only the information that is relevant to helping them decide what should happen next. Reports contribute to different but specific decisions. Their content needs to be tailored accordingly, with the proviso that they do not lose a sense of balance and fairness.

Reports: the qualities that make a difference

In the changing context of criminal justice, what constitutes quality in a report may be open to discussion and debate (Downing and Lynch, 1997; Tata et al, 2008; Gelsthorpe et al, 2010). There are, however, different and useful perspectives about report writing in a justice setting which help to build a picture of what a good report, prepared with integrity, may look like. Other chapters also explore the idea of integrity (for example, Chapter Seven looks at professional integrity in the context of multi-agency working), but for the purposes of this discussion integrity relates to the transparency and thoroughness of the investigative process and to the degree of honesty with which information is interpreted and articulated.

Reflection

If you were judging the quality of a report in a youth justice context, what would you base your judgements on?

- Would you draw on your experience as a reader of reports, discussion with colleagues, policy documents, and feedback from decision makers and/or inspections?
- Are you aware of people holding differing views about quality?
- What issues cause debate?

Notions of quality derive from a combination of guidance and policy, quality assurance processes and the opinions of audiences. We consider this mix of perspectives and explore the practical implications for practitioners.

Guidance

Some guidance on the attributes of good reports (that is, reports that will be fit for purpose) has been provided by government (Scottish Executive, 2004; YJB, 2010b). This indicates that, as well as being written to a consistent format, reports should be balanced, impartial, timely, focused and analytical, free from discriminatory language or stereotypes, verified and factually accurate and understandable to the young person and their parents/carers. In addition, NACRO (2003) has included satisfying statutory provisions, meeting the requirements of national standards, contributing to the aim of preventing offending, embodying effective and anti-discriminatory practice, taking account of welfare and being consistent with children's rights.

Quality assurance processes

There are a variety of quality assurance processes associated with assessment and report writing, ranging from routine gate-keeping of reports to broader inspections of practice. These are informed by national policy and guidance. In relation to the gate-keeping of Pre-Sentence Report (PSR) compilation, for example, the YJB recommends a two-tiered approach focusing on the pre-report stage (the process) and then upon the report itself (the product).[2]

Key issues prioritised in relation to the pre-report stage include:

- bringing together relevant professionals to discuss the issues, needs and risks in order to agree a potential package to be proposed;
- the importance of engaging management support – reports belong to the team not just the individual;
- gathering a range of information to help make resource decisions early in the process.

Implicit here is a view of quality which recognises that report compilation is not just about assessment of what *is*, but it is also concerned with decisions about the future and about the capacity of the practitioner and agency to provide relevant services.

In relation to the report itself, quality assurance aims to 'maximise the chances of the sentencing outcome being in line with the PSR proposal', enhancing the credibility of both practitioner and agency. In addition to the indicators of quality identified in national standards described above, guidance also emphasises the centrality of the young person's perspective by encouraging the use of the 'What do YOU think?' self-assessment form to complement interviews and the professional assessment in *Asset* (YJB, 2006). Local quality assurance procedures and tools should be informed by national standards and guidance.

Inspections start with an evaluation of the reports themselves; on this basis they then identify what might need to be done differently to improve future outcomes. At the level of team practice, inspections of reports have identified several key areas for development (HMIP, 2008; 2009a). These relate to achieving accuracy in gathering information, better analysis of that information to explain offending behaviour in context, attention to diversity, clarity about concepts and definitions, especially in relation to risk, and conciseness in writing and presentation.

What the audience values

Recognising that reports will differ in style and content, dependent upon the audience, is important in enhancing the effectiveness of their influence on decision makers. There is some limited research evidence about what audiences value in reports and how far they contribute to decisions (sentences or agreements made at panel meetings) (Jones and Roberts, 2006; McNeill et al, 2009; Phoenix,

2010). Research suggests that courts are generally satisfied with the quality of the background information in reports. However, like court users across the justice system, those in youth courts identify having confidence in the sentencing proposals, how realistic these proposals are, and whether the report writer has credibility with the court as significant factors in influencing their perception of reports (Tata et al, 2008; YJB, 2009b; Field and Nelken, 2010).

Confidence and credibility are not straightforward qualities, however. They are subjective judgements which certainly reflect the quality of the reports but may also reflect the concerns and biases of the reader, the context in which decisions are made, how sentencers and panel members perceive their responsibility to the community, or the interventions available. So while the skills of report writers are important, relationships between practitioners and their different audiences (sentencers and advocates, for example), will also have a bearing. Reports are one very important part of the decision-making process but there are also a multitude of other influences on the sentencing process which can affect how reports are written and received (Morgan and Haines, 2007). Practitioners and managers would do well to try to understand 'the mechanisms and influences that drive decision making' (YJB, 2009b, p 12) in order to maximise the impact of their reports. One issue to consider relates to how effective liaison is between practitioners and court users or panel members, particularly in informing them about the range of specific interventions available and their potential benefits in reducing offending behaviour and meeting the needs of young people. In addition, consideration needs to be given to how effective staff are in the court setting, including whether practitioners attend court to speak to their reports, if necessary.

What all this means for report writers

The messages for practitioners emerging from guidance, quality assurance processes and their audiences fall into three broad areas:

1. *Understanding the audience and the legal and practice context*: including legislation, agency policy and procedures, and the requirements of decision makers.
2. *Analysing, selecting and editing information* to make sense of that information in a way that is helpful to all readers and conveys an understanding of the behaviour within the context of an individual's lived experiences and needs. This includes what information appropriately forms the evidential base of the report and relevant decisions and interventions flowing from it.
3. *Presenting information in a manner appropriate to the setting in which it is to be used* and contributing to a decision-making process that is clear, fair, respectful and transparent. This relates not just to the structure and content of the report but also the language and style of the writer.

> ## Reflection
>
> Think back to earlier chapters, particularly the content relating to the assessment process as a whole in Chapter One, analysis and decision making in Chapter Two and the use of tools in Chapter Four.
>
> ■ How might some of that material help report writers in addressing the second point in the list above?

With the exception of the NACRO good practice guide (2003) and limited material relating to training (for example, Whitehead and Thompson, 2004, in relation to probation trainees; Dalzell and Sawyer, 2007, in relation to social workers; YJB, 2008a, in relation to YOTs), there is little, however, by way of help for practitioners as to how quality in these areas can be developed. The following sections explore what practitioners might need to know or do in order to produce persuasive and relevant reports.

The legal and practice context: roles and responsibilities

In courts the youth justice practitioner is not normally a lead decision maker; they are there to assist and influence decisions so that the outcome is 'the most suitable method of dealing with a young person who has offended' (Criminal Justice Act 2003, section 158). This is 'a critical principle in the court's sentencing decision' (YJB, 2009b, p 107) and ultimately the court holds '(j)udicial ownership of the allocation of punishment' (Tata et al, 2008, p 848). By contrast, the use of Referral Orders for young people entering the court system for the first time in England and Wales represents a decision-making process where responsibilities are shared between the court, which decides on the length of order, and the community panel, which decides on the interventions to be undertaken within the order.

Practitioners work in a variety of settings and adopt a variety of roles, therefore. They may be servants of the court (PSRs or Social Enquiry Reports), consultants who inform and guide (Youth Offender Panel reports), enforcers or prosecutors (breach reports), or advocates (for example, reports to Youth Inclusion Support Panels). Whatever the particular context, however, the youth justice practitioner can act as an 'expert', sharing their knowledge in order to help others make appropriate decisions.

The court setting

Courts have ultimate responsibility in determining sentences and are bound, firstly, by legal constraints in terms of the sentencing options open to them, along with the sentencing principles that are there to guide their decisions. These include the key principle of proportionality, which means that sentencing should reflect the seriousness of the offending, having taken account of all the circumstances of the case. Sentencing options open to courts in England and Wales were formally redefined in the Criminal Justice and Immigration Act 2008 and include the YRO, the standard generic community sentence for young people who offend. This comprises a 'menu' of interventions that can be imposed, proportionate to the seriousness of the offence and dependent upon the assessed level of risk (YJB, 2010a).

In making referrals for reports, courts will give some indication of what their concerns are, certainly in relation to seriousness and also where they intend to make a judgement about dangerousness (YJB, 2010e). The messages, formal and informal, that come from the court are a useful indicator of the types of questions sentencers might have in mind and should be an initial guide for report writers about how to respond most appropriately in terms of content and tone. Where specific issues relating to 'dangerousness' are raised by Youth Courts (in England and Wales) the report writer must address this in their offence analysis and assessment of risk, but definitive judgements about 'dangerousness' remain the court's responsibility (YJB, 2010e).

Courts are also expected to take account of the age of the young person, the seriousness of his/her offences, the likelihood of reoffending and the extent of harm that might result from any further offences. Sentencers are advised to consider individual characteristics which might hinder the effectiveness of a sentencing decision and factors which might mitigate the young person's behaviour (Sentencing Guidelines Council, 2009). Without the PSR, sentencers are unlikely to be able to individualise sentences in this way, but report writers should also recognise that individualisation takes place within relevant legislative boundaries.

A common perception among sentencers, in Youth Courts and Crown Courts, is that, where the young person is on the cusp between a community or custody disposal, reports are less helpful; readers 'part company with' writers because, it is argued, practitioners are reluctant to address the possibility of custody and therefore diminish the realism and credibility of their arguments (Field, 2007; YJB, 2009b). Report writers may not agree with initial indications from the court about what might happen, but risk undermining the influence of reports if they ignore them.

Reflection

Are you aware of common differences of perspective between youth justice practitioners and courts? How might the following strategies help to manage those differences:

- the reports themselves – through their evidence and argument?
- personal contacts between youth justice practitioners/managers and courts?

Community panels in England and Wales

In all cases the decision as to the length of the order is the responsibility of the courts. What is at issue for Youth Offender Panel members is the content of the order and the intensity of work to be undertaken, proportionate to the seriousness of the offence and the level of risk posed (including both likelihood of offending and risk of serious harm to others). It is also expected that panel members will bring their own local knowledge and experience to the process.

The report writer has a responsibility to inform panel members, who are lay volunteers, about key risk factors and the range of interventions available, appropriate to prevent future offending. Reports for panels are likely to be informative rather than prescriptive. The emphasis is upon explaining behaviour, outlining potential options and suggesting 'what *might* happen *if* ...'. Their persuasiveness will lie in the quality of information provided (including local knowledge about services and resources for young people who offend), and how material is presented, conveying important messages without taking over or dominating the panel meeting (YJB, 2007a). Jones and Roberts (2006) suggest that attention could be paid to putting more practical detail in these types of reports, but this should be balanced against the need for succinctness and concern about the sheer volume of what is included, bearing in mind the time available to panel members to read and digest key pieces of information.

The youth justice practitioner's role as 'expert'

In all settings reports 'should ... establish and confirm the expertise of the writer, and ... demonstrate with concise and logical argument, the rationale for the assessment made and the outcomes which follow from it' (Swain, 2005, p 46). The youth justice practitioner's realm of expertise is in understanding offending behaviour (as explored in Chapter Three) and employing their skills in working with young people to achieve and communicate that understanding (see Chapter Eight).

Their role is to apply this expertise to help courts or panels understand why the individual offended and how best their future risk(s) can be reduced. They bring the young person 'alive' for their audiences, providing what Gorman describes as 'a coherent personal story, which endeavours to make sense of past mistakes/ misdeeds, integrat(ing) present strengths, difficulties and contradictions' and proposing a vision for a non-offending future (Gorman, 2006, p 114).

By concentrating on this endeavour, rather than becoming preoccupied by how best to satisfy their audience or simply adhering to templates and standards, the report writer is more likely to produce a document which engages and persuades (Gorman, 2006). Reports which genuinely reflect the writer's opinions, where the writer specifically 'owns' those opinions (using 'I' statements, for example) and demonstrates through clear, reasoned argument the value of those opinions, are less likely to be regarded as 'unrealistic' and more likely to hold the reader's attention (Tata et al, 2008). Like many other 'expert' contributors to judicial court processes, youth justice practitioners should value and have confidence in their own specialist knowledge and experience (David, 2004). However, Swain also argues that 'the report writer must be prepared to have both the assessment and the basis on which it is made challenged ... and should be able to respond to that challenge' (Swain, 2005, p 56). If their reports are based on in-depth assessments undertaken with the range of knowledge and skills discussed throughout this book, practitioners should be well prepared to respond to challenges and be confident in their role as expert.

Assessment to report: a critical and systematic approach

Reports do not stand alone from the core assessment process, and structured tools (see Chapter Four) lend a basic 'professional framework' (Swain, 2005) to the investigation process. They help practitioners to record and scrutinise information, distinguishing between fact and opinion, between concrete evidence that can be verified and speculation or hypothesis based upon the particular knowledge of the assessor.

Even with the use of tools, however, there is still an editorial role for the report writer to prune and tune the content of assessments to the needs of their audience, while remaining 'true' to the core assessments upon which they are based (Dalzell and Sawyer, 2007). This is so even in an environment where reports are expected to conform to a formal structure or where there is the facility, via IT systems, to populate reports directly from the basic assessment. A summative process is required that highlights the key information, lending it narrative or meaning so that it can be more relevant to an audience's deliberations.

In this editing process it is important that the young person is not 'lost in translation'. As we argue elsewhere (Chapters Three, Five and Eight, for example), the young person's perspective is essential to understanding their behaviour, deciding what to do about it and engaging them productively in the process. Reports should not simply summarise information, they should also try to capture the spirit of the young person, including both their weaknesses and those strengths (or protective factors) which might support change in the future.

Staging the report-writing process

Key complementary skills in selecting and editing material for reports are analysing and synthesising (see Chapters Two and Four). A staged approach to the task is encouraged which involves working through key sections of reports to arrive at conclusions which flow logically from the main content.

The report introduction

A report should provide readers with an insight into the assessment process itself, including any challenges associated with gathering information from a range of sources. There may be contradictory information or opinions about an individual and these should not be overlooked; as well as editing information, report writers should cast a critical eye upon it and be prepared to present evidence which may both support and/or dispute their own judgement (Dalzell and Sawyer, 2007; Hoge and Andrews, 2010). The self-confidence required to do this comes not just from their professional expertise, but also from feeling secure and supported in their role (see Chapter Nine, which explores the importance of supervision). An explicit weighing of evidence will be reflected in the conclusions and proposal, demonstrating that the writer has taken a balanced approach to their information.

Offence analysis

The first step in selecting relevant content to be included in the report is to draw on an analysis of the offending.[3] This should be one of the outcomes of a core assessment and the cornerstone of any report. The offence analysis is distinct from the official prosecution account of events or the account given by a young person, both of which are often repeated uncritically and in too much detail in assessments and reports. It should be derived from the analytical process of breaking down the offending behaviour into a number of interconnecting elements (see, for example, the ABC model in Chapter Three) and then pulling these elements together to arrive at a professional explanation of the behaviour in context. The model in Chapter Five describing the *Asset* framework and illustrating the interactions between risk factors can also serve as an analytical tool. A useful offence analysis would include the following four dimensions:

- the key direct and indirect influences upon the young person
- any patterns of behaviour that are apparent over time
- circumstances that trigger offending or other anti-social behaviour
- how the young person's thinking (or lack of) affects their behaviour.

All of the above applies equally to offence analyses recorded in assessments and those shared in reports. It is important that, for inclusion in a report, the writer reviews and edits the assessment-based analysis in the light of the specific purpose of the report and the specific audience who will read it.

Relevant information about the young person and assessment of risk

Each of the dimensions of the offence analysis can be applied to the selection of relevant information about the individual and help inform the assessment of risk in relation to likelihood of reoffending and risk of serious harm to others. By using the offence analysis to help guide the selection of the background details, this body of information assumes some shape and narrative, becoming not just interesting but useful. Information should be selected to expand upon the main elements of the offence analysis, to give it depth and detail, and then to begin to explore the implications for the future and the most appropriate next steps. Information should be included on the basis of relevance to offending, not the general welfare or character of the young person. If, for example, the young person steals to finance a drug habit, it would be pertinent to include further background information about their drug use. If, on the other hand, it emerged in the assessment that they were a social user of cannabis but this had no connection to their offending, the writer would need to think about if and how they included this information, and to ask themselves whether it would unduly prejudice the court or panel members, resulting in unfair decisions or inappropriate interventions.

In addition to explaining the offending behaviour, the report writer is asked to provide information about anything that might, while not condoning the behaviour, provide a realistic understanding of why it occurred. They will also consider aspects of the young person's life that might affect their welfare (in accordance with the Children and Young Persons Act 1933, section 44), put them at risk or influence their ability to respond to future interventions. The report writer therefore undertakes a second stage of selection to bring in any additional information about the young person's wider life experience and personal characteristics. This includes factors (both positive and negative) and personal resources which are likely to help or hinder future work with the young person (relevant to responsivity and motivation).

At this stage writers will apply their knowledge and theoretical understandings (as discussed in Chapter Three) in order to identify key messages from the information collected. When communicating their judgements about the young person's behaviour they may also need to consider how much detail to give about the knowledge base and the theoretical perspectives underpinning their thinking. Referring to any tool(s) used in the core assessment may lend authority to the report's arguments, for example, but on the other hand it may not be appropriate to go into too much detail about how any numerical scores were derived from the tool. Similarly, examples of research about the characteristics of young people who become involved in different types of offences, especially if this has also influenced the choice of intervention, can support arguments in later sections.

Communications about risk

In relation to risk it is particularly important that the practitioner is clear about terminology (for example, being specific about what types of risk are being discussed) and evidences important points in order to avoid misunderstanding or misinterpretation (Carson and Bain, 2008; Hoge and Andrews, 2010). It is not enough to describe someone as 'high risk'; far more helpful is to talk about how likely a specific event or behaviour is to occur, in what circumstances and why, to justify and explain succinctly the reason for your judgement. This is important in all cases, but particularly so in situations where a judgement about 'dangerousness' is being made (YJB, 2010e).

Conclusions and proposals

The final element of a report should be a realistic, logical conclusion about what should happen next. The report writer applies their understandings about effective interventions (see Chapter Five) to issues that have emerged from their investigation, bearing in mind the legal context governing the sentences available. The conclusion brings together the strands of the narrative that began with the offence analysis. There should be no surprise endings.

Conclusions should return to the reasons why a report was requested in the first place (including any initial messages from sentencers) and address them constructively and realistically without overstepping the report writer's responsibility or usurping that of the decision makers (NACRO, 2003). Courts expect a detailed and well-argued proposal about what will be done by the youth justice practitioner and his/her team, including consideration of the range of relevant options. A review of PSRs in Wales concluded that conclusions were 'strong and cogent' (NACRO Cymru, 2003, p 5) when report authors:

- presented and discussed objectively a range of options;
- offered firm, clear-reasoned proposals;
- plainly described what work would be undertaken with the young person on the preferred community sentence;
- were explicit about negative impacts on the young person of not pursuing a particular course of action;
- clearly explained the potentially negative outcomes of custody for a young person;
- acknowledged concerns about the ability of the young person to comply and identified steps that might encourage their compliance;
- used positive language and addressed issues in a factual and objective manner;
- clearly indicated how the proposed community sentence would reduce further offending and why it was appropriate.

By contrast, community panel members expect an indication (still well argued) of what might be offered, subject to their discussion with the young person, his/her carers and, sometimes, the victim. The tone of the conclusion may need to be more provisional so that the practitioner does not appear to be dominating what is intended to be a negotiated process.

Table 6.1 represents this staged approach to compiling reports. It emphasises the fundamental importance of the core assessment, but encourages a critical use of that assessment to produce a document that is relevant to the decision-making process and coherent in terms of how it summarises key information and presents its arguments. The content of the table incorporates the key aspects of quality discussed earlier in the chapter and also draws on the knowledge base described in Chapter Three.

The following activity is the first of two that can be used to review reports.

Activity: Reviewing reports 1

Use Table 6.1 as a checklist to review the content of reports that you or others have completed.

Presentation and writing

Formal reports often have prescribed structures with common sections and headings (YJB, 2010d), aimed at ensuring a consistent approach which can, in turn, support fairness and transparency. They also help to prevent the report writer straying from their purpose and support a logical follow-through of themes from beginning to end. Such structures are intended to facilitate ease of navigation, but can also detract from the content and hinder the communication between writer and audience. As with the formal tools which underpin assessments, report frameworks can cause the writer to lose the sense of narrative and the reader to read only the parts they want to read (Tata et al, 2008). A further challenge of these required formats for practitioners lies in avoiding the routinisation of the writing process. There is a danger that report writing becomes part of a process of moving information around under different headings, encouraging a 'cut and paste' approach to report compilation, as opposed to the combination of analysis and synthesis required for making a report relevant and convincing. IT programmes designed to draw down information directly from assessments, although having the advantage of saving time and the duplication of effort, can also increase this risk.

In its presentation and style of writing, the report also needs to be clear, transparent and readily accessible to all readers (from magistrates speed-reading in the retiring room, to the young person unaccustomed to formal documents and distracted by the court setting). It needs to engage and persuade readers (Gorman, 2006), be they decision makers or young people expected to sign up to suggested interventions. It therefore needs to demonstrate respect for both the formal decision-making processes and the young person. Concerns about the genuineness of the involvement of young people in the report-writing process and the subsequent development of the intervention plan or contract have been highlighted in recent research (Jones and Roberts, 2006; Hart and Thompson, 2009). Some of the challenges of encouraging participation in statutory processes are explored further in Chapter Eight.

In order for reports to provide a meaningful 'communication process' (Tata et al, 2008) the report writer should try to ensure that everyone, professionals and non-professionals alike, really does understand the content of the report by keeping the message clear and avoiding lengthy, convoluted sentences or digressions (HEA,

Table 6.1: From assessment to report

	Core assessment	Report				
		Introduction	Offence analysis	Relevant information	Risk	Conclusion and proposal
Task	Gathering and analysing information	Summarising the information-gathering process and the evidence base	Explaining the behaviour	Selecting relevant information to put the behaviour in context	Distilling particular issues relating to risk	Providing a logical, 'cogent' conclusion and relevant valid proposal
Process: Pay attention to ...	• Range, sources and quality of information • Verification • Is specialist assessment needed? • Identifying key influences on behaviour • Making judgements about likely future behaviour	Explaining the assessment process: • how information was gathered and evaluated	Whether you have covered: • the important direct and indirect influences upon the young person • patterns of behaviour apparent over time • the circumstances that trigger offending • how the young person's thinking affects their behaviour	Aspects of the young person's life that are: • associated with the offending • likely to lead to them experiencing harm or other adverse outcomes • potential obstacles to positive engagement • suggestive of welfare issues • potential protective factors	Being clear about: • different types of risk • levels of risk (how do you evidence these?) • triggers and context • how you think it should be reduced and/or managed	• Initial messages from court • Legal options available • Your responsibilities • What you can realistically offer • Consequences of all options • Which are most likely to be effective and why • NO SURPRISES!

At each stage:
• Note key points you want to communicate.
• Evaluate information to ensure relevance and accuracy and to avoid repetition.

online reference). Careful editing that excludes unnecessary information will optimise the clarity of presentation (Morris and Mason, 1999).

There is also an obligation for writers to avoid discriminatory and stereotypical language or forms of expression (NACRO, 2003, p 50). Limited research from small-scale studies in the probation context has highlighted problems of bias and stereotyping in reports written on adult offenders from minority groups (Power, 2003; Hudson and Bramhall, 2005), suggesting that practitioners need to be as precise and careful as possible in expressing professional opinions. It is important to evidence those opinions transparently, avoiding irrelevant and prejudicial information (Hoge and Andrews, 2010) and generalised statements which can (particularly in relation to girls and young black offenders) reinforce prejudices or lead to ill-targeted and disproportionate sentencing decisions (Farrow et al, 2007).

Reports are part of the official record about an individual and can 'stay' with someone as they move through the justice system. Thus, as we have argued in earlier chapters, care needs to be taken with the nuances of language and style and with the way that information and opinions are recorded and presented (see Chapter Four).

All of this suggests that, while fluency and logic of argument is important, a wonderful facility for words or the well-turned phrase is not essential to producing a thoughtful, purposeful and effective document. Readers need to be clearly informed both about the subject of the report and about the reasoning and evidence that has influenced the report writer. In presenting their 'findings' and conclusions, writers should aim for an approach that pares down rather than embellishes or risks 'fudging' issues.

Activity: Reviewing reports 2

The last activity reviewed the content of the report; this activity is more concerned with how that content is presented.

- Were the key points expressed clearly and directly?
- Are there examples of simple everyday and non-discriminatory language (as opposed to professional jargon)? (YJB, 2008a)
- Are the professional judgements evidenced and justified?
- Did the writer demonstrate ownership of their opinions (for example by using 'I' statements)?
- Were specific statements used rather than generalised comments?

Other audiences – other reports

Our focus has been predominantly upon reports for courts and lay panels at the point of sentencing and decisions about the content of orders. A systematic approach is equally relevant to other reports. Some additional reflection about parole and breach reports is worthwhile, since both draw not only on the core assessment but, just as importantly, on ongoing assessments of progress to reduce and manage risk.

Breach reports

Breach proceedings illustrate the balance that practitioners sometimes have to hold between enforcement and compliance. Initially, the YOT practitioner assumes the role of prosecutor. Having justified and evidenced the initial decision to enforce an order, they then step back from the decision-making process to resume their role as expert advisor to the court, handing over the ownership of the sentencing decision to the court. The breach report again considers the young person's behaviour in context, as well as summarising the work done so far, and suggests in the proposal what should now happen to prevent reoffending, either by arguing for a continuation of the existing order or exploring the options realistically available if the court were to resentence.

The report should draw on ongoing assessments and increasing knowledge about how the young person has responded to interventions (what has helped, what have been the barriers to engagement and how compliance could be encouraged in the future) to arrive at a firm proposal about what interventions are likely to have a realistic prospect of success. Issues relating to the management of the young person's behaviour, their motivation and commitment and suitable methods will be central to this proposal. In this instance the young person is an important reader of the report; what is said, the tone in which it is said and the proposal itself are part of the wider breach experience which will affect their future engagement with the youth justice system.

Parole reports

The Parole Board is likely to be particularly influenced by the practitioner's assessment of risk and how that can realistically be managed, since youth justice services will have primary responsibility for supervision in the community following a young person's release. Once again, understanding the young person's behaviour, particularly how s/he has responded to the custodial measures, is central. This will provide indications not only about the likelihood of future offending but also on the strategies that may be required to manage effectively their risk to others in the community.

The report will need to make arguments about the wisdom of releasing an individual on parole and make specific commitments about what services can be provided when they return to the community.[4] Parole reports will typically emphasise risk to the public more than other types of reports, and inclusion of risk management plans will be the norm. These will often formalise the responsibilities of other agencies also, in relation to either risk management or providing services to support the young person. As with PSRs, the parole report forms part of the written record of a defensible decision-making process that is open to scrutiny, and in effect the practitioner is an expert 'witness'. Both the quality of information (sources and standard of verification) that underpins the writer's judgement and the reliability and realism of the conclusions are particularly significant. There is an expectation that '[w]here a YOT is recommending the release of a young person in this situation *the report should clearly spell out the reasons for this and provide full details of the risk management plan*' (YJB, 2010f, forthcoming).

> **Activity**
>
> - Compare reports written for different audiences: a PSR with a referral order report, or a breach report with a parole report, for example.
> - Do the differences you find in the reports appropriately match the different needs of the intended audiences?

Conclusion

As well as undertaking a systematic, multi-faceted assessment, the report writer will be helped by having an understanding of decision-making processes, in particular how these are informed by evidence (Chapter Two); be able to construct plans which are relevant to individual young people (Chapter Five); and be able to work effectively with other agencies in compiling the assessment and delivering the plan (Chapter Seven).

Reports should summarise and communicate the key points of an assessment in order to engage persuasively with the decision-making process. It is important to remember that the story or narrative within the report should be helpful to everyone in determining what should happen next (Milner and O'Byrne, 2009). They are professional documents for a sometimes non-professional audience. Furthermore, they are not the end of the story. They are fixed in time and therefore may be incomplete and leave the reader with unanswered questions. A realistic, evidence-based document that inspires confidence in the reader can recognise and live with uncertainty. At the same time, it should suggest positive and helpful ways of working with a young person to address what *is* known and to plan and manage for what is not.

Notes

[1] Reports are also written to advocate for resources from other agencies or to secure inter-agency collaboration. The complexities of working with other agencies will be covered in Chapter Seven.

[2] See www.yjb.gov.uk

[3] For practitioners using *Asset*, this will mean using the 'offence analysis' section of the Core Profile, for example.

[4] Guidance about the required content of parole reports is provided in *Guidance on 'Release and Recall Provisions for Young People Serving Long Term Custodial Sentences'* (YJB, 2010f).

SEVEN

Communication and working with other agencies

[I]n inter-professional work, specialist expertise becomes more rather than less important, as does the need to be quite clear about the limits of one's expertise and to know when to work with others. (Edwards et al, 2009, p 10)

Introduction

The requirement to communicate and work with other agencies has become integral to assessment, planning and service delivery in youth justice. Multi-agency approaches are now embedded in practice with young people who offend (Johnstone and Burman, 2010). The Crime and Disorder Act 1998, which fundamentally restructured youth justice in England and Wales, established multi-agency YOTs in April 2000 (Goldson, 2007). These teams included representatives from a number of agencies and were intended to encourage a shared approach to the work, avoiding duplication and inconsistency (Home Office, 1997).

This Act established 'preventing offending by children and young persons' (section 37(1)) as the principal aim of the youth justice system. However, it was recognised that young people who offend also 'need support to lead crime free lives' (YJB website). They remain young people with a range of needs (Whyte, 2004) and the teams were set up to reflect this, including, for example, professionals from health, education and social work services. While the same structural and legislative changes do not apply in Scotland or Northern Ireland, in all jurisdictions multi-agency approaches are now encouraged. The 'two hats' worn by youth justice services (Sutherland, 2009b, p 49), that is, balancing the needs of the child with a responsibility to protect the public, necessitate a range of responses to youth crime which will require the involvement of a number of different agencies (Burman et al, 2007; Fielder et al, 2008).

Youth justice services have a sometimes complex relationship with other agencies when working together to assess and plan interventions for young people. Williams, writing about offender health, suggests that 'working across the "care control" divide potentially involves a greater number of agencies with an even greater divergence of professional cultures' (I. Williams, 2009, p 573). It is possible to argue that YOTs are in a singular position, straddling the structural divisions between community safety and children's services (Fielder et al, 2008). This offers both opportunities for, and threats to, delivering outcomes for young people who offend and has implications for practitioners in managing the processes and relationships involved.

> ## Reflection
>
> Think about the 'two hats' of youth justice. To what extent, in your experience, does the 'care/control' divide influence responses to young people from a range of agencies?

Clarification of terms

It should be acknowledged that in discussions of working with other agencies, language is often used loosely. Brown and White, for example, considering integrated children's services, list a number of terms used without clear definition: 'partnership working, joint working, joined up working, interagency working, multi-agency working, multi-professional working, inter-agency communication, intra and inter-organisational collaboration and collaborative working are often used interchangeably' (Brown and White, 2006, p 6). Generally in the literature, inter-agency working is used to refer to relationships between agencies in a multi-agency context, that is, where several agencies are involved, whereas intra-agency refers to relationships between professionals within an individual agency. This differentiation is complicated by the nature of teams like YOTs which include staff from a number of agencies. This chapter therefore makes use of two specific terms to structure some later discussion. Morris (2008) differentiates between:

- '**Collaborative working**. ... the sharing of professional responsibilities to deliver a service with mutually agreed outcomes' (p 168, emphasis added), which best describes the structures of YOTs in England and Wales, where workers are seconded from other agencies and work in the same location to common objectives, and
- '**Multi-agency working**. ... where services come together to plan and deliver services that have shared aims and outcomes' (p 167).

Collaborative teams then also have to work with a wide range of other agencies, for example, when a YOT is involved with looked-after children.

Relationships with the wider community

The agencies that youth justice practitioners work with will often be other statutory bodies, but will also include voluntary organisations. As Gough (2010) points out, this carries some threats to those organisations if, in delivering services for the state, they lose some of the creativity and independence that they brought to the task.

Youth justice practitioners also work with families and with community members, and these relationships throw up their own opportunities and challenges.

Jones and Roberts (2006), for example, highlight some of the complexities of the involvement of community volunteers in Youth Offender Panels and the difficulty of finding panel members who are truly representative of the young person's community. The importance of building social capital, raised in Chapter Five, suggests, however, that community involvement is important. Even where there is a risk of serious harm to others, greater consideration is now being given to finding more integrative ways of managing that risk in the community (Kemshall, 2008a). The focus of this chapter is predominantly on working with other statutory agencies, but at the time of writing it is clear that relationships with other community groups are likely to remain a key part of practice and perhaps become more important.

Reflection

What experience do you have of working with non-statutory agencies and community members in the broad context of youth justice?

Based on that experience, what do you find most useful about:

- the perspectives that they bring to working with young people?
- the resources they provide to support young people?

Why working with others matters

Young people who offend can, like many other young people, be involved with a number of services. The agencies concerned need to share information to ensure that assessments are accurate and that plans address significant needs, build strengths and capabilities and provide opportunities for development, but also avoid any unnecessary duplication. Sometimes specialist assessment is required, for example with young people who sexually offend or young people with mental health difficulties, and this may involve other agencies, as might planning for the delivery of multi-modal interventions, discussed in Chapter Five (Print et al, 2001; McGuire, 2002).

At one level, increased working across agencies is seen to 'make a lot of sense' (Balloch and Taylor, 2001, quoted in Morris, 2008, p 170), but it is important to consider what happens in practice and whether it can actually make a difference to outcomes for young people. There are some promising findings from YOTs (Burnett and Appleton, 2004), although it is difficult to link this directly to reductions in offending. This reflects a wider issue, that evaluations of multi-agency approaches have tended to focus on processes and structures rather than outcomes, so there is limited evidence so far about their effectiveness.

Achieving positive outcomes for young people

In order to tackle what was seen as the fragmentation of services for young people, government initiatives have established common goals for all agencies working with children in the Every Child Matters/Getting it Right for Every Child agendas across the United Kingdom (HMG, 2003; Scottish Government, 2008; Welsh Assembly Government, 2009). These were intended to ensure that positive outcomes for children and young people are sought by all organisations working with them (Hughes and Owen, 2009). The Children Act 2004 provided a legislative framework for working between agencies (in England), including the setting up of children's trusts, with 'all services working with children in a local area to work together to develop an integrated approach to delivering positive outcomes for children through the children's trust arrangements' (Fielder et al, 2008, p 4). Section 10 of the Act places a reciprocal duty to cooperate on YOTs and local authority children's services.

The developing preventative agenda also supports the seeking of positive outcomes for young people at risk of becoming involved in offending (Audit Commission, 2004). These developments all support the idea that young people, wherever they are located in the criminal justice process, should be assessed as young people with a range of strengths and needs, not just as offenders. Plans that improve access to mainstream services are, then, important in achieving the goals of supporting desistance, developing strengths and promoting rehabilitation (McNeill et al, 2005; see also Chapter Five).

Safeguarding and protecting young people

'We need to see individuals under supervision as both potential future offenders and as potential future victims of harm' (HMIP, 2009b). This highlights the overlap between young people who offend and those receiving services as children at risk or in need. 'Children who commit offences are usually children with a range of needs, such as mental health problems, or exclusion from school' (Fielder et al, 2008, p 3). This is the case for many young people receiving custodial sentences (Hart, 2006). Working with others should help to assess and meet the needs of those young people.

'YOTs have a duty to make arrangements to ensure that their functions are discharged with regard to the need to safeguard and promote the welfare of children' (HMG, 2010, p 1) and must cooperate with LSCBs. Secure children's homes, Secure Training Centres and Young Offender Institutions also have responsibilities for safeguarding. A review of practice in the secure estate found mixed results, with both policy and practice needing further development (YJB, 2008b).

There has been concern, however, about the failure of services to protect children and young people at risk adequately. Inquiries into fatal child abuse have repeatedly highlighted difficulties in communication and working relationships between agencies as being significant elements of ineffective practice (Reder and Duncan, 2004a). How to remedy these failures remains contested. Driscoll argues that 'perhaps more investment in professionals would have reaped greater rewards than a focus on structures and systems' (2009, p 342). Later in this chapter consideration is given to how to improve communication between professionals.

Safer communities

YOTs typically work with other professionals, through Community Safety Partnerships, for example to achieve the objective of reducing offending in a local area (Home Office and Ministry of Justice, 2010). Multi-agency working is also particularly important in relation to protecting the public from those who might commit serious sexual and violent offences, and youth justice services have to work with other criminal justice agencies, for example through MAPPA for those offenders considered to pose a risk of serious harm to others (Jones and Baker, 2009). Inquiries into cases where young people under statutory supervision have committed serious crimes have revealed weaknesses in this area (Blyth, 2007). Deficiencies in communication between youth justice services and firms providing electronic monitoring, for example, were a factor in the Peter Williams case (HMIP, 2005) and this, along with the lessons learned from other incidents (YJB, 2009a), illustrates the need for improvements in this aspect of practice.

Reflection

Based on experiences you have had in youth justice with multi-agency teams and/or working across organisational boundaries, can you find evidence to suggest that these relationships have been helpful for:

- achieving positive outcomes for young people?
- safeguarding young people at risk?
- promoting public protection?

Your own experience probably provides some evidence to support the usefulness of working with other agencies, as well as highlighting some concerns and difficulties.

Working with integrity

In order to work effectively with a range of other agencies to assess, plan and deliver services, practitioners need a clear sense of the contributions they can make and of their own professional integrity. Banks (2009) identifies three aspects of professional integrity:

- **conduct**, that is, following accepted professional guidelines and codes of ethics;
- **commitment** to the ideals or principles of the profession;
- **capacity** to reflect on practice, being willing to re-evaluate and if necessary give up previously held ideals and principles.

None of the above is sufficient on its own and the practitioner has to be able to demonstrate and hold in balance all three. Banks suggests that committed professionals stand up for their own judgements, but properly respect the judgements of others, acting in ways that avoid inflexibility, while at the same time avoiding superficiality and weakness.

When working across professional boundaries, practitioners nevertheless still have to comply with their own agency's policies and procedures. While at times it may feel as if these constrain practice, they do have an important role to play in ensuring accountability and in 'sustaining the professional identities of the practitioners who work in them and undertake often risky work with clients' (Edwards et al, 2009, p 117). Edwards et al go on to suggest that more rigid structures can 'inhibit the reciprocity needed' (p 126) for inter-agency work, but they also recognise that practitioners may become vulnerable without such support. To forge successful relationships, therefore, it is important that each agency, or professional grouping, has a clear sense of its own expertise, knowledge base and skills, and has the ability to understand and communicate within the language of others. Professional integrity needs to function to avoid the danger that 'organizational scripts' take priority over the needs of service recipients (Bates, 2004, p 61); and Howard (2010) argues that reflection, focused on outcomes for service users, is an important component of multi-agency working. It is also particularly crucial to keep a balance between discretion or creativity and accountability (Eadie and Canton, 2002; Pycroft, 2010), as discussed in Chapter Two.

Working with others: demands and limitations

Merely stating the principle of inter-agency cooperation is not enough; to be effective it requires 'constant attention, re-motivation and energy' (Murphy, 2004, p 143). One reason for this is that 'service delivery within a multi agency context increases the complexity of the tasks at hand in terms of the numbers of people and processes involved and ... an increase in complexity leads to an increase in unintended or unpredictable outcomes' (Pycroft, 2010, p 8). Similarly, Murphy argues that inter-agency work doesn't make a difficult task easy, or solve all problems, but if done well it can 'increase the likelihood that the task will be completed to a high standard' (Murphy, 2004, p 130).

The legislative framework for communication

The process of working with others is shaped by legislative and practical issues around sharing sensitive information. The Data Protection Act 1998, the Human

Rights Act 1998 and Article 8 of the European Convention of Human Rights are all significant. Guidance for practitioners helps to address the balance that has to be struck between protecting an individual's rights to privacy and the need to share information to prevent crime or protect vulnerable people, including young offenders themselves (YJB, 2005a; DCSF, 2008). Good practice principles stress the importance of seeking the consent of the person about whom you wish to communicate, but it is clear that information sharing without the subject's consent is lawful and sometimes necessary, in the context of youth justice.

> Exchanging personal and sensitive personal information between agencies, without the consent of the data subject, is seen as difficult and this is often used as an excuse for not doing it. However, in the context of preventing or reducing crime and disorder, and given the legislative framework within which the agencies referred to in this guidance operate, such exchange of information can, in fact, normally be done lawfully. (YJB, 2005a, p 2)

Important elements of the legislation to be taken into account are the exemptions from restrictions that apply in exchanging information for the prevention or detection of crime (Data Protection Act 1998, section 29) and the requirement to consider the necessity and proportionality of any disclosure.

Working within collaborative teams

The collaborative model should not be seen as providing a complete answer to the challenges of ensuring effective assessment, planning and service delivery for young people. In a review of partnership working in relation to young offenders with substance misuse problems, for example, Minkes et al (2005) suggest that while collaborative approaches may sometimes be the most helpful, they are not the only valid approach. Burnett and Appleton (2004) expressed a concern, for example, that in collaborative teams like YOTs there would be a de-professionalisation of practice and a greater emphasis on the monitoring of performance. In considering services for offenders with addiction problems, Rumgay (2000) expressed concern about the potential for workers to lose their professional identities. Burnett and Appleton did find support for this, with some YOT practitioners feeling that they had lost contact with their parent agency and a more generic YOT worker mantle was being adopted by staff.

One of the conundrums in collaborative teams is deciding to what extent specialist knowledge and skills are retained and how they are owned and shared (Edwards et al, 2009). Another study suggested that the extent to which staff retained distinct professional identity within a YOT put into question the success of the reconfiguration of youth justice services. 'Without some degree of generic YOT identity, the absorption of staff from different agencies into a single team created scope for inter-agency conflict' (Souhami, 2007, p 24). Differences are essential in developing new ideas and approaches, but too much conflict is likely to be counterproductive. A balance (like those discussed in Chapter Two) between complete absorption into a generic identity on the one hand, and absolute retention of professional identity on the other, needs to be held along a continuum, as shown in Figure 7.1.

Figure 7.1: Professional identity continuum

```
        Generic                           Distinct
   <─────────────────────────────────────────────>
        YOT identity                      Professional
                                          identity
```

Drawing on a study of a collaborative team delivering services to older people, Hudson (2005) suggests the following key elements for success:

- parity of esteem within the team;
- acceptance of the judgement of others: mutual respect among team members for each other's contribution;
- reorientation of professional affinity to the new team.

One of the benefits found in Burnett and Appleton's study was that services for young people were more quickly and easily available, as a result of the multi-agency make-up of the team. Anecdotally, this would be supported by the authors' contacts with practitioners. However, this advantage cannot be taken for granted, or understood simplistically. There are dangers that the easy availability of some services within teams, such as a substance misuse specialist, might encourage staff to assess with that in mind. If the problem you identify during assessment has an easily accessible local solution, there is at least a temptation to see that as more important than other, more intractable difficulties. Another danger of collaborative teams is proposed by Sutherland (2009b), who suggested that the composition of YOTs can sometimes lead to an assumption that other multi-agency structures like MAPPA have little to offer them, with the consequence that thinking and practice become too insular and lack challenge from other viewpoints.

Reflection

Use the continuum above to think about collaborative teams you have had experience of.

- What balance did they strike, and did that change over time?
- What effect did that have on relationships within the team?

Multi-agency working

Closer working relationships with other agencies, statutory and non-statutory, outside of collaborative teams, have the potential to help practitioners assess and provide services for young people, as illustrated, for example, by the role of the voluntary sector in work to reduce the over-representation of black and ethnic minority (BME) people in the criminal justice system (Hilder, 2010). The evaluation by Fielder et al, however, found that 'closer work was most apparent in preventative work and was less evident with young people who had committed several offences, or who were in custody' (Fielder et al, 2008, p 41).

The importance of wider services, for example to address significant mental health needs in young people who offend, and the need for joint planning between a number of organisations to ensure adequate employment and training provision is widely acknowledged (Edcoms, 2008). However, in advocating for young people attempting to access mainstream services, youth justice practitioners often encounter significant obstacles. 'Some older adolescents are beyond the reach of existing services and their vulnerability is not being recognised or taken sufficiently seriously by professionals' (Brandon et al, 2008a, p 9). Where youth justice services are seen as the responsible agency, it can be hard to persuade other agencies to help to meet the needs of some young offenders. 'Although agencies are aware of the need to co-operate, this division of responsibilities can still lead to conflict between services about whose job it is to meet different aspects of need' (Fielder et al, 2008, p 41). Similarly, Sutherland (2009b) discusses some of the difficulties for YOTs in working within MAPPA if different obligations are not clearly understood and articulated. There is a need for clarity about the core business of each agency and who is responsible for meeting different elements of need.

The thresholds for agencies to take action vary. A very common frustration expressed to the authors by practitioners relates to the difficulties of persuading health and children's services that young people in the youth justice system have needs sufficient to trigger their involvement. In relation to children's services, Driscoll documents widespread concerns that 'a high proportion of "at risk" cases are not deemed to be of sufficiently high priority to be allocated resources' (Driscoll, 2009, p 336). A recent inspection report on safeguarding found that other agencies were also experiencing problems in the response to referrals to children's services (Joint Chief Inspectors, 2008). Those working with young people in the secure estate can encounter real difficulties in accessing appropriate services on release (Hart, 2006; NACRO, 2008). Similarly, evaluations of MAPPA suggest that just having structures and policies in place is not sufficient. They have found that, in general, YOTs were not well embedded into the MAPPA structure and were finding it difficult to work within those arrangements (Kemshall et al, 2005; Sutherland and Jones, 2008). Again, this may in part be about thresholds, because 'when compared to the local adult population, young people seem less "risky" and thus may not be referred' (Sutherland, 2009b, p 53).

Other factors can also hinder multi-agency working. Hilder, for example, suggests that smaller, voluntary sector, community-based agencies, may lose some of the characteristics that made them appropriate to BME young people because of what she calls 'cultural transference as part of a statutory partnership contract' (Hilder, 2010, p 71). A focus on targets and output-based performance management has also, arguably, damaged relationships between agencies. Commentators have suggested, in the context of child protection, that there has been too mechanistic an approach and an overemphasis on thresholds (Brandon et al, 2008b; Deveny, 2008). This can distort practice, making it less focused on engaging with the complexities of some young people's needs.

Reder and Duncan expressed concern about the tendency of responses to inquiries to 'concentrate their implications down to a series of policy statements or tasks that could be audited' (Reder and Duncan, 2004b, p 97). Instead, like Driscoll cited earlier, they suggest that greater attention should be paid to the individual professionals involved, focusing on their skills, knowledge and working environment. They draw attention to the importance of practitioners understanding why they are carrying out particular tasks and being aware that, when sharing information with other professionals, they need to communicate both facts and the meanings that they have attributed to those facts. This echoes some of the discussion in Chapter Two and leads now to a consideration of how to improve working relationships between professionals.

Sustaining and developing professional relationships

Despite all the attention now given to working in collaboration, there is often still a lack of clarity about what constitutes a good inter-agency relationship (Murphy, 2004; Glennie, 2007). In response, Murphy et al (2006) have proposed eight standards for inter-agency practice, relating to areas such as: clarity about roles and responsibilities; consultation and communication; reviews; and recording of inter-agency collaboration. These standards have implications for policy, for how organisations are led and managed and for how individual practitioners work and interact with young people and each other. Guidance on the skills required by the children's workforce reflects similar themes (DCSF, 2010a).

Effective working with other professionals needs a set of personal skills and understandings. McKimm and Phillips (2009) discuss the importance of emotional intelligence for collaborative leadership. They identify three important components: the drivers – what motivates us to make the effort; the constrainers – what helps to make sure our motivation is put into practice with integrity; and the enablers – the skills that facilitate our efforts. Adapting that idea, this chapter suggests that to work and communicate well with other professionals:

- One of the drivers should be a desire among practitioners to use and develop their individual expertise and that of others, a belief that harnessing a range of expertise will be best for young people.

- Multi-agency practice needs to be delivered with integrity, with practitioners remaining reflective and willing to question practice in order to avoid insular practice or simplistic solutions.

Developing and sharing professional expertise

To work well with others a practitioner needs a secure sense of self-efficacy; that is, they should be clear about their skills and confident that they can use those skills, in context, to achieve the desired outcomes (Bandura, 1997). Where this is lacking, problems may arise. In child protection settings, for example, it has been found that inexperienced practitioners or those who are under-confident are less likely to play a full part in safeguarding and less likely to challenge the decisions of others (Brandon et al, 2005).

Murphy cautions against inter-agency efforts being dominated by a particularly powerful perspective (2004), and Leadbetter against guarding particular elements of practice (2008). A challenge for all staff, therefore, is to foster professional efficacy, while also remaining open to the expertise of others (Edwards et al, 2008). Practitioners who are most secure in their skill base should, arguably, be the most likely to recognise the skills of others without feeling threatened. It is important, instead, to know what other practitioners can offer, how to access their expertise and then how to coordinate and bring together different elements of practice. Edwards et al talk about being 'professionally multilingual' (2009, p 61), that is, knowing enough about the work of others and their professional language to be able to communicate effectively and to respect the work that they do.

Table 7.1 (loosely derived from a table in Brandon et al, 2005) summarises some of the range of knowledge that confident youth justice practitioners need. The row labels list the areas covered in an *Asset* assessment, broadly divided into four sections. The column titles are different kinds of expertise:

- knowledge of legislation, processes and how agencies work;
- expert knowledge deriving from professional background and qualifications;
- knowledge that derives from working experience, such as being aware of 'who knows who' in a neighbourhood, for example.

The first section of the table is completed to provide one example and is written from the point of view of a probation officer newly seconded into a YOT, who is working with a young person at the stage of the PSR.

The example illustrates that this professional has some real strengths to draw on in assessment but that they also need to make use of the expertise of others to supplement their thinking and practice. If they were completing the rest of the table, they might realise, for example, that while they had an expert understanding of cognitive deficits in young people they had much less knowledge about how these operated in practice for young people in this particular community. One of the challenges for this practitioner, as they develop a broader range of youth justice skills, is to remain as open as they are here. They will need less advice, but should remain aware of times when they need the expertise of other professionals. Working with others requires those concerned to have a clear idea about what they contribute to the process and what they can learn from others, and a real desire to do both of those things.

Table 7.1: Developing professional expertise

	Procedures and protocols	Expert knowledge	'On the ground' knowledge
Families and personal relationships	The probation officer knows about child protection procedures and MAPPA processes relevant to an adult in the family, but less about the CAF which has been completed on this young person. They ask a social worker in their team to give them some advice about the CAF process.	They have a good understanding of the criminality of this young person's father and older siblings and its significant impact on this young person. There are, however, worries about the child's emotional well-being in the family and while understanding some of this, they also contact a social worker involved with the family, to get a more complete picture. In turn they are able to help the social worker better understand the young person's offending.	They know about the pressures facing families with multiple difficulties and how hard parents can find it to cope. They are not used to being in a family situation engaging with young people too, so do a joint home visit with a parenting worker. Both workers learn from the skills and understandings of the other.
Neighbourhood and life-style			
Health – mental and physical/serious substance misuse			
Young person's attitudes, thinking and behaviour			

Activity

Use Table 7.1 to review your own, or another practitioner's, expertise and confidence in using that expertise most appropriately. Identify:

- areas of knowledge, strengths, and gaps
- where to turn in order to fill the gaps
- when knowledge should most helpfully be shared with others.

Self-awareness in working with others

It is important to be self-aware about the processes that affect how working relationships play out in practice. One of the influences on professional practice and on discussions between professionals is the way in which practitioners understand their role. In a study of an organisation working with homeless women, Juhila (2009) identified 'interpretive repertoires' used by workers to conceptualise their role in practice, including caring, assessment, control, therapy, service provision and fellowship. Similarly, Taylor (2006) identified a range of 'paradigms' or interpretations of the practitioner's role in the long-term care of older people. The repertoire, or paradigm, being used at any one time will affect how professionals make sense of roles and responsibilities. Given the dual focus of youth justice, one meeting might include workers who are operating on a predominantly caring paradigm, alongside others whose paradigm is around control and yet others who are thinking in a therapeutic way. All may be appropriate and helpful, provided workers are sufficiently explicit about their perspectives and the individuals concerned are able to act with integrity and listen to each other.

These different repertoires of understanding are in part a reflection of the roles and responsibilities of different professionals and can be seen in concrete form in the range of plans young people are subject to. One young person may have a plan as a looked-after child, alongside a MAPPA risk management plan and an intervention plan in youth justice. Partly because these plans may be rooted in different paradigms, there may be a tension between them and the professionals involved will have to work together to make sure that conflicts are worked through and don't impact unhelpfully on the young person.

Earlier sections of the chapter have explored the need for, and role of, professional integrity in multi-agency working, but maintaining that integrity while working in groups of professionals is not always straightforward. Meetings allow for the sharing of knowledge and expertise and sometimes of resources. However, they can also become ends in themselves, with safe practice being seen as having held the meeting rather than 'whether intelligent discussion took place' (Munro, 2008b). It has also been suggested that decision making in groups can give the illusion of fairness and objectivity, but groups, like individuals, are still prone to bias and error (as briefly discussed in Chapter Two). For example, groups are more likely to reach agreement around a high- or low-risk assessment than a moderate one

(Munro, 2008a). Groups can be closed minded and avoid conflicting views and contain within them a pressure towards conformity. Nash (2010) suggests that there are dangers that multi-agency working can lead to a single, mono–agency view of a problem. In a survey of practitioners involved in MAPPA, he found that some did not value the expertise of other agencies. In general, practitioners agreed about the importance of sharing information, but rated listening to the perspectives of others less highly.

Similar processes can apply in one-to-one inter-professional decision making. In a study involving approved social workers and psychiatrists making decisions in pairs, Peay (2003) found good practice, but also similar problematic processes, including decisions being seen as the only choice even when there were unexplored alternatives to consider, and strong opinions were sometimes dominating the discussion. It is therefore the responsibility of every practitioner to maintain professional integrity, resist pressures from closed and unhelpful interpersonal processes and really listen to and value different perspectives.

Activity

Use the following questions to review a meeting that included a number of agency and/or professional perspectives.

- How successful was the discussion in striking an appropriate balance between enabling participants to put their own perspectives and encouraging openness to the perspectives of others?
- Did one or more particular viewpoint(s) dominate and, if so, what effect did this have?
- What interpretive repertoires or paradigms could you identify among the participants in the discussion? What effect did they have?
- If there were a number of plans for a young person, was relevant attention paid to ensuring that they all worked together and didn't conflict?

Communicating effectively

As will be evident from the discussions so far, communication is essential to effective practice in working with others. It affects all stages of the assessment and planning process, from gathering information, through to analysing its meanings and then writing reports or sharing information with colleagues and decision makers (as discussed in Chapter Six, for example). 'Front-line practitioners need to be supported to talk across professional boundaries' (University of Birmingham, 2005, p v), not least because of the problems that can arise where communication is inadequate. Case reviews, for example, regularly identify poor communication as a contributory factor to serious incidents (Reder and Duncan, 2004a; Brandon et al, 2005).

Practitioners need to be able to articulate the evidence and knowledge base for their practice decisions (Osmond and O'Connor, 2004). Guidance on multi-agency working in the children's workforce emphasises communication skills such as 'listening and ensuring you are being listened to', providing 'timely, appropriate, succinct information' (DCSF, 2010a, p 18) and being 'able to use clear language to communicate information unambiguously' (p 21). Communication is easy to identify as essential, but harder to achieve in practice, and the reasons for that are complex. It is, however, an area where individual practitioners can consciously seek to develop their skills (see also Chapter Eight).

A model of communication

A well-known model of communication summarises the process of transmitting information from a source to a receiver (Donnelly and Neville, 2008). It includes:

- the cognitive content of the message;
- the process of transmitting it;
- the channel chosen for that transmission (your voice or a written document, for example);
- the receiver of the message and their cognitive response.

Donnelly and Neville expand the model to include an understanding that messages are not unidirectional, but pass backwards and forwards between the participants, affecting how the communication is received, developed and understood. The model also incorporates the idea of noise – something that disrupts the communication and that can include:

- physical factors, for example noisy offices or pressure of time affecting attention;
- psychological factors, for example anxiety and stress;
- semantic factors, for example a lack of clarity about how terms are used.

One suggestion for improving communication and reducing 'noise' involves asking the following questions (YJB, 2005c; drawn from the 5WH model of open questioning discussed in Chapter Eight):

- Who needs the information?
- Why do they need it?
- What do they need to know?
- When do they need to know it?
- Where will they receive it?
- How do I want them to use it?

A transmitter should think about their audience and why they are communicating with them. If it is just as an end in itself, or for 'back covering', how helpful is that communication likely to be? All of the potential routes for communication should be considered, alongside the detailed content, including analysis and judgement about the meaning of facts.

Disagreements may often be about meaning, rather than facts themselves; for example, the transmitter may think the facts suggest mental health needs, whereas the recipient sees them as suggesting a need for additional controls on a young person's behaviour. The urgency or otherwise of the communication should be taken into account, as this affects the choice of appropriate channels. Urgency might dictate a telephone call, but significance might indicate a follow-up in writing. For example, a violent step-parent has returned unexpectedly to the family home. A youth justice worker might immediately telephone other agencies to alert them to an imminent risk, but would follow this up as soon as possible with a written confirmation, possibly including a more formal request for a review of the situation.

All the time it is important to think about the recipient and about the context where the communication is being received. In MAPPA, for example, many participants may be focused on adult offenders and may not fully understand issues for young people. As is suggested in Chapter Four, it is important not to assume that just because a worker uses one assessment tool they will understand all possible tools; a social worker using a CAF may not understand *Asset* and vice versa. Careful thought about all of those elements should help to minimise 'noise'.

Once communication is embarked upon, it has the potential to be a two-way process, so the final question of how the information should be used is crucial. If the transmitter wants the recipient to take action and the latter is tasked by their agency with holding to thresholds, the response may not be all that was hoped for. The transmitter should think ahead about how to respond if this occurs.

As a recipient of communications from others, it is just as important to be alert to roles and responsibilities, to listen and to make best use of the information received, being pro-active in seeking clarification. Recipients may distort the meaning of some communications – for example, if they conflict with decisions already made (Chapter Two has a fuller discussion of this process of confirmation bias). A youth justice worker needs to understand, and value accordingly, different kinds of communications received about young people and the strengths and weaknesses of each. For example, the different status of police intelligence and a formal assessment by a social worker will affect how those communications should be recorded and acted upon.

Activity

Use the following table to analyse a particularly difficult experience of communicating, in order to identify what might be done differently.

What did the transmitter actually do?	What did the receiver hear and do?	What could be done to improve communication next time?
To whom was the information given, and why?		
What information was given? (Think about both facts and meaning.)		
When and where was the information provided and in what form?		
What action was hoped for from the receiver? Was that made explicit to the receiver?		

Sharing meanings and understandings

In an analysis of reviews of child deaths and serious injuries, Brandon et al (2005) make the point that what is most helpful to share is information not just about symptoms, but also about their impact on behaviour. Similarly in youth justice, being able to communicate specific and helpful information and insight to others is essential for good assessment. For example, a young person may have substance misuse problems; aside from that information, what may be more valuable to share for one young person is that those problems lead to aggression, whereas for another they lead to passivity and reluctance to act.

At the outset of this chapter there was an attempt to clarify the terms of this discussion. There is also potential for confusion around terms used to communicate and reach decisions about young people, such as 'risk' and 'harm'. For example, workers in the community and those in the secure estate may have very different perspectives on the kinds of issues captured by those terms. The former may be largely thinking about reoffending, the latter about risks to the safe running of the institution.

Youth justice practitioners have a responsibility to think about how to explain their roles and processes to others; for example, how someone from another agency might be helped to understand what is meant by a risk of serious harm classification. Equally, if a practitioner is unsure about the language used by another agency, they have a responsibility to say so and ask for clarification.

Conclusion

Working and communicating with other agencies is a central component of assessment in youth justice. Practitioners need to have well-developed skills in listening and in sharing decision making with other professionals, and be good at reflecting on their own practice and their professional relationships. They also need to be clear about their own expertise and open to the contributions of others. Achieving all this requires a commitment to the ongoing development of skills (Chapter Eight) and appropriate organisational support (Chapter Nine).

Part Three
Skills and practice development

EIGHT

Skills in assessment

[T]he skills required in assessment are slowly acquired through training and experience. (Davies, 1985, p 157)

Introduction

Using tools can be a dangerous business. In the wrong hands, tools can cause the user or others serious damage. You or I using a saw, for example, might risk injury. The outcome for a carpenter, however, should be a chair that will work reliably as a piece of furniture and, if making furniture is the carpenter's livelihood, can be reproduced to meet customer demand, time and again, with some degree of accuracy. The quality of the product will depend upon the knowledge, practical expertise, skills and problem-solving abilities of the carpenter. He or she will understand how wood responds to different tools, will choose the best tool for the desired outcome, and will also need to have dexterity in manipulating the wood and the tools to achieve that outcome.

Similarly, in youth justice, it isn't just about selecting the right tool for the job (see Chapter Four) or having theoretical and research-based knowledge about young people and offending (Chapter Three). In order to achieve the outcomes of assessment in youth justice, the practitioner also needs a set of skills in terms of the methods they employ and the way in which they process information (Skills for Justice, 2008). Developing proficiency in assessment and planning through the acquisition of these skills is a shared responsibility between individuals and organisations (see Chapter Nine).

Professional expertise in working with children and young people is widely understood to derive from a combination of factors (McNeill et al, 2005; Munro, 2008a; Whyte, 2009; DCSF, 2010a). These include: the skills that practitioners routinely employ in their work with young people, especially in relation to communication with others and problem-solving; personal qualities, such as appropriate values, emotional insight and reasoning skills (Trevithick, 2000; Lefevre, 2010); formal knowledge (as described in Chapter Three); and practical experience. Expertise, like knowledge, is not static; it can be developed or enhanced by training and experience, through working with others, by the capacity to reflect on practice and by learning from studies which focus on what practitioners actually do in real-life day-to-day work (Bonta et al, 2008; Forrester et al, 2008; Trotter and Evans, 2010).

Some of the skills required for assessment have already been discussed in earlier chapters, for example, the critical thinking needed to interpret and analyse information (Chapter Two), the ability to work in a structured and systematic way to produce plans and reports (Chapters Five and Six), and the ability to communicate and work with professionals from other organisations (Chapter Seven). This chapter complements these earlier discussions by looking, firstly, at practical skills in preparing for and organising assessments. It then turns to the enquiry process, focusing on how interviews are conducted and how young people can be encouraged to participate in the process. The chapter also offers some practical ideas about recording information and ends with consideration of reviews, given that (as described in Chapter One) assessment is an ongoing activity.

Reflection

Take time to think about the skills that you use in your work with young people and others that have already been touched upon in this book.

- What do you think your strengths are?
- Where assessments have been effective, what did you do that made a difference?
- Are there any skills in which you are less confident? If so, think about how you might begin to change that.

A planned and reflective approach

Formal tools can alleviate some of the pressure when planning which issues to address in assessments and can certainly act as aides-mémoires (see Chapter Four). However, to rely too heavily upon the tool may lead to an approach in which assessment is treated as an event rather than a process (see Chapter One). Tools root assessments in a specific context and provide a broad map for the assessor, but are, and can only be, half the story. The other half of the story is how practitioners approach the task. With assessments having to vie for attention with other equally urgent priorities, the time to use a thoughtful and skilled approach is sometimes squeezed out by everything else that needs to be done. Practitioners and, perhaps just as importantly, managers need to find ways of giving priority to a planned and systematic, but also reflective, approach; this is likely to be more effective than a reactive, piecemeal one.

An assessment that is planned and organised:

- is more likely to be purposeful, focused and accurate (Coulshed and Orme, 2006);
- can help the assessor recognise the limitations of their assessment, to identify gaps in their knowledge;
- supports positive engagement with young people, who will be helped to respond appropriately and positively if they know what is expected of them and why (Parker and Bradley, 2007);

- can help practitioners begin to compile information and marshal arguments when preparing reports or communicating with other agencies to access resources.

The need for preparation

Chapters One and Four have highlighted the importance of preparing for assessments, and this is explored further here. There are, for example, aspects of the environment in which assessment takes place in youth justice which underline the importance of practitioners taking a measured and organised approach.

The quality of the relationship established between a practitioner and a young person is a critical factor in the accuracy and effectiveness of the assessment (McNeill et al, 2005; Ellis and France, 2010). However, assessments require young people to talk about their behaviour to unfamiliar adults who are in positions of authority. These conversations often take place in formal and, for some, uncomfortable surroundings – interview rooms in busy offices, secure establishments, courts or police stations. In many instances participation is compulsory and involuntary and cooperation is, to some degree, coerced. This may be unavoidable but can hinder the positive engagement necessary to promote change (Hörnqvist, 2007; Barnett and Mann, 2010; Farrow et al, 2011). As noted in Chapter One, McNeill argues that practitioners should try to 'anticipate the types of aspirations and concerns that the offender may bring to the supervision process' (McNeill, 2009a, p 31) and then plan ahead accordingly.

Assessment also takes place in a multi-agency context. While the focus in this chapter is upon enquiries involving the young person and their family/carers, assessments necessarily entail gathering information from other professionals and agencies. This raises many issues about status, relationships and the quality of information sharing which were explored in Chapter Seven. For our purposes here, the key point relates to the need for preparation. Pre-planning, knowing what questions to ask and being clear about roles, responsibilities and boundaries will all contribute to productive professional conversations.

The need for planning and organisation is further highlighted by issues arising from what practitioners themselves bring to the equation. They may be subject to deadlines and formal requirements which can produce a sense of pressure or powerlessness (Lefevre, 2010). They may feel uncomfortable working with a particular offender or dealing with certain types of offences. Alternatively, they may feel less skilled or knowledgeable in communicating with particular groups, such as minority ethnic young people and their families (de Vries, 2008). Their confidence can be enhanced by developing their communication skills, but will also be helped by their being clear about the purpose of their enquiries and what type of information they are looking for.

In youth justice, therefore, the practitioner is not simply a neutral interviewer, a compiler of data; when preparing to undertake assessments there are sensitivities to be addressed, environments to be managed and the effects of potentially unhelpful power dynamics to be recognised and allowed for. A systematic and reflective approach is not simply about handling sometimes complex information from a range of sources, but is an important foundation for ensuring that the assessment process is ethical and transparent and that the information gathered is of sufficient relevance, depth and detail.

Being systematic and organised

Being systematic means recognising the importance of time management; prioritising and sequencing activities; organising and recording data; reliability; and attention to detail (Trevithick, 2000; Parker and Bradley, 2007). Consequently, a number of practical questions need addressing before you embark on the assessment itself. The following list suggests some simple steps that should be part of an organised approach:

- Be clear about deadlines and plan accordingly (taking account of other work commitments that might get in the way).
- Note what information you need to gather from whom, where and how, and leave enough time to accomplish this.
- Think ahead to the need for home visits or office interviews and about the availability of interviewing space.
- If you anticipate difficulties, for example, in getting pre-convictions or information during school holidays, plan ahead.
- Consider beforehand whether there are any particular issues relating to the young person's age, maturity, background or capabilities which will influence how information is communicated.
- Allow time for thinking and reflecting before interviews and as the process goes on. Use this time to structure your own thinking and ongoing planning and to reflect on the engagement of the young person in the process.
- Look ahead to any help you may need, including the services of an interpreter, specialist assessments or consultation with colleagues and managers. Leave enough time for them to do their jobs.
- Allocate sufficient time for recording and report writing.

It may not be possible or necessary to apply such a detailed planning process in every case. The steps listed above, however, represent a checklist or framework that, over time and with practice, might be absorbed into the practitioner's body of expertise, becoming their routine way of approaching assessment.

Activity

Use the list above to review the planning that went into an assessment. Identify what was helpful, and also any gaps in the preparation.

Paying attention to power and powerlessness

In preparing for any discussion with children and their families, thought needs to be given to the dynamics of power and authority, as these can influence if, and how, information is exchanged. Ideally, effective assessors would provide 'a listening ear and a sounding board that is free of compulsion and fear' (Barry, 2007, p 47). With 'the duality between the enforcement and enabling functions of the youth justice system' (Hart and Thompson, 2009, p 4), however, some degree of compulsion is inevitable. However, the fear and potential imbalances of power attached to this do need to be addressed in how the assessment and planning process is managed (Jones, 2003). Assessors need to be alert, for example, to the fact that young people may exercise their own (limited) power or influence by saying nothing and resisting the interview process. While this might sometimes be interpreted as showing lack of insight or remorse, it might equally be indicative of cynicism about the process and how they can contribute to it (Luckock et al, 2006; Milner and O'Byrne, 2009).

The right of children to be consulted and listened to is embodied in statements of intent and legislation (Article 12 of the UN Convention on the Rights of the Child, the Children Act 2004 and, in Scotland, the Commissioner for Children and Young People (Scotland) Act 2003). In this context, there has been increased interest in encouraging participation by young people in the decisions that affect their lives (Hart, 1997; SPICe, 2002; Hart and Thompson, 2009; Wood and Hine, 2009) and in exploring what qualities they value in those who have responsibility for making decisions about their lives (see, for example, Morgan (2006) on young people's views about what they value in social workers).

One theme that has emerged is the danger, particularly in contexts such as youth justice, where participation is often involuntary, that the exchange of information may be tokenistic (Fleming and Hudson, 2009); that children and young people are asked to say what they think about an issue but have little or no choice about how their views are then expressed or acted upon (Mitchell et al, 2009). One example here would be about how much weight is given to self-assessments completed by young people in the justice system.[1] The extent to which an assessor reflects on the issues raised and explores differences in perspective with the young person will send messages about how seriously his/her views are taken. The self-assessment, even where formalised in tools and procedures, can still be seen as 'going through the motions' unless the assessor's response is individualised and interactive.

In planning interviews (at whatever stage in the assessment process), and before asking any questions, assessors must be interested in the answers that might be given (Trevithick, 2000, p 86). This kind of genuine engagement seems to be essential to effective and empathic communication (Forrester et al, 2008) and will mean being prepared to take the answers seriously, however unexpected they might be or however much we might disagree with them. In some cases this may not be immediate but will occur later in the ongoing assessment process. Once you begin to talk about children's subjective experiences, as opposed to factual information, answers are more likely to be provisional and incomplete and may only be explored properly as the relationship between worker and young person develops.

Encouraging and managing expectations

Hart and Thompson (2009) suggest that young offenders have particularly low expectations about their ability to influence decisions. It is perhaps even more important, therefore, to encourage genuine contribution, to listen, and not to be tokenistic. It is also important for the assessor to be clear with the young person that while their story is central, it is not the whole story. The assessor will, in gathering information and compiling their assessments, be employing skills in 'analysis and interpretations ... which ... demand different knowledge than that generally available to children' (Harden et al, 2000, para 2.20). There is a balance to be struck between taking the young person's version of events seriously and evaluating it alongside other information to produce a balanced, professional assessment. Just as tokenistic approaches can produce cynicism and disengagement, so too can raising unrealistic expectations about how far the young person can influence the outcome of the process. Setting clear boundaries within the interview is therefore essential, especially where, in some cases, you may have to make professional decisions which may ultimately restrict a young person's freedom or which they perceive as intrusive (see also the section on involuntary clients in Chapter Five).

Reflection

Put yourself in a young person's shoes and think about how they feel about being asked to talk about difficult subjects.

- What can be done to reduce their unease and lack of power in the situation?
- How do they know that an interviewer is genuinely interested in their story?

The enquiry process 1: assessment interviews

Assessments should draw upon a range of sources, and this wider information can help assessors to evaluate the young person's perspective; it complements, sheds light, adds depth and supports professional understandings and judgements. Interviews and the quality of the information they generate remain fundamental, however, as it is the information gleaned from the young person that provides access to the way they make sense of their own experiences and social worlds. Interviews are undertaken in different settings, formal and informal, and can employ a multitude of methods and techniques which go beyond a simple question–answer format.

The importance of everyday skills

The 'everyday' professional skills (Munro, 2008a) relevant to all interactions with young people are not left at the door when undertaking assessments. In communicating with children and young people, the practitioner needs to have good listening skills; to be culturally sensitive (Kadushin and Kadushin, 1997; Luckock et al, 2006; Dalzell and Sawyer, 2007; Milner and O'Byrne, 2009); to be able to empathise and put themselves in another person's shoes; and to be able to demonstrate the specific 'communication process or skill' (Mason and Prior, 2008, p 28) of showing genuine interest in what young people have to say.

Skills aimed at building trust are also core to work with children and families (DCSF, 2010a), and the aim should be to create 'rapport', which Trevithick helpfully defines as: 'the favourable conditions necessary for people to be able to discuss and reveal problems or difficulties, successes or failures, and strengths or weaknesses in ways that aid understanding and allow for a realistic plan of action to be created' (2000, p 76). From the initial contact with a young person a tone is being set. Not only do you want to obtain the best possible information, you also want to lay the foundations for future interventions (YJB, 2008a). The satisfaction of service users, voluntary or involuntary, 'hinges significantly upon the interpersonal behaviour of the staff they encounter' (Koprowska, 2010, p 34). This behaviour includes what the practitioner says, how they say it and what they do, from meeting and greeting the young person in the first place, through to the assessment conclusion and decision-making process. It is important that the practitioner communicates a professional approach that is disciplined and rigorous, demonstrates care, concern and competence (Trevithick, 2000) and models the values and behaviours that they would expect from the young people (Trotter, 2006).

In work with involuntary clients, Trotter identifies 'role clarification' as a key skill, addressing the questions: 'What are we here for? What do we hope to get out of this? What do we have to do? What do we have a choice about?' (2006, p 65). Attention is paid to the purpose of the assessment, what both worker and young person can expect, how information will be used and issues of confidentiality (Luckock et al, 2006). Clarity and transparency are also important attributes (Koprowska, 2010) and, when applied in the assessment, are the basis of an ethical foundation for what will be a professional 'conversation with a purpose' (Trevithick, 2000, p 69). When talking to young people and their parents/carers at the information-gathering stage, therefore, practitioners should aim:

- to explain the purpose of the interview and assessment process (Hutton and Partridge, 2006), including what will be done with the information gathered;
- to clearly describe roles and responsibilities;
- to be clear about what is expected of the young person and how they can participate in the assessment and planning process (taking care, as noted above, not to raise false expectations);

- to clarify boundaries and limits to confidentiality;
- to describe how the interview will be managed, including timings and any ground rules about how people should contribute or listen to each other. It might be helpful to build in some 'thinking time' when you could take a break to take stock (either together or separately) of what you know, to see whether there are any important questions still to be asked and to consider next steps;
- to keep the purpose modest and of 'manageable proportions' (Kadushin and Kadushin, 1997, p 93) so as to avoid being over-ambitious about what can be achieved in a limited time period.

It can also be helpful to everyone to acknowledge the artificiality of the interview setting, which might make some people feel awkward about talking. The assessor needs to remember that a successful interview isn't always about the words that are said; silence or the young person's behaviour can be just as informative. It can be reassuring to explain to the young person that they do have some choice in what information to confide.

How these key points are communicated (the style, tone and language that the practitioner uses) will influence how the information is received and understood, which in turn sets the tone for the conversation to follow. Practitioners should always aim to use language that can be understood by the interviewee(s) (Coulshed and Orme, 2006; YJB, 2008a; Communication Trust, 2009), for example:

- Be as specific and straightforward as possible, avoiding jargon and overly negative, problem-oriented language which could increase the young person's anxiety.
- Use a language and tone that is appropriate to individual children, being sensitive to their situation and their level of understanding (Luckock et al, 2006, p 25).
- Be alert to the dangers of a mismatch in dialogue styles between adults and children (Jones and Roberts, 2006) and the associated risk of discussions being primarily between the adults (including parents/carers), thus marginalising the young person.

The following is the first in a series of activities that can be used to structure observations and feedback about assessment interviews.

Activity: Reviewing an interview 1

Arrange to observe someone else carrying out an interview, or ask someone to observe you. Use the following questions to structure some observations and feedback.

- How were the interviewees welcomed and helped to feel at home?
- How were they helped to understand the process and what was expected of them?
- How was language adjusted – for example, to explain technical or legal issues – without patronising participants?
- If adults were present, how were they included? What balance was struck between their contribution and that of the young person?

Questions

Interviews are a time for exploration, and asking questions is therefore at the heart of an interview. Kadushin and Kadushin describe asking questions as a 'multipurpose intervention' (1997, p 235) which helps the interviewee to begin to organise the presentation of their ideas and include all relevant material in their responses.

There are different types of questions that are each best suited to specific purposes.

- **Closed questions**, for example, are used to obtain and check out basic factual information: the content of the questions is tightly defined by the practitioner, with the interviewee giving straightforward responses that often demand little reflection. Beyond refusal to answer a question or giving incorrect information, the interviewee has limited control over the content or direction of the conversation. Closed questions are most relevant when seeking concrete information and verifying its accuracy.
- **Open questions**, on the other hand, recognise that the other person has detailed knowledge about their own situation and seek to elicit this perspective. Open questions are exploratory, aiming to develop depth, understanding and meaning. They are often captured under the 5WH heading: who, why, what, where, when, how. It is usually difficult to give one-word answers and the interviewee has to think about their response. In this case the young person has more active control over what information they share.

Closed questions may be more characteristic of the 'questioning model', whereas open questions are associated more with the 'exchange model' (these different approaches to assessment were discussed in Chapter One). Assessors need to know how and when to use both types of question appropriately.

When using open questions, the practitioner needs to steer the interview so as to ensure that it retains an appropriate focus. They will listen accurately and respond appropriately, perhaps with further questions to probe beneath the surface and to help the interviewee develop their thinking, or by clarifying and reflecting back what they take to be the meaning of what is said. They will also use their observational skills to gauge the behavioural response of the young person. Sometimes there can be a disjunction between what is said, how it is said and the general demeanour of the young person. A young person might minimise the impact of their actions on a victim, suggesting a lack of remorse. Signs of embarrassment or upset, however, might also be an indication that this verbal minimisation is masking real ambivalence and unease, which can then be explored with follow-up questions.

The three complementary skill-sets discussed below can help assessors to expand upon the young person's initial response to open questions and to take opportunities to get 'below the surface'.

Socratic questioning

This helps to 'create a dialogue and helps the other person to work through information and arrive at their own answers' (Callahan et al, 2009, Theory disc: 18) to *explore* issues. A Socratic dialogue is particularly useful as the young person begins to talk about their offending and difficulties associated with it. Socratic questions encourage greater honesty and depth of information, helping the young person 'to move beyond habitual responses … [and to concentrate] … on the attitudes and beliefs underpinning statements' (Kemshall et al, 2007). They can be used to achieve a range of purposes:

- probing reasons for beliefs and the evidence that supports them (for example: How do you know that? What might change your mind about this?);
- making a young person think about different perspectives on their situation (for example: What would your mum think or do in that situation?);
- prompting reflection upon the consequences of their behaviour (for example: What if you continue to solve your problems in this way?);
- unpicking beliefs and attitudes (for example: When you said … what did you mean?).

Assumptive questions

In contrast to Socratics, assumptive questions are designed to challenge and expand upon the young person's account of events. They are a technique which should be used sparingly in order to extend knowledge, not as the main means of obtaining it. They can also be used as a means of assisting the young person to move beyond a tendency to avoid responsibility that might, understandably, be inherent in their account of their own behaviour (Vrij, 2002). Asked with care, they can encourage the individual to talk about issues which they find awkward, uncomfortable or embarrassing. There is, however, a balance to be struck between not allowing the young person to avoid talking about a subject and unnecessarily breaking down their defences. This is an exploratory process rather than an inquisition, with the aim being to achieve a more accurate understanding of the behaviour in context and of its consequences.

These questions draw upon the assessor's knowledge about young people's offending (see Chapter Three) and contain within them an implicit assumption about the situation. Examples could include:

- 'How many times a week would you guess you use cannabis?' instead of 'Do you use cannabis?' (Assumption = this young person is more likely than not to use cannabis.)
- 'What bothers you about your behaviour?' instead of 'Are you bothered about your behaviour? (Assumption = the young person will be concerned, this is normal but difficult to express.)
- 'Why was your dad so upset about …?' instead of 'Was your dad upset?' (Assumption = The young person's behaviour is having an upsetting effect on others.)
- 'When you were walking past the house, what made you think it would be OK or safe to go in?' instead of 'What happened next?' (Assumption = burglaries involve some element of forethought.)

Active listening

The practitioner's response to answers to Socratic and assumptive questions could usefully draw upon motivational interviewing skills (Miller and Rollnick, 2002), particularly those skills associated with (really) active listening:

- Reflecting back meaning as well as content; for example: 'When you said "they asked for it" [be careful to use the words of the young person as accurately as possible] … I thought that meant you weren't really in the wrong in acting in this way.'
- Making observations about behaviour as well as what was said; for example: 'When we were talking about your mum you looked worried – I wondered if that was because you are concerned about her giving up on you?',
- Accurate summarising and thoughtful paraphrasing; for example: 'So … you are telling me that you are most likely to commit offences when you are with your mates and are bored?',

The attentiveness of the practitioner is demonstrated through the questions they ask and the accuracy of their responses; this needs to be based on an empathic and sensitive understanding of the young person's experience and its meaning for them.

Activity: Reviewing an interview 2

As in the earlier activity, the following questions could be used to provide in-depth review and feedback on a real interview.

- Note examples of closed questions used appropriately to obtain and check facts.
- Note some examples of good open questions used to develop depth and detail.
- Note examples of Socratic questions used to explore the young person's experience and understanding.
- Note examples of assumptive questions used to challenge or expand upon the young person's perspective.
- Think about the balance between different types of questions and whether this is appropriate.
- Were any types of questions overused or used inappropriately.
- Were questions used at the right time in the interview and in a helpful order?

Varied and interactive methods

While asking 'good' questions is essential, effective interviewing goes beyond this in order to engage young people, and practitioners need to be able to draw on a variety of approaches, not just relying solely on verbal and language-based interaction (Mason and Prior, 2008). Sometimes we can perceive interviews which seem to lack depth of response and rapport as being less 'successful'. We risk assuming that the best kind of information comes from talking, and the more 'talk' the better (the information). In fact, children and young people may talk less than adults in formal settings, especially with unfamiliar adults, about difficult, sensitive topics (Harden et al, 2000). Research also suggests that young people are not as likely as adults to give long answers, so stimulus material and other prompts that can be used alongside careful questioning can help to encourage their positive engagement (Punch, 2002).

Methods such as drawing timelines, cartooning an event, using spider diagrams, constructing family trees or friendship circles all have their place at the assessment stage (Hutton and Partridge, 2006; Callahan et al, 2009), as does the use of technology. These are not designed simply to keep young people engaged. If chosen appropriately, taking account of the child's age, culture and abilities as well as the nature and pattern of their offending, they can support a Socratic dialogue which captures both detailed information about events and the significance of these events (Baker and Kelly, 2011). In addition, using a variety of methods and observing how the young person responds to different approaches (Borenstein, 2002) can give an insight into which approaches are likely to be effective in future interventions.

Some studies suggest that young black offenders appreciate and respond best to active, inclusive and inquisitive approaches (Tuklo Orenda Associates, 1999). These principles are also relevant to work with other young people, and such participative approaches can help to improve outcomes (Hart and Thompson, 2009). For practitioners this means using methods that:

- encourage the active participation of young people and reinforce their sense of agency (see Chapter Five);
- recognise the diverse needs and abilities of young people, increasing the possibility of their positive response to the assessment process;
- demonstrate a genuine interest in young people's lives, and in the depth and detail of their individual experiences (Callahan et al, 2009).

Activity: Reviewing an interview 3

As in the earlier activities, use the following questions to review and feed back on a real interview.

- What (if any) 'active' approaches were used?
- Why do you think they were used in this case?
- What effect did they have?

Use this last set of observations to think about what other approaches might have been tried and to think about what approaches might work best for different young people.

Note taking

During an interview, capturing and recording relevant information needs to be done in a way that doesn't impede the communication process. One helpful approach is the technique of summative note taking, which can be used to support motivational methods such as clarifying and reflecting back information. At intervals throughout the discussion the assessor summarises what has been said, checking with the young person that the information and the interpretation of it is accurate and recording those summaries in written form. This process of recording is more transparent but it is also a more time-consuming method and may be over-formal for some young people.

Note taking in general could be structured around the topic areas to be covered. While formal tools are not to be used as interview schedules, they can form the basis of simplified interview templates to be used to record information. An example of such a template is the diagrammatic version of the *Asset* framework (described in Chapter Five), which has also been developed into an activity that can be shared with a young person where they help to record the discussion alongside the assessor (Callahan et al, 2009). Other visual, interactive methods described earlier can also provide collaborative and open means of recording information and accompanying discussions. For example if a young person has completed a cartoon of an offence, this provides part of the record and can be returned to and worked on in more depth at a later date.

The enquiry process 2: 'cause and effect' thinking

Following the process of exploration that occurs during interview, it is then necessary to think about actions and solutions. Chapter Five emphasised the importance of understanding the interactions and effects of a range of factors in a young person's life in order to guide planning. Some specific skills and strategies can help the assessor, and sometimes the young person, to think through the causes of problematic behaviour and a range of potential consequences.

Understanding problems and identifying solutions

Chapter Two considered some of the 'shortcuts' that people commonly use when making decisions, with one example being our tendency to focus too quickly on familiar explanations or what would seem to be 'common sense' courses of action. Root cause analysis (Gano, 2008) is one example of an approach which can help to ensure that all the potential factors contributing to offending behaviour are considered, rather than just the most obvious ones. It is particularly useful for multi-dimensional, sometimes seemingly intractable, issues: it helps practitioners to deconstruct problems by asking questions about a range of causes, both immediate and more distant, and then identifying potential solutions, some of which may be contingent upon each other.

The principles have been adapted to develop problem-solving frameworks (Tooth, 2000), and also a model for working with young people involved in youth justice known as the 'Why? What if? Tree' (YJB, 2004; Callahan et al, 2009). This is a visual approach to plotting the cause and effect of problems, and the process can be shared with young people in order to help them seek realistic solutions. Figure 8.1 provides a partially worked example (from Callahan et al, 2009, p 103). Using the approach, the practitioner, with the young person, maps the roots (the 'Whys') of the presenting issue (stealing to buy drugs). The young person is helped to identify the most immediate obvious causes, in this case having no money and needing a fix. They are then helped to think about the causes of those causes and so on, continuing back as far as is useful. Some causes will be STOP points, causes that realistically can't be changed; others will be things they can do something about. This approach helps because it challenges existing perceptions of the problems, stretching the thinking of young person and worker alike. It allows the young person to think about a range of causes and makes them more likely to 'buy in' to solutions. It also helps to ensure that causes are addressed in the right order – so not being able to get up in the morning, for example, might need to be worked on before aiming to get a job.

The approach also recognises the value of everyone's contribution, and Gano (2008) emphasises the importance of incorporating a range of perspectives in unpicking problems and identifying solutions. It is, therefore, a model that is helpful in a range of situations and with diverse young people. In the event of breach action for non-compliance, for example, this method could be used to understand the reasons for the non-compliance, helping to see solutions that might make compliance more likely in the future. The approach can also be used, as the figure suggests, to think through the consequences (the 'what ifs') of an issue, including those that might be less immediately obvious to a young person.

Figure 8.1: The 'Why? What if?' tree

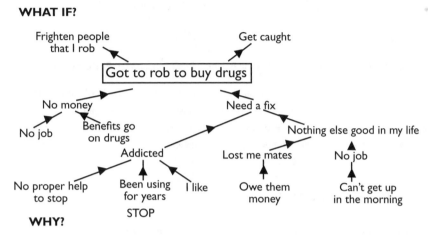

Where difficult decisions in high-risk situations such as child protection or parole are being considered, a similar but more detailed and technical approach using decision trees may be useful (Munro, 2008a). These have the advantage of allowing assessors 'to speculate more rigorously about the outcomes of their decisions on users and others, and to weigh more transparently and empirically the decision choices available to them' (Kemshall, 2008a, p 9).

Looking to the future

Since assessment is ongoing and young people's lives (and our understanding of them) keep developing, even well-structured plans can go wrong or encounter unexpected obstacles. To some extent this is unavoidable, but thinking ahead and planning for a range of contingencies can help, particularly in complex high-risk cases.

One method which can be used to help achieve that is to imagine a number of possible future scenarios that might (plausibly) happen. This process can then be used to think about additional elements to be included in plans. Imagine a young person who has been seriously violent to peers and to adults in authority; the risk-management plan might include a curfew to keep them away from pubs and clubs. The practitioner, knowing what the young person has done before, now thinks about what they might do in the future. This will involve considering whether the young person might be violent in different locations or towards different victims. This young person might be violent at home, for example, and the practitioner thinks about what might realistically trigger such behaviour and how serious it might be. This might lead them to consider that a curfew could result in a parent having to act more authoritatively and therefore becoming more at risk of violence from the young person. This consideration would then inform their planning; for example, they might build in additional support strategies for the parent. A much more detailed account of scenario planning for offenders who pose a particularly significant risk of harm to others can be found in materials published by the Scottish Risk Management Authority (2007b).

> **Activity**
>
> Look for opportunities to try out one or both of these approaches. For example:
>
> - the 'why?' tree could be used to analyse a case or included as part of a discussion with a young person to actively think through a range of causes and solutions;
> - thinking about future scenarios could be used in a case discussion about a young person who may present a risk of serious harm to others.

Reviewing assessments

Ongoing assessment and review is essential because practitioners 'neither have a crystal ball, nor do they know everything there is to know about past, present or the likely future' (Dalzell and Sawyer, 2007, p 89). The purpose of review is to fill gaps in knowledge, develop understanding and refine judgements and decisions so that interventions remain relevant, progress is reinforced and new problems are identified. There will usually be formal procedures and guidance relating to review, but ongoing assessment is a 'dynamic, self-questioning process' (Tuddenham, 2000, p 174) relying as much on the reflective and critical mindset of the practitioner as on these formal frameworks. Review is a professional task, not simply a monitoring process. As well as using tools and adhering to procedures, other important elements of review are:

- Young people should be involved. Assessments often increase in depth and accuracy as the relationship between practitioner and young person develops, highlighting progress as well as new areas of need.
- Assessments should be kept up to date, irrespective of formal and minimal required timescales.
- Using systematic approaches such as scenario planning (above) can enhance a practitioner's alertness to the possibility of change.
- Practitioners need to be both willing and able to reflect on their own practice and be open about and learn from their mistakes. In accepting that the truths of assessment are rarely finite and often provisional, the practitioner is more likely to be able to see and address problems as they develop, to shift perspective and learn from their mistakes or errors of judgement (Milner and O'Byrne, 2009).

• Reviewing assessments should also include an appraisal of the skills/methods employed so as to identify what was effective (or not) and to determine what needs to be done differently in future.

Reflection

Think about how work with individual young people is actively reviewed throughout their supervision.

- How have reviews helped you to develop your understanding of a young person?
- How have you used reviews to inform the content and direction of your interventions?

Conclusion

The skills discussed in this chapter provide an essential foundation for working with young people who offend and should underpin the use of assessment tools and formal frameworks. The context for practice is constantly changing, however, so that these, and the other skills covered in earlier chapters, will need to be continually developed and refined for use in new situations or with different groups of young people. Chapter Nine goes on to consider some of the ways in which both practitioners and organisations can achieve this.

Note
[1] Such as the 'What do YOU think?' self-assessment component of *Asset*.

NINE

Developing assessment practice

> People in organizations construct and enact worlds that, in turn, affect their behavior. What they study is what they become knowledgeable about and skilled in carrying out. (Cooperrider et al, 2008, p 33)

Introduction

A recurring theme of previous chapters has been the importance of professionalism and what this means in terms of, for example, the knowledge base required for assessment practice (Chapter Three), how assessment tools are used (Chapter Four) and the skills required for working with young people (Chapter Eight). A desire and commitment to improve practice is a further hallmark of professionalism and is the focus of this chapter.

There is a danger that talking about 'improvement' brings to mind ideas about audit or quality assurance processes which (because they tend to be seen as dull or bureaucratic activities) may put people off thinking about what can be done to develop assessment and planning practice. This is unfortunate because learning about how to improve what you do can, and should, lead to better outcomes for young people and communities, alongside a greater sense of professional satisfaction. Reflective questions have been used throughout the book to prompt thinking about both theoretical and practical aspects of assessment. In this chapter, the use of questions to develop practice is explored further because inquisitive questioning can be a key mechanism for producing change. It helps to open up opportunities for learning and can be useful in a range of contexts, for example, for evaluating both good and poor practice and identifying lessons for the future.

As noted in previous chapters, the decisions and choices made by individual workers are shaped by numerous practical, cultural and organisational factors (Calder, 2008a; 2008b; Carson and Bain, 2008; Wilson, 2009). Although the focus of attention often seems to rest on individuals (particularly when things go wrong), 'recent work on reducing errors in high-risk organisations recognises that the individual is only one causal factor in a complex social and technological network' (Munro, 2008a, p 125). A systems perspective implies that there are shared personal and corporate responsibilities for developing practice. Individuals need to be active in reviewing and improving their work, but organisations also have a reciprocal obligation to operate in a way that encourages and facilitates learning. This link between individual and organisational development is highlighted by Senge, who argues that '[a]n organization's commitment to and capacity for learning can be no greater than that of its members' (Senge, 2006, p 7). Positive practice development does not happen accidentally, but instead requires deliberate choices, decisions and commitment to learning.

Organisational culture and the learning environment

Whyte argues that 'in youth justice, the organisational context is as relevant to practitioners as the social context is to young people' (Whyte, 2009, p 177). Organisational factors affecting how staff undertake assessments can include very practical issues like resources, not just in terms of caseloads, but in relation to whether practitioners have adequate access to expert advice and specialist services. They also include less tangible factors, such as shared assumptions or common (mis)perceptions within a team, which can affect how assessment tools are used (Gillingham and Humphreys, 2009). Other aspects of organisations that influence day-to-day assessment practice will include the various policies, procedures and guidance documents in place (as described in Chapter Three).

All of these are important, and changes in these areas can help to promote better practice. The main focus of this chapter, however, will be on the development of practice *through learning*. Individual practitioners need to take responsibility for learning and '[m]anagers should be actively striving to help their staff understand how good they are at risk decision-making, and how they might improve' (Carson and Bain, 2008, p 63). Understanding the ways in which organisational structures and cultures can either help or hinder practice development is therefore essential because, as Munro explains, '[w]e need to learn and, so, need organisations that encourage learning' (2010, p 15).

Identifying good practice

In a study looking at the use of the OASys assessment tool in one probation area, Crawford noted that '[b]ecause there is no formal procedure to respond to instances of good practice, this is not routinely acknowledged' (Crawford, 2007, p 162). This reflects a common pattern in which attention tends to be focused on problems, rather than investment being made in identifying and sharing good practice. But, as Carson and Bain rightly argue, looking at good practice is an essential aspect of learning. 'How do we continue to learn new skills and improve old ones? Do we learn best by having our errors, failings and inadequacies pointed out to us? To an extent, but surely the best, and most, learning comes from being shown what works, how and why it is correct, and what is good practice' (2008, p 61).

To do this requires more than just vague expressions of interest in good practice, but rather 'an organisational interest not only in whether good quality products and outcomes have been produced but also in finding out *how* these have been achieved' (Fish, 2009, p 8). It means having systems and feedback mechanisms in place to identify when good practice occurs, what supports it and what might make it more difficult to attain in particular cases or situations.

The value of 'thinking time'

Munro argues that '[l]earning requires not only experience but reflection on that experience' and consequently that 'workers who hurry from one task to the next without time for reflection fail to develop wisdom from their work' (Munro, 2009, p 1019). Individuals and organisations need to understand the value of thinking time and find ways of building this into regular work routines in order to reflect on a range of topics, including:

- assessments and decisions made in specific cases
- patterns or recurring issues in practice over time
- personal and emotional reactions to the work (for example to undertaking risk assessments with young people displaying sexually abusive behaviour).

Improving rather than blaming

Organisations – particularly those under pressure from the media and public – can easily slip into operating with a blame culture. Sometimes this can occur because a focus on defensibility has been misunderstood or misapplied (as discussed in Chapter Two), thus leading to practice which is defensive and concerned more with reputational risk than with the quality of services provided (Baker and Wilkinson, 2011). A blame culture will restrict learning, firstly, because it discourages people from disclosing potential problems (before the event) which could provide triggers for change, and secondly, because it is likely to reduce the willingness of staff to learn from difficulties or serious incidents that have occurred (after the event). Barry argues that 'systems can either encourage learning or openly allocate blame/responsibility' (2007, p 31), and one of the key steps for moving away from a blame culture involves creating a working environment in which 'mistakes may be perceived as *opportunities for learning*' (Beddoe, 2010, p 11, emphasis added).

Trust, openness and respect

Organisational structures can sometimes impede learning. In settings with a hierarchical approach, for example, research suggests that willingness to learn from others can be affected by status, with those in positions of power sometimes reluctant to learn from people they perceive as being below them in the pecking order (Miller, Freeman and Ross, 2001). In situations where multi-agency working is required, inter-professional suspicion or rivalry can prevent staff from valuing the views of practitioners from other organisations (Nash, 2010). There may also be more personal reasons why workers are sometimes reluctant to identify their need to learn: for example, 'an experienced worker may also feel more reluctant to ask for help or reveal their ignorance because they feel they are supposed to understand already' (Cousins, 2004, p 182).

Issues about role and status can be particularly significant in collaborative or multi-agency settings (see Chapter Seven), where there may be reluctance to trust or learn from staff from other professional backgrounds. For example, youth justice services have sometimes been characterised by mistrust between those working in the community and those based in custodial establishments. However, 'learning in the workplace requires a flow of information' (Taylor, 2004, p 84) and a culture in which all grades and groups of staff are open to learning from each other.

Reflection

In your experience of workplaces in youth justice, what are the particular factors which promote or discourage learning? How would students or new staff learn about good assessment practice?

In your own workplace what opportunities for learning are you:

■ taking?

■ making?

■ ignoring?

Asking perceptive (and sometimes awkward) questions

One useful approach to developing a learning culture within organisations is to consider the role of questions and questioning. Chapter Eight considered the value of different types of questions for helping young people to understand their behaviour, and there are parallels here with the way that questioning can help organisations to move forward in their practice. 'The questions we ask, the things that we choose to focus on, and the topics we choose to ask questions about determine what we find' (Cooperrider et al, 2008, p 103).

Using questions to best effect

Questions will be most useful if they focus on a clearly defined field of enquiry. This means being clear about:

- *What needs to be improved*. This might cover: all assessments; assessments in relation to specific types of offences; assessments for particular groups of young people; intervention plans for those assessed to present a risk of serious harm to others.
- *Who needs to be asked questions*. Options include: one practitioner, all practitioners in a team, specialists, managers, other agencies, young people, parents/carers, IT suppliers, community/secure estate staff, courts or other stakeholders.

When thinking about how to improve assessment quality, questions are likely to be used for several key purposes: to *describe*, to *evaluate* and to *explain*. This applies whether it is one practitioner reflecting on their own practice or a manager reviewing practice across an organisation. Different types of questions are best suited to these various purposes. The 5WH headings (who, why, what, where, when, how) were discussed in Chapter Eight. 'What' and 'when' questions would be useful for describing practice, whereas 'why' questions are likely to be more useful for finding explanations.

A range of activities is required to answer these different types of questions. For example, monitoring and data collection can be useful for answering the 'what' and 'when' type questions. However, since 'formal documentation is not able to explain *why* people act the way they do and what factors influence them for good or ill' (Fish, 2009, p 10) the 'why' type questions may be better addressed through discussion, supervision and critical reflection. Behaviour that may appear irrational or just as 'practitioners being difficult' might often have a reasonable explanation if people are given an opportunity to explain why they do or don't do something. For example, research suggests that practitioners don't always use assessment tools in the way the designers intended because of factors such as workload pressure or inadequate IT systems (Gillingham and Humphreys, 2009). Asking 'why' questions is therefore essential for understanding and improving practice. Some more examples of how 5WH questions can illuminate practice are provided in later sections of the chapter.

The model of appreciative inquiry (AI) provides another helpful approach to using questions. This is based on the assumption that 'every organization has something that works well, and those strengths can be the starting point for creating positive change' (Cooperrider et al, 2008, p 3). The model then involves asking questions grouped into four areas (the 4Ds):

- *discovery*: appreciating the best of current practice;
- *dream*: envisioning new possibilities and considering 'what might be';
- *design*: finding out how the new possibilities can be incorporated into everyday work;
- *destiny*: empowering staff and sustaining the changes through collective action.

A distinctive feature of AI is that all the questions asked under these headings should be positive. For example: What works well? Which approaches to assessment seem to help young people engage more actively with the process? How have intervention plans improved since this time last year? If 'the appreciative eye takes nothing for granted' (Cooperrider et al, 2008, p 7), this kind of approach can help people take a fresh look at what happens on a day-to-day basis and can be particularly useful for identifying examples of good practice. Although the 4D model has typically been used to promote organisational change, the core principles could also be used by individuals reflecting on their own work.

Asking awkward questions

Much of the face-to-face work between practitioners and young people is unobserved, which means that there is often little questioning of how individuals go about some of the most important aspects of their work. If, as suggested earlier, the questions we ask shape what we find, then it will also be the case that the areas we *don't* ask questions about will remain hidden and not understood. It is important therefore to consider which aspects of practice are rarely questioned or challenged. Examples of this could include: assessments which contain assumptions or judgements about behaviour by members of particular ethnic groups which are not questioned for fear of seeming racist; or decisions made by practitioners who have been in the team a long time which are not challenged because they are seen as being the most experienced and therefore 'above criticism'.

Activity

If we accept that some questions are used much more often than others, it can be useful to try to identify examples – for a specific team or context – of which ones are often asked, which ones are sometimes asked and which ones are rarely asked. The table below has some examples of each type.

- Do these match your experience? What other examples have you seen?
- What does the balance of questions reveal about an organisation's priorities?
- Identify some questions that are rarely asked but which you think should be used more often.

	Questions individuals ask themselves about their own practice	Questions asked by others (for example, managers or inspectors)
Often asked	Can I get this finished in time?	Have you met national standards?
Sometimes asked	Have I covered everything?	How difficult did you find this to complete?
Rarely/never asked	How could I have done that interview in a more engaging way?	How might you have done this better?

If the balance and frequency of questions were altered, how might that help to improve practice?

Learning through critical reflection

Regular review of cases will normally be built into organisational procedures (such as national standards). In addition to this, however, practitioners need time and space for more rigorous in-depth reflection: the importance of such 'thinking time' was noted above and this section considers some ways of achieving this.

Supervision

While '[t]he single most important factor in minimising errors is to admit that you may be wrong' (Munro, 2008a, p 125), evidence also shows 'how hard it is for people to correct their own intuitive errors' (Munro, 2009, p 1019). This reluctance to change opinions was discussed in Chapter Two and is one reason why supervision is so important. In addition, supervisors who 'model seeking advice' when they are unsure of something (Cousins, 2004, p 182) can help to create a learning culture.

Supervision is not simply the same as line management (which typically may focus more on administrative and procedural compliance or performance monitoring). This is not to say that managerial oversight is unimportant – organisations clearly need to have systems of accountability – but that it is not sufficient on its own to improve practice. For example, getting a manager to countersign a RoSH form can provide an initial quality check but does not necessarily contribute to increased learning about how to undertake a more thorough risk assessment. Similarly, in a study of the use of OASys, Crawford found that probation officers generally held the view 'that counter-signature reduces opportunities to learn, previously facilitated through face-to-face discussion' (Crawford, 2007, p 162).

The literature on supervision (particularly in social work) has long noted that it tends to have multiple purposes relating, in particular, to education, administration and support (Jones, 2004). Beddoe argues that it should also be a process to assist practitioners 'to manage emotions and uncertainty' and a 'place for rekindling hopefulness' (Beddoe, 2010, p 10). However, the shift in recent years has been for supervision to become more focused on checking that workers are following procedures and meeting performance indicators, so that time for reflective and critical thinking is reduced.

The diagram in Figure 9.1 builds on the discussion in Chapter Two about the balance within organisations between accountability and discretion, narrowing the focus down to how this will affect the goals and activities of supervision.

Figure 9.1: The focus of supervision

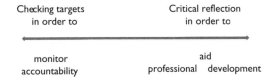

Given time and resource constraints, the opportunities for purely reflective discussion may sometimes be limited and it might be more realistic to expect supervision to cover a mixture of performance monitoring and developmental discussions. The level of attention give to each will vary over time to reflect particular practice issues that arise. The key, however, is to ensure that there is always a balance and that thinking time is seen as a core supervision activity rather than an optional extra.

Reflection

'The ideal supervision process would create a safe environment for people to "discover their learning edge", build competence and utilise the energy generated by excitement and challenges in practice.' (Beddoe, 2010, p 8)

In your experience, to what extent does supervision of staff match that description? What more could be done to make the most of supervision as an opportunity for learning?

■ How should practitioners and supervisors prepare for supervision?
■ What should they bring with them?
■ What questions might be most helpful to consider?

Encountering unexpected views and opinions

The desire for social approval and the (often understandable) temptation to 'give the audience what they want to hear' will inevitably affect the process of assessment. One of the consequences of this can be that assessors take account of a limited range of information or focus on the most obvious explanations but avoid some of the more complex aspects of analysis (Tetlock, 1997; Baker and Wilkinson, 2011). Examples in youth justice could include: tailoring court reports to fit the anticipated views of local sentencers (see Chapter Six); or adjusting assessment scores to match the expectations of colleagues from other professional backgrounds. The impact of the desire for social approval affects groups as well as individuals (as discussed in Chapter Two) and can result in a tendency to avoid disagreement or debate. An example would be a risk-planning forum where people go along with the accepted or predominant 'line' without challenging it, even though they may have serious doubts about it.

Encountering audiences who have unknown or unexpected opinions can therefore be a useful learning opportunity because it encourages people to think in different ways. Options for achieving this include making sure that gate-keeping of assessments and reports is done by different people so that responses are not always predictable. In team discussions, 'group leaders therefore have to challenge themselves to encourage dissent and be open to challenge, sometimes even appointing a "devil's advocate"' (Burton, 2009, p 11). Listening to the views of visitors, new staff or volunteers can also provide a fresh take on things. For example, Thomas suggests that 'students are perceived as supporting learning within organisations' (2004, p 106) because their questions about how and why things work the way they do can prompt more experienced staff to reflect on aspects of practice that might typically be taken for granted.

Reflection

Think about some opportunities that might exist to be a (constructive) 'devil's advocate' to help practitioners and managers think in different ways about their own and others' assessment practice.

Learning from monitoring, audit and data

Although activities such as monitoring, audit or data analysis sometimes seem overly technical or remote from the realities of practice, using information skilfully should be a core feature of youth justice organisations. This links back to the discussion about questioning earlier on, and suggests an approach which focuses on seeing data as a tool to trigger further enquiry and exploration of practice. A helpful question to consider at this stage would be: 'Is your organisation understanding that data helps you to ask intelligent and pertinent questions rather than just providing a complete picture?' (Fish, 2009, p 12).

As noted in Chapter Three, different types of data are useful for different purposes. One benefit of collecting 'hard' data is that it can complement the 'softer' information that practitioners use on a day-to-day basis. For example, analysis in a court report tends to reflect the assessor's own judgements and perceptions about a young person's offending behaviour. Analysis of aggregate data, however, can add to this by illustrating 'how typical their criminality is in characteristic, in its operation in time, its enactment in geographical space or its social relationship, or when set against local or national crime data' (Whyte, 2009, p 183). Having this more objective data for comparison can help to provide a much more complete account.

Organisational monitoring systems, such as the *Youth Justice Performance Improvement Framework* (YJB, 2010g) for example, can contribute to this if they are designed in a way that prompts questioning, rather than just presenting requests for data to feed into a central system. Sometimes, however, these systems are used and completed by only a few people in the team, with the result that other staff may not be aware of what the information indicates about local practice.

Table 9.1 illustrates questions that can be used to interrogate local data to uncover useful information about practice that can be of interest to all staff. The first column relates to assessment *processes*, which covers topics such as completeness, accuracy and the timeliness of assessments and plans. The second column deals with *outputs* and includes questions about, for example, the scores, ratings, classifications and plans that are produced from assessments. These can be particularly useful for exploring whether there are differences in the assessments and plans produced for different groups of young people (for example by age, gender or ethnicity). The final column concerns the *outcomes* of assessments and this is important because individuals within organisations may not always experience the consequences of some of their decisions (Senge, 2006, p 23). This may occur where assessment teams are separate from intervention teams, for example. If it is difficult for practitioners to see the results of their actions, then organisations need to have systems for monitoring outcomes and giving feedback to decision makers. Systematically asking these kinds of questions can help to ensure that organisations have 'good feedback loops' (Munro, 2010, p 14), but to gain maximum benefit the questions need to prompt further exploration of 'why' the data show particular patterns. Answers to these *why* and *how* type questions will most likely be found through the processes of supervision and critical group discussion discussed earlier. In order to be of value, any such investigation of data must then lead to action to change practice.

Table 9.1: Examples of questions to ask about monitoring, audit and data

Processes	Outputs	Outcomes
• At which times of the year are completeness and timeliness better or worse? • Is there any significant difference in levels of completeness between different types of cases? • Which sources of information do practitioners draw on most frequently? Which ones are rarely/never used? • Which items of information are most prone to error/inaccurate recording? • How often do young people complete self-assessments?	• What proportion of group X is classified as having a high likelihood of reoffending and how does this compare to group Y? • Are scores for particular sections of *Asset* typically higher/lower for BME young people than for white young people? • Which types of interventions appear most frequently on intervention plans for female/male/older/younger offenders? • Are there are any interventions which are never recorded in the plans for young people convicted of certain offences, for example burglary, violence or sexual offences? • Do the scores/ratings change more often for some groups than for others?	• Are there high drop-out rates from a particular programme which might indicate that young people were wrongly assessed as suitable to attend? • Are there differences between groups in terms of how quickly young people reoffend following interventions, e.g. between those classified as having a 'high' or 'low' likelihood of reoffending? • Is there any noticeable difference in the assessments/plans in cases where young people have completed a self-assessment as compared to those who didn't? • What were young people's views about the relevance of their intervention plans?

Learning from serious incidents and 'near misses'

When problems occur – such as a death in custody or a young person under supervision committing a very serious offence – there will normally be a range of reports and inquiries which have the potential to provide learning points for practice. However, it is also fair to say that reviews often have other purposes – reassuring the public, protecting an organisation's reputation by being seen to be 'doing something' – such that they are not always written in ways that are the most useful for promoting learning (Cambridge, 2004). Their value for improving practice will depend both on how they are written (whether are they focused on blame or on identifying areas for development) and on the culture of the organisations that receive them.

Serious incidents

Reviews of serious incidents involving young people under supervision in the community in England and Wales[1] have highlighted a number of concerns in relation to assessment and planning (Blyth, 2007; YJB, 2009a) including:

- assessments which were cloned (i.e. duplicated and redated without any changes or revisions) when there should have been a reassessment;
- failure to complete additional and/or specialist assessments when triggered;
- assessment scores not adequately linked to the evidence provided;
- poor communication with other agencies;
- poor management oversight of assessment;
- intervention plans not being completed until several months into an order;
- a mismatch between the factors identified in the assessment and those prioritised for action in the subsequent plan.

Similar problems with the collection, recording and analysis of information have been found in reviews of serious incidents committed by adult offenders (HMIP, 2006; 2008) and in numerous child abuse inquiries (Reder, Duncan and Gray, 1993; Reder and Duncan, 2004a; Ofsted, 2009). Chapter Seven considered the implications of these reports for inter-agency working. This section now looks at how an individual practitioner, team or organisation can use these reviews to develop their own practice. The similarities in the findings from inquiries over many years present something of a paradox. On the one hand, it seems clear that these reports can provide 'an invaluable source of teaching and learning material' (Balen and Masson, 2008, p 129). On the other hand, the fact that reports keep identifying similar problems suggests that this learning is not really happening in practice. Some of this may be down to the style of the reports, and this is not something that front-line staff can influence. Nevertheless, organisations do have a responsibility to learn from the available information wherever possible and this requires understanding the focus and purpose of the different types of reports. Some relate to individual cases, for example:

• Local Management Reports (England and Wales): the primary focus of these reports is the activity of the YOT (YJB, 2007b);
• Inspectorate, LSCB or Care Commission (Scotland) reports;
• MAPPA Serious Case Reviews: the focus here is on how the different agencies involved in MAPPA worked together (Ministry of Justice, 2009).

Other reports or reviews take a wider look at the common lessons emerging from a number of cases over time, for example the Youth Justice Board's annual review of serious incidents that have occurred involving young people under statutory supervision in the community (YJB, 2009a). In addition to understanding the purpose of reports, time needs to be allocated to thinking about the implications for practice. Questions to consider might include:

• Are the reports and findings accessible in our team?
• What are the similarities/differences between the context in which the serious incident(s) occurred and the local practice context here?
• In what way is our assessment/planning practice more rigorous than that described in the report?

'Near misses'

One aspect of review and monitoring often overlooked in youth justice, but found in other spheres, ranging from healthcare to aviation (Barach and Small, 2000; DH, 2000b), is that of encouraging people to report near misses. A 'near miss' can be defined as 'an incident where something could have gone wrong but has been prevented or did go wrong but no serious harm was caused' (Bostock et al, 2005, p vi).

Relevant examples for youth justice might include a young person associated with a particular gang being placed on a group work programme which brings him/her into close proximity with members of a rival 'postcode' gang. The initial assessment process failed to pick this up, but the issue is subsequently identified and alternative action taken before any harm has been caused. Or a situation where a young person with complex health needs is sentenced to custody but some key details were not recorded in the assessment or post-court report. A medical practitioner in the secure establishment subsequently identifies the relevant needs but the young person had for a while been placed at risk of experiencing unnecessary health complications. A third example might be where an electronic monitoring supplier fails to notify the case-worker that a young person has breached the conditions of their tag. There is concern that s/he may have been involved in a serious offence that occurred while her/his whereabouts were unknown although this is subsequently shown to be unfounded when it is discovered that s/he had simply been staying with a friend to get away from tensions at home.

Learning can occur either from single incidents or from 'clusters' of near misses (Calder, 2008a, p 145), which can be a warning sign that problems need to be addressed. There needs to be a balance between taking account of near misses while not being so overly preoccupied with the fear of mistakes that people become reluctant to take action. Questions to consider could include:

- Was this near miss an exceptional event that couldn't have been predicted or were there signs/triggers that we didn't identify quickly enough?
- If there has been a cluster of near misses, what are the common themes?

This section has focused on learning from serious problems, which inevitably creates something of a negative tone. This is not intended to emphasise failure but rather to recognise that in the complex world of youth offending some things will go wrong. It is important to learn from these events, and this needs to be done alongside the work of identifying good practice highlighted earlier. By focusing on learning rather than blaming, organisations can move towards a culture in which '[t]he aim is to make it harder for people to do something wrong and easier for them to do it right' (Institute of Medicine, 1999, p 2, cited in Munro, 2010, p 7).

Striving for 'deep learning'

All of the activities and processes described above are likely to reveal gaps in knowledge and skills, for both individuals and organisations, that need to be addressed if practice is to develop. In thinking about how to promote improvement, Whyte provides a helpful reminder that 'practitioners require what has been described as "deep" as opposed to "surface" learning' (2009, p 203). This involves many of the elements outlined in earlier chapters – understanding theory, knowing the local context for practice, reflecting on successes, problems and near misses and then applying all of this appropriately to each individual young person. Achieving this kind of depth in practice requires a combination of individual knowledge and experience plus an organisational commitment to promoting and applying learning, as illustrated in Figure 9.2.

The diagram suggests that individuals need to take personal responsibility for learning, for putting their learning into practice and for reflecting on that practice. It is also then important that this individual learning is supported within teams and by supervisors. In addition, organisations have responsibility for promoting knowledge and enabling staff to keep up to date with new thinking through the provision of training and opportunities for academic study. All these things have to work together. For example a training event (organisation) should be followed up by reflection in supervision and peer discussion with colleagues (team) as well as by the practitioner (individual) consciously putting the learning into practice.

Plans should also then be made (organisation) for implementing and monitoring subsequent changes in practice.

Figure 9.2: The 'deep learning' triangle

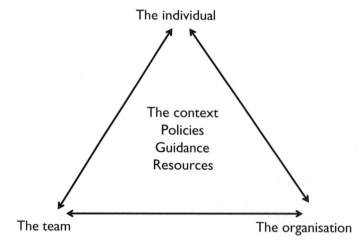

Source: Adapted with permission from Kemshall et al (2007)

Acquiring knowledge

Chapter Three looked at the knowledge base required for undertaking assessments. Acquiring this knowledge is not always easy for practitioners, however, with factors such as the 'culture gap' between the academic world and front-line practice presenting a barrier to the effective transmission of knowledge. One issue to consider, therefore, is simply the extent to which practitioners have access to knowledge – including guidance, policies, legislation, local data, research findings and evaluations. How easy is it for you and people in your team to locate and read each of these different types of knowledge?

Increasing attention is now being given to finding creative and effective ways of bridging the gap between evidence and action. One example would be that of identifying knowledge champions or 'knowledge brokers' (Ward et al, 2009), who would be responsible for keeping up to date with developments in a particular field (for example, offending by girls or violent offending). This could be done at team or organisational level, depending on the size of the agency, but in either case, the knowledge broker would be responsible for sharing new information with colleagues. Supervisors should then take opportunities to discuss it with practitioners, and individuals would have a responsibility to incorporate these developments into their work. A second example involves the role of technology and its ability to facilitate the sharing of knowledge through virtual practitioner networks or communities (LaMendola et al, 2009).

Consideration also needs to be given to how well training contributes to the transmission of knowledge. For example, Bonta et al (2001) suggest that training about an assessment tool is more likely to be effective if it includes:

- time devoted to summarising the research supporting the assessment tool (and any associated procedures for planning or supervision) so participants know that the recommended ways of working are reasonable and empirically defensible;
- theoretical explanations of offending behaviour (so that practitioners have confidence in assessing the unusual and exceptional cases which, by definition, training manuals are unlikely to address).

Training (whether it is e-learning, group based or one to one) that only focuses on processes is less likely to have an impact than training which also includes presentation of relevant theory and research. In addition to training that is specifically about assessment or use of structured tools, training on many other topics should of course also contribute to improving assessment practice (for example, increased knowledge about particular types of offences can improve the information-collection process by enabling assessors to focus more clearly on key factors). Useful questions to ask of any training event or training pack could therefore include:

- How will this help to improve the collection and recording of information?
- How will this help to improve analysis and decision making?
- How will this improve the quality of intervention plans or risk-management plans?

Applying knowledge

To develop deep knowledge, practitioners need opportunities to try out their knowledge in action. This is an integral part of learning in many fields, for example, 'in education for the fine arts, we find people learning to design, perform and produce by engaging in design, performance and production' (Schön, 1987, p 16). To continue with the example of training in the use of assessment tools, this should not only help to disseminate knowledge but should also include opportunities to 'try out' a tool. This should involve practical activities during training, followed by opportunities to use the tool in practice, perhaps supported or overseen by a more experienced colleague.

Testing out knowledge in practice should not be a one-off activity. Assessors need to be able to apply their knowledge and practise their skills with a variety of cases that present different challenges. Options for incorporating this into regular work routines can include videoing interviews, observation, shadowing, mentoring, co-working and learning from specialists. These can be relevant both for new staff and for more experienced practitioners. If it is true that 'we learn an art or craft by doing the things that we shall have to do when we have learnt it' (Aristotle, *Nicomachean ethics*), then practitioners need to be looking out for new ways to practise skills and managers need to provide appropriately supported opportunities for staff to 'try out' their knowledge.

Activity

In your experience of a particular working context, what learning opportunities are provided for staff?

	Current good points	What could be improved
Access to knowledge and academic resources relating to assessment and planning		
Provision of theoretically based/evidence-informed training to support assessment		
Follow-up and review of training		
Opportunities for peer discussion about specific assessments		
Other opportunities to practise skills and develop expertise in assessment and planning		

Learning should never be dull

The mention of 'learning' or 'training' may induce feelings of despair or boredom in some readers (in much the same way that audit and quality assurance will do for others, as discussed earlier). This is partly because they have sometimes been presented as rather passive activities which occur away from the workplace with little connection to the everyday challenges of assessing young people who offend. This is not always true, of course, and some training and learning material will be of excellent quality. But this view does reflect a wider social trend in which 'learning has come to be synonymous with taking in information' (Senge, 2006, p 13). This is problematic, because real learning requires much more than this. It should be an active, purposeful process that takes you towards greater proficiency in assessing young people and planning meaningful interventions. As such, it should be interesting and challenging, not dull and passive!

Taking in information (whether that is basic guidance on using an assessment tool or complex data about patterns of offending) will be a necessary *but not sufficient* condition for effective practice. Assessment and intervention planning are not tick-box or technical activities but require professional expertise that needs to be continually honed and refined. And no matter how experienced you are, there will always be some way that you can extend your knowledge and skills and go deeper into the learning process.

Inquisitiveness in action

This chapter has shown a variety of ways in which questioning and learning can help to improve assessment and planning practice. Now we can draw some of these threads together and look at how they might work in combination, using a specific example, that of assessments of the risk of serious harm posed by young people involved in serious violent offending. The list below gives some examples – for the different types of learning discussed in this chapter – of questions that a practitioner could ask in order to improve their practice in this area:

- **Supervision**: What are my emotional reactions to this offending? How do I deal with the uncertainty and concern for the safety of self/others?
- **Acquiring knowledge**: What is the evidence about the links between substance use and violence? Or between mental health problems and serious violence? Do I fully understand the strengths and limitations of the assessment tools I use for assessing this type of offending?
- **Monitoring, audit and data:** What is the prevalence of this type of violence in this locality? Who are the typical perpetrators and victims? What information is there locally about successful completion of programmes by young people displaying violent behaviour?
- **Serious incidents**: Are there common patterns/events/triggers seen in offenders prior to their committing a serious violent offence while under supervision?
- **Applying knowledge**: What opportunities are there for shadowing or learning from more experienced colleagues? How can I improve the way I ask questions in interviews with young people who display threatening and intimidating behaviour?

This is by no means a complete list, but is a way of illustrating how a range of questions and approaches can inform the development of a specific area of assessment practice. This example relates to an individual practitioner seeking to improve their own practice, but a similar approach can be used by managers or teams as a whole.

Activity

Consider an area of assessment practice that you think should be improved (be specific; for example, assessments of girls, younger offenders, fire setters, or young people susceptible to becoming drawn into violent extremism).

Use the table to identify action that could be taken by any of the role holders listed in the top row to improve learning and practice in your chosen area.

	Practitioner	**Manager**	**Information/data manager**
Supervision			
Hearing unfamiliar views			
Monitoring, audit, data:			
processes			
outputs			
outcomes			
Serious incidents			
Near misses			
Acquiring knowledge			
Applying knowledge			

Conclusion

In the complex world of youth justice assessment and planning, promoting and developing 'the capacity to think' (Reder and Duncan, 2004b, p 109) is essential. This chapter has shown that developing assessment practice requires both that organisations provide a learning environment in which questions are encouraged and seen as a prompt for improvement, and that individual practitioners make the most of the opportunities available to further their knowledge and skills.

There are many examples of good assessment and planning practice in youth justice and we should not lose sight of that. However, there are also some problems that need to be addressed and, even where practice is generally good, there will always be scope for improvement, or new developments to be taken into account. That is the challenge – and interest – of professional practice with young people who offend.

Note

[1] Serious incidents are defined by the Youth Justice Board as the death or attempted suicide of a young person under supervision or where a young person under supervision commits or is the victim of one of the following offences: murder, attempted murder, manslaughter, rape, torture, kidnapping, false imprisonment, firearms offences (YJB, 2007a).

Conclusion

Assessment has become so much a part of the routine of everyday youth justice work in the UK that there is a danger of its becoming something that is just done because it has to be, without much thought necessarily being given to its purpose or to how to approach the task. It is one example (a similar argument has been made in relation to record keeping) of an activity which may superficially be viewed as boring and bureaucratic but actually presents a complex range of challenges when people stop to think about it (O'Rourke, 2010). As the preceding chapters have shown, however, the authors consider that assessment is not only a critical aspect of practice but also an activity that demands considerable knowledge and skill. The purpose of assessment, namely, that it should lead to action to help reduce offending and enable young people to develop their potential and make a positive contribution to society, needs to be kept in mind at all times so as to ensure that it is seen as a meaningful task rather than one that has to be done just for the sake of it.

The Introduction set out five key principles and the subsequent discussions have sought to illustrate their implications in practice. The exploration of theory and practice has highlighted the many and varied elements of assessment and planning in youth justice. These include the types of knowledge required (theory, research, local knowledge); the types of judgements to be made and thinking styles used (analytical and intuitive); the types of activities involved (interviewing, describing, analysing, interpreting, persuading); types of communication (verbal and written, formal and informal); the significance of relationships (engaging a young person, working with professionals from other agencies); and the need for critical reflection (reviewing one's own practice and challenging/being challenged by others).

Achieving the impossible

In a study of recording practice in social work, many of the difficulties reported by practitioners related to the competition between the purposes of the activity and the multiple audiences that had to be considered. On the one hand, for example, assessors felt that they had to make a client's problems seem as serious as possible in order to have any hope of getting the resources they felt were needed, but on the other hand, writing in such a negative way could damage the worker's relationship with the client, who might feel that they had been described inaccurately. It seems at times to be an 'impossible task' (O'Rourke, 2010, p 164), and similar problems can arise with assessment in youth justice, where there are competing demands and expectations placed on practitioners (Baker and Kelly, 2011).

As this book has shown, youth justice workers need to manage different priorities, such as balancing public protection with promoting the welfare of young people, and also face challenges relating to the process – the 'how' – of assessment, for example:

- enabling young people to make a meaningful contribution to the assessment process, while remaining analytical and taking account of other perspectives;
- using information about the past, while remaining alert to new information and changes in circumstances or behaviour;
- working consistently within shared frameworks for practice, yet avoiding the drift towards standardised descriptions of young people that can occur if a common language becomes 'little more than a sentence bank' (White et al, 2009, p 1212);
- making decisions promptly in order to take required action, while not damaging the relationship with a young person by being seen as too intense or personal at an early stage of contact (Yates, 2009);
- recording assessments for a range of audiences – colleagues, young people, parents, courts, managers, inspectors.

Achieving all this is difficult and is why, throughout the book, the responsibility of organisations has been emphasised alongside that of practitioners. This kind of practice requires skilled staff working in supportive and flexible environments.

Enabling assessment practice to flourish

Faced with the complexities of practice and the potential for very hostile criticism when things go wrong, one of the key organisational responses of recent years has been to encourage increasing structure and standardisation in practice (as discussed in Chapters One and Four, for example). This can have some advantages but, contrary to the focus of much of the debates about assessment frameworks, these are not primarily to do with the predictive validity and reliability of structured tools. Instead, the authors would agree that the real strength of standardised approaches is in their 'transparency in identifying which individual domains practitioners associate strongly with criminality, evidence that can be accepted or challenged, and the degree to which those identified "needs and risks" can then be incorporated meaningfully into an action plan which is dynamic, open to revision and for which service providers as well as service "users" are accountable' (Whyte, 2009, p 85).

The authors also believe that professional discretion remains a central aspect of practice. Even where there are structures and frameworks, practitioners retain considerable discretion over how these are applied (Evans and Harris, 2004; Baker, 2008), and various informal and local approaches inevitably develop (Horlick-Jones, 2005; Gillingham and Humphreys, 2009; Kemshall, 2010). For example, there may be local agreement over which items of information are essential and must be completed for all assessments and which could be completed at a later date if time for the initial assessment is very limited. Another example would be a team deciding to adapt the self-assessment section of *Asset* to make it more visual and interactive for young people to use. As argued in Chapter Two, discretion is essential but needs to be balanced with proper systems of accountability. The question that constantly needs to be asked is whether (and how) a particular localised approach, or a variation from a common practice framework, will really improve the quality of service that a team provides to young people, courts, partner agencies and other stakeholders.

Earlier chapters have looked at a number of factors in organisations that affect the ability of staff to learn and to develop practice. If we had to summarise the key features most conducive to the flourishing of assessment practice and highlight the essential points to make most strongly to teams and senior managers, it would be that '[t]he culture of the team or agency that practitioners work within, the expectation they have of each other and that their managers have of them, all need to allow priority to be given to *practitioners taking time to think carefully and to record this thinking usefully*' (Dalzell and Sawyer, 2007, p 6, emphasis added). This careful thinking then needs to lead to action, if it is to make a difference to young people and their communities.

Where do we go from here?

Writing in the context of work with adult offenders, Burnett et al (2007) show how assessment has remained a core element of practice over time but, alongside this continuity, there have also been significant changes in how the task of assessment has been perceived. The emphasis in probation has moved from determining which offenders were 'reformable' (McWilliams, 1986), through a phase of identifying who might be 'treatable', to the current focus on assessing 'risk'. In youth justice, a similar theme of continuity and change also seems likely to apply. Assessment will continue to be a critical foundation for practice but there will almost inevitably be changes in purpose and processes. The shape of these developments is not yet clear and will depend on political priorities, but possibilities include a move away from an essentially deficit-led approach, as at present, to one that takes greater account of strengths and aspirations, with the consequent revisions to assessment tools and frameworks which this would require.

In this constantly changing context, a mechanical approach to the use of tools or procedures will never be enough. Instead, as argued throughout the book, practitioners need to be able to apply professional knowledge and skill, supported by organisations that encourage continual learning and practice improvement. The common mistake of equating learning with taking in information was noted in Chapter Nine, and reading a book about assessment will not necessarily make people into good assessors. For this to happen, the ideas need to be absorbed and applied. In keeping with the emphasis on critical reflection throughout the book, therefore, three final questions are included here:

Reflection

- Which positive aspects of your practice/approach to assessment and planning have been reinforced through reading this book?
- What have you learned that has been new?
- How will this knowledge be applied in practice?

There is much about the complexities of offending by young people – and the types of responses needed to support them in moving towards a non-offending life-style – which this book has not been able to cover. As noted in Chapter Three, knowledge about young people's offending is continually expanding and youth justice professionals have a responsibility not only to develop their own understanding and keep up to date with developments in theory and research, but also to contribute to building this knowledge base actively through recording their own insights and practice experiences.

At the start of the book, we made the assumption that readers care about practice and want to improve outcomes for young people. We hope that the discussions have provided much food for thought and introduced new perspectives which can provide the foundations for an approach to assessment practice that will lead to better decision making and, hopefully, better outcomes for young people and communities. In addition, we hope that the book will be a 'springboard' that prompts continued inquisitiveness on the part of those working in youth justice and greater determination to apply the knowledge thus acquired to assessment practice with young people involved in anti-social and offending behaviour.

Assessment tools – additional references

Chapter Four refers to a number of assessment tools currently in use in the UK. For those who are interested in looking in more detail at the evidence from evaluations of these tools, some additional references are provided below. These relate to studies in the UK.[1]

AIM2

Griffin, H. and Beech, A. (2004) *Evaluation of the AIM framework for the assessment of adolescents who display sexually harmful behaviour*, London: Youth Justice Board.

Print, B., Griffin, H., Beech, A., Quayle, J., Bradshaw, H., Henniker, J. and Morrison, T. (2007) *AIM2: An initial assessment model for young people who display sexually harmful behaviour*, Manchester: The AIM Project.

Asset

Baker, K., Jones, S., Roberts, C. and Merrington, S. (2003) *Validity and reliability of ASSET*, London: Youth Justice Board.

Baker, K., Jones, S., Roberts, C. and Merrington, S. (2005) *Further development of Asset*, London: Youth Justice Board.

SAVRY

Dolan, M. and Rennie, C. (2008) 'The Structured Assessment of Violent Risk in Youth (SAVRY) as a predictor of recidivism in a UK cohort of adolescent offenders with conduct disorder', *Psychological Assessment*, vol 20, no 1, pp 35–46.

Rennie, C. and Dolan, M. (2010) 'The significance of protective factors in the assessment of risk', *Criminal Behaviour and Mental Health*, vol 20, no 1, pp 8–22.

[1] Readers should note that, particularly for SAVRY and YLS/CMI, there are more papers available relating to studies of the use of these tools in other countries.

YLS/CMI

Marshall, J., Egan, V., English, M. and Jones, R. (2006) 'The relative validity of psychopathy versus risk/needs-based assessments in the prediction of adolescent offending behaviour', *Legal and Criminological Psychology*, vol 11, no 2, pp 197–210.

Rennie, C. and Dolan, M. (2010) 'Predictive validity of the youth level of service/case management inventory in custody sample in England', *Journal of Forensic Psychiatry and Psychology*, DOI: 10.1080/14789940903452311 .

Glossary of useful terms and abbreviations

AIM	Assessment, Intervention and Moving on: an initial assessment model for young people who display sexually harmful behaviour.
Asset	The structured tool used by YOTs in England and Wales (and some local authorities in Scotland) for assessing young people who offend.
CAF	Common Assessment Framework: a standardised approach to conducting assessments of children's additional needs and deciding how these should be met.
dangerousness	The Criminal Justice Act 2003 defines 'dangerousness' in the context of offenders who have committed a specified or serious specified offence (these are defined in the Act) and who have been assessed by a court as presenting 'a significant risk to the public of serious harm'. Due to the potential for confusion, it is best to avoid the term unless using this specific legal definition.
defensible decisions	Decisions which will stand up to 'hindsight scrutiny' should a further offence of serious harm occur. Such decisions must demonstrate that 'all reasonable steps' have been taken.
HMIP	Her Majesty's Inspectorate of Probation: an independent Inspectorate, funded by the Ministry of Justice, and reporting directly to the Secretary of State on the effectiveness of work with individual offenders, children and young people
LSCB	Local Safeguarding Children Board: the key statutory mechanism for agreeing how the relevant organisations in each local area will cooperate to safeguard and promote the welfare of children, and for ensuring the effectiveness of what they do.
MAPPA	Multi-Agency Public Protection Arrangements: statutory arrangements for managing sexual and violent offenders. MAPPA is not a statutory body in itself but is a mechanism through which agencies can better discharge their statutory responsibilities and protect the public in a coordinated manner.
NACRO	National Association for the Care and Resettlement of Offenders
National Standards	The National Standards for Youth Justice Services outline the minimum standards for youth offending team (YOT) managers, YOT practitioners and other relevant partners delivering services within the youth justice system.
OASys	Offender Assessment System: a structured assessment tool used in England and Wales to assess adult offenders in the community and in custody.
Parole Board	An independent body that works to protect the public by risk assessing some prisoners, including a small number of young people serving long custodial sentences, to decide whether they can be safely released into the community

PSR	Pre-Sentence Report prepared for the Youth Court, magistrates' court or Crown Court in England and Wales by the Probation Service or Youth Offending Service as an aid to sentencing.
Referral Order	A sentence given to a young person who pleads guilty to an offence when it is his/her first time in court. Its primary aim is to prevent young people reoffending and provide a restorative justice approach within a community context. Young people receiving a Referral Order are referred to a panel made up of community volunteers who agree a contract with them.
Referral Order report	Report prepared by a member of the YOT to help the Referral Order panel agree a contract.
RoSH form	Risk of Serious Harm to Others form: part of the *Asset* assessment process designed to help assessors analyse whether a young person may pose a risk of serious harm to others.
safeguarding	Protecting children from maltreatment, preventing impairment of children's health or development, ensuring that children are growing up in circumstances consistent with the provision of safe and effective care.
SAVRY	Structured Assessment of Violence Risk in Youth: structured professional judgement tool designed to assist with assessing and making judgements about a young person's risk for violence.
scaled approach	A tiered approach to interventions that varies the intensity of intervention according to the level of risk and seeks to ensure that interventions are based on an assessment of the risks and needs of an individual young person.
secure estate	Establishments for young people serving custodial sentences (this includes young offender institutions, secure care homes and secure training centres).
SER	Social Enquiry Report: prepared for the Children's Hearings and Courts in Scotland by criminal justice social workers as an aid to decision making.
serious harm	Harm to others which is life threatening and/or traumatic and from which recovery, whether physical or psychological, can be expected to be difficult, incomplete or impossible.
SIFA	Mental Health Screening Interview for Adolescents: a detailed interview designed to be completed by specialist health staff in YOTs for assessing mental health needs. May form the basis for a referral to the Children and Adolescent Mental Health Service.
SQIFA	Mental Health Screening Questionnaire Interview for Adolescents: a short screening tool attached to *Asset* to help YOTs identify whether further assessment of a young person's mental health needs is required.
YJAA	Youth Justice Agency Assessment: assessment framework (adapted from *Asset*) used in Northern Ireland.

YJB	Youth Justice Board for England and Wales: the YJB is an executive non-departmental public body and oversees the youth justice system in England and Wales. Board members are appointed by the Secretary of State for Justice.
YLS/CMI	Youth Level of Service/Case Management Inventory: assessment tool (adapted from the Level of Service Inventory (LSI) tool for adult offenders) used by some youth justice services in Scotland.
YOT	Youth Offending Team: there is a YOT in every local authority in England and Wales. They are made up of representatives from a number of agencies including the police, Probation Service, children's services and health.
YRO	Youth Rehabilitation Order: the new generic community sentence for children and young people who offend (in England and Wales). It replaces a number of previous sentences, combining them into one generic sentence with a menu of 18 different requirements that sentencers can select. It will be the standard community sentence used for the majority of children and young people who offend.

References

Aas, K.-F. (2004) *Sentencing in the age of information: From Faust to Macintosh*, London: The Glasshouse Press.

Adcock, M. (2001) 'The core assessment: how to synthesise information and make judgements', in J. Horwath (ed) *The child's world: Assessing children in need*, London: Jessica Kingsley, pp 75-97.

Andrews, D.A. and Dowden, C. (2006) 'Risk principle of case classification in correctional treatment: a meta-analytic investigation', *International Journal of Offender Therapy and Comparative Criminology*, vol 50, no 1, pp 88–100.

Andrews, D.A., Bonta, J. and Hoge, R. (1990) 'Classification for effective rehabilitation: Rediscovering psychology', *Criminal Justice and Behavior*, vol 17, no 1, pp 19–52.

Ansbro, M. (2008) 'Using attachment theory with offenders', *Probation Journal*, vol 55, no 3, pp 231–44.

Ansbro, M. (2010) 'The nuts and bolts of risk assessment: when the clinical and actuarial conflict', *Howard Journal*, vol 49, no 3, pp 252–68.

Aristotle, *Nicomachean ethics*, Book 2, 1103a, 30.

Armstrong, S. (2009) 'Managing meaning: metaphor in criminal justice policy'. Accessed on 30 December 2009 at http://ssrn.com/abstract=1508340.

Attrill, G. and Liell, G. (2007) 'Offenders' views on risk assessment', in N. Padfield (ed) *Who to release? Parole, fairness and criminal justice*, Cullompton: Willan, pp 191–201.

Audit Commission (2004) *Youth justice 2004: A review of the reformed Youth Justice System*, London: Audit Commission.

Aye-Maung, N. and Hammond, N. (2000) *Risk of reoffending and needs assessments: The user's perspective*, Home Office research study 216, London: Home Office.

Babchishin, K. and Hanson, R. (2009) 'Improving our talk: moving beyond the "low", "moderate" and" high" typology of risk communication', *Crime Scene*, vol 16, pp 11–14.

Bailey, S. (1996) 'Adolescents who murder', *Journal of Adolescence*, vol 19, no 1, pp 19–39.

Bailey, S. (2003) 'Young offenders and mental health', *Current Opinion in Psychiatry*, vol 16, no 5, pp 581–91.

Baker, K. (2004) 'Is *Asset* really an asset? Risk assessment of young offenders', in R. Burnett and C. Roberts (eds) *What works in probation and youth justice: Developing Evidence-based practice*, Cullompton: Willan, pp 70–87.

Baker, K. (2005) 'Assessment in youth justice: professional discretion and the use of *Asset*', *Youth Justice*, vol 5, no 2, pp 106–22.

Baker, K. (2007) 'Risk in practice: systems and practitioner judgement', in M. Blyth, E. Solomon and K. Baker (eds) *Young people and 'risk'*, Bristol: The Policy Press.

Baker, K. (2008) 'Risk, uncertainty and public protection: assessment of young people who offend', *British Journal of Social Work*, vol 38, no 8, pp 1463–80.

Baker, K. (2010) 'More harm than good? The language of public protection', *Howard Journal*, vol 49, no 1, pp 42–53.

Baker, K. and Kelly, G. (2011) 'Risk assessment and young people', in H. Kemshall and B. Wilkinson (eds) *Good practice in assessing risk: Current knowledge, issues and approaches*, London: Jessica Kingsley.

Baker, K. and Sutherland, A. (eds) (2009) *Multi-agency public protection arrangements and youth justice*, Bristol: The Policy Press.

Baker, K. and Wilkinson, B. (2011) 'Professional risk taking and defensible decisions', in H. Kemshall and B. Wilkinson (eds) *Good Practice in Assessing Risk: Current Knowledge, Issues and Approaches*, London: Jessica Kingsley.

Baker, K., Jones, S., Roberts, C. and Merrington, S. (2003) *Validity and reliability of Asset*, London: Youth Justice Board.

Balen and Masson (2008) 'The Victoria Climbié case: social work education for practice in children and families' work before and since', *Child and Family Social Work*, vol 13, no 2, pp 121–32.

Ballucci, D. (2008) 'Risk in action: the practical effects of the Youth Management Assessment', *Social and Legal Studies*, vol 17, no 2, pp 175–97.

Bandura, A. (1997) *Self-efficacy: the exercise of self control*, New York: Freeman.

Banks, S. (2009) 'Integrity in professional life: issues of conduct, commitment and capacity', *British Journal of Social Work*, doi:10.1093/bjsw/bcp 152 (accessed 13 August 2010).

Barach, P. and Small, S. (2000) 'Reporting and preventing medical mishaps: lessons from non-medical near miss reporting systems', *British Medical Journal*, vol 320, no 7237, pp 759–63.

Barnett, G. and Mann, R. (2011) 'Good lives and risk assessment: collaborative approaches to risk assessment with sexual offenders', in H. Kemshall and B. Wilkinson (eds) *Good practice in assessing risk: Current knowledge, issues and approaches*, London: Jessica Kingsley.

Barrow Cadbury Trust (2008) *Coping with kidulthood: The hidden truth behind Britain's abandoned adolescents*, London: Barrow Cadbury.

Barry, M. (2006) *Youth offending in transition: The search for social recognition*, London: Taylor and Francis.

Barry, M. (2007) *Effective approaches to risk assessment in social work: An international review of the literature*, Edinburgh: Scottish Executive.

Barry, M. and McNeill, F. (eds) (2009) *Youth offending and youth justice*, London: Jessica Kingsley.

Barter, C. (2009) 'In the name of love: partner abuse and violence in teenage relationships', *British Journal of Social Work*, vol 39, no 2, pp 211–33.

Batchelor, S. (2005) '"Prove me the Bam!": victimisation and agency in the lives of young women who commit violent offences', *Probation Journal*, vol 52, no 4, pp 358–75.

Batchelor, S. (2009) 'Girls, gangs and violence: assessing the evidence', *Probation Journal*, vol 56, no 4, pp 399–414.

Batchelor, S. and Burman, M. (2004) 'Working with girls and young women', in G. McIvor (ed) *Women who offend*, London: Jessica Kingsley, pp 266–87.

Bates, J. (2004) 'Embracing diversity and working in partnership', in R. Carnwell and J. Buchan (eds) *Effective practice in health and social care: A partnership approach*, Maidenhead: McGraw-Hill, pp 51–64.

Beckett, C. (2008) 'Risk, uncertainty and thresholds', in M. Calder (ed) *Contemporary risk assessment in safeguarding children*, Lyme Regis: Russell House Publishing, pp 40–51.

Beddoe, L. (2010) 'Surveillance or reflection: professional supervision in the risk society', *British Journal of Social Work*, vol 40, no 4, pp 1297–313.

Beech, A. and Mann, R. (2002) 'Recent developments in the successful treatment of sex offenders', in J. McGuire (ed) *Offender rehabilitation and treatment*, Chichester: Wiley, pp 259–88.

Bhui, H. (2001) 'New probation: closer to the end of social work?' *British Journal of Social Work*, vol 31, no 4, pp 637–39.

Blyth, M. (2007) 'Serious incidents in the youth justice system: management and accountability', in M. Blyth, E. Solomon and K. Baker (eds) *Young people and 'risk'*, Bristol: The Policy Press, pp 73–84.

Boeck, T. (2009) 'Social capital and young people', in J. Wood and J. Hine (eds) *Work with young people*, London: Sage, pp 88–103.

Boeck, T. and Fleming, J. (2011) 'The role of social capital and resources in resilience to risk', in H. Kemshall and B. Wilkinson (eds) *Good practice in assessing risk: Current knowledge, issues and approaches*, London: Jessica Kingsley.

Boeck, T., Fleming, J. and Kemshall, H. (2006) 'The context of risk decisions: does social capital make a difference?' *Forum: Qualitative Social Research*, vol 7, no 1, www.qualitative-research.net/index.php/fqs/article/view/55.

Bonta, J. (1996) 'Risk-needs assessment and treatment', in A. Harland (ed) *Choosing correctional options that work: Defining the demand and evaluating the supply*, Thousand Oaks, CA: Sage, pp 18–32.

Bonta, J., Bogue, B., Crowley, M. and Motiuk, L. (2001) 'Implementing offender classification systems: lessons learned', in G. Bernfeld, D. Farrington and A. Leschied (eds) *Offender rehabilitation in practice: Implementing and evaluating effective practice*, Chichester: J. Wiley & Sons, pp 227–46.

Bonta, J., Rugge, T., Scott, T., Bourgon, G. and Yessine, A. (2008) 'Exploring the black box of community supervision', *Journal of Offender Rehabilitation*, vol 47, no 3, pp 248–70.

Bordin, E. (1979) 'The generalizability of the psychoanalytic concept of the working alliance', *Psychotherapy*, vol 16, no 3, pp 252–60.

Borenstein, L. (2002) 'The impact of the therapist's curiosity on the treatment process of children and adolescents', *Child and Adolescent Social Work Journal*, vol 19, no 5, pp 337–55.

Borum, R. (2003) 'Managing at-risk juvenile offenders in the community: putting evidence-based principles into practice', *Journal of Contemporary Criminal Justice*, vol 19, no 1, pp 114–37.

Borum, R., Bartel, P. and Forth, A. (2003) *Manual for the Structured Assessment for Violence Risk in Youth (SAVRY) Version 1.1*, Tampa, FL: University of South Florida.

Bostock, L., Bairstow, S., Fish, S. and MacLeod, F. (2005) *Managing risk and minimising mistakes in services to children and families*, London: Social Care Institute for Excellence.

Boswell, G. (1996) *Young and dangerous: The backgrounds and careers of section 53 offenders*, Aldershot: Avebury.

Bottoms, A., Shapland, J., Costello, A., Holmes, D. and Muir, G. (2004) 'Towards desistance: theoretical underpinnings for an empirical study', *The Howard Journal*, vol 43, no 4, pp 368–89.

Bouhana, N. and Wikström, P.-O. (2008) *Theorising terrorism: Terrorism as moral actions*, London: Jill Dando Institute.

Bowlby, J. (1988) *A secure base: Clinical applications of attachment theory*, London: Routledge.

Bowling, B. and Phillips, C. (2002) *Racism, crime and justice*, London: Longman.

Brandon, M., Dodsworth, J. and Rumball, D. (2005) 'Serious case reviews: learning to use expertise', *Child Abuse Review*, vol 14, no 3, pp 160–76.

Brandon, M., Belderson, P., Warren, C., Howe, D., Gardner, R., Dodsworth, J. and Black, J. (2008a) *Analysing child deaths and serious injuries through abuse and neglect: What can we learn?*, London: DCFS.

Brandon, M., Belderson, P., Warren, C., Gardner, R., Howe, D., Dodsworth, J. and Black, J. (2008b) 'The preoccupation with thresholds in cases of child death or serious injury through abuse and neglect', *Child Abuse Review*, vol 17, no 5, pp 313–30.

Brezina, T., Tekin, E. and Topalli, V. (2009) '"Might not be a tomorrow": a multi-methods approach to anticipated early death and youth crime', *Criminology*, vol 47, no 4, pp 1091–129.

Broadhurst, K., Hall, C., Wastell, D., White, S. and Pithouse, A. (2010) 'Risk, instrumentalism and the humane project in social work – identifying the informal logics of risk management in children's statutory services', *British Journal of Social Work*, vol 40, no 4, pp 1046–64.

Brookman, F., Maguire, M., Pierpoint, H. and Bennett, T. (2010) *Handbook on crime*, Cullompton: Willan.

Brown, K. and White, K. (2006) *Exploring the evidence base for integrated children's services*, Edinburgh: Scottish Executive.

Brown, S. (2009) 'The changing landscape of youth and youth crime', in M. Barry and F. McNeill (eds) *Youth offending and youth justice*, London: Jessica Kingsley, pp 17–37.

Bryan, K. (2004) 'Preliminary study of the prevalence of speech and language difficulties among young offenders', *International Journal of Language and Communication Disorders*, vol 39, no 3, pp 391–400.

Burman, M. and Batchelor, S. (2009) 'Between two stools? Responding to young women who offend', *Youth Justice*, vol 9, no 3, pp 270–84.

Burman, M., Armstrong, S., Batchelor, S., McNeill, F. and Nicholson, J. (2007) *Research and practice in risk assessment and risk management of children and young people engaging in offending behaviours*, Paisley: Risk Management Authority.

Burnett, R. (2000) 'Understanding criminal careers through a series of in-depth interviews', *Offender Programs Report*, vol 4, no 1, pp 1–16.

Burnett, R. (2004) 'One-to-one ways of promoting desistance: in search of an evidence base', in R. Burnett and C. Roberts (eds) *What works in probation and youth justice: Developing evidence-based practice*, Cullompton: Willan, pp 180–97.

Burnett, R. and Appleton, C. (2004) 'Joined-up services to tackle youth crime: a case study in England', *British Journal of Criminology*, vol 44, no 1, pp 34–54.

Burnett, R. and McNeill, F. (2005) 'The place of the officer–offender relationship in assisting offenders to desist from crime', *Probation Journal*, vol 52, no 3, pp 221–42.

Burnett, R. and Maruna, S. (2006) 'The kindness of prisoners: Strengths based resettlement in theory and in action', *Criminology and Criminal Justice*, vol 6, no 1, pp 83–106.

Burnett, R., Baker, K. and Roberts, C. (2007) 'Assessment, supervision and intervention: fundamental practice in probation', in L. Gelsthorpe and R. Morgan (eds) *The handbook of probation*, Cullompton: Willan, pp 210–47.

Burrowes, N. and Needs, A. (2009) 'Time to contemplate change? A framework for assessing readiness to change with offenders', *Aggression and Violent Behaviour*, vol 14, no 1, pp 39–49.

Burton, S. (2009) *'The oversight and review of cases in the light of changing circumstances and new information: How do people respond to new (and challenging) information?'*, London: Centre for Excellence and Outcomes in Children and Young People's Services (C4EO).

Bush, J. (1995) 'Teaching self-risk management to violent offenders', in J. McGuire (ed) *What works: Reducing reoffending*, Chichester: Wiley, pp 139–54.

Calder, M. (2008a) 'Organisational dangerousness: causes, consequences and correctives', in M. Calder (ed) *Contemporary risk assessment in safeguarding children*, Lyme Regis: Russell House Publishing, pp 119–65.

Calder, M. (2008b) 'Professional dangerousness: causes and contemporary features', in M. Calder (ed) *Contemporary risk assessment in safeguarding children*, Lyme Regis: Russell House Publishing, pp 61–96.

Calder, M. (2009) *Sexual abuse assessments*, Lyme Regis: Russell House.

Callahan, D., Kelly, G. and Wilkinson, B. (2009) *The jigsaw approach: A programme for young people in the community*, Manchester: Youth Justice Services and KWP.

Cambridge, P. (2004) 'Abuse inquiries as learning tools for social care organisations', in J. Manthorpe and N. Stanley (eds) *The age of the inquiry*, London: Routledge, pp 231–54.

Carson, D. (1996) 'Risking legal repercussions', in H. Kemshall and J. Pritchard (eds) *Good practice in risk assessment and risk management*, vol 1, London: Jessica Kingsley, pp 3–12.

Carson, D. and Bain, A. (2008) *Professional risk and working with people*, London: Jessica Kingsley.

Case, S. (2007) 'Questioning the "evidence" of risk that underpins evidence-led youth justice interventions', *Youth Justice*, vol 7, no 2, pp 91–105.

Case, S. and Haines, K. (2009) *Understanding youth offending: Risk factor research, policy and practice*, Cullompton: Willan.

Chambers, J., Eccleston, L., Day, A., Ward, T. and Howells, K. (2008) 'Treatment readiness in violent offenders: the influence of cognitive factors on engagement in violence programs', *Aggression and Violent Behaviour*, vol 13, no 4, pp 276–84.

Chapman, T. and Hough, M. (1998) *Evidence based practice: A guide to effective practice*, London: Home Office.

Cherry, S. (2006) *Transforming behaviour*, Cullompton: Willan.

Coe, R. (1996) 'Metaphor', in T. Enos (ed) *Encyclopaedia of rhetoric and composition: Communication from ancient times to the information age*, New York: Garland, pp 438–43.

Cohen, L. and Felson, M. (1979) 'Social change and crime rate trends: a routine activity approach', *American Sociological Review*, vol 44, no 4, pp 508–608.

Collins, R. (2008) *Violence: A micro-sociological theory*, Princeton, NJ: Princeton University Press.

The Communication Trust (2009) *Sentence trouble*, London: The Communication Trust.

Cooperrider, D., Whitney, D. and Stavros, J. (2008) *Appreciative inquiry handbook* (2nd edn), Brunswick: Crown Custom Publishing.

Cornish, D. and Clarke, R. (eds) (1986) *The reasoning criminal: Rational choice perspectives on offending*, New York: Springer-Verlag.

Coulshed, V. and Orme, J. (2006) *Social work practice: An introduction* (4th edn), Basingstoke: Macmillan.

Cousins, C. (2004) 'Becoming a social work supervisor: a significant role transition', *Australian Social Work*, vol 57, no 2, pp 175–85.

Craissati, J. and Sindall, O. (2009) 'Serious further offences: an exploration of risk and typologies', *Probation Journal*, vol 56, no 1, pp 9–27.

Crawford, A. (2007) 'What impacts on quality assessment using OASys?', *Probation Journal*, vol 54, no 2, pp 157–70.

Cross, W. (1980) 'Models of psychological nigrescence: a literature review', in R. Jones (ed) *Black Psychology* (2nd edn), New York: Harper & Row, pp 81–98.

Dalzell, R. and Sawyer, E. (2007) *Putting analysis into assessment: Undertaking assessments of need*, London: National Children's Bureau.

David, T. (2004) 'Avoidable pitfalls when writing medical reports for court proceedings in cases of suspected child abuse', *Archives of Disease in Childhood*, vol 89, no 9, pp 799–804.

Davies, M. (1985) *The essential social worker: A guide to positive practice* (2nd edn), Aldershot: Wildwood House.

De Vries, A. (2008) 'Working with interpreters in pre-sentence report interviews', *Probation Journal*, vol 55, no 2, pp 153–60.

Dent, R. and Jowitt, S. (2003) 'Homicide and serious sexual offences committed by children and young people: findings from the literature and a serious case review', *Journal of Sexual Aggression*, vol 9, no 2, pp 85–96.

DCSF (Department for Children, Schools and Families) (2008) *Information sharing guidance for practitioners and managers*, London: DCSF.

DCSF (2009) *Common assessment framework practitioners' guide*, London: DCSF.

DCSF (2010a) *Common core of skills and knowledge for the children's workforce*, London: DCSF.

DCSF (2010b) *Working together to safeguard children: A guide to inter-agency working to safeguard and promote the welfare of children*, London: DCSF.

Deveny, J. (2008) 'Challenging output based performance management in child protection', in M. Calder (ed) *Contemporary risk assessment in safeguarding children*, Lyme Regis: Russell House Publishing, pp 15–24.

DH (Department of Health) (2000a) *Framework for the assessment of children in need and their families*, London: The Stationery Office.

DH (2000b) *An organisation with a memory: Report of an expert group on learning from adverse events in the NHS*, London: Department of Health.

Dodge, K. (2006) 'Translational science in action: hostile attributional style and the development of aggressive behaviour problems', *Development and Psychopathology*, vol 18, no 3, pp 791–814.

Donnelly, E. and Neville, L. (2008) *Communication and interpersonal skills*, Newton Abbott: Reflect Press.

Douglas, K. and Kropp, P. (2002) 'A prevention-based paradigm for violence risk assessment', *Criminal Justice and Behavior*, vol 29, no 5, pp 617–58.

Downing, K. and Lynch, R. (1997) 'Pre-sentence reports: does quality matter?', *Social Policy and Administration*, vol 31, no 2, pp 173–90.

Driscoll, J. (2009) 'Prevalence, people and processes: a consideration of the implications of Lord Laming's progress report on the protection of children in England', *Child Abuse Review*, vol 18, no 5, pp 333–45.

Duffy, M., Schaefer, N., Coomber, R., O'Connell, L. and Turnbull, P. (2008) *Cannabis supply and young people: 'It's a social thing'*, York: Joseph Rowntree Foundation.

Eadie, T. and Canton, R. (2002) 'Practising in a context of ambivalence: the challenge for youth justice workers', *Youth Justice*, vol 2, no 1, pp 14–26.

Edcoms (2008) *Education, training and employment: Source document*, London: Youth Justice Board.

Edwards, A., Apostolov, A., Dooher, I. and Popova, A. (2008) 'Working with extended schools to prevent social exclusion', in K. Morris (ed) *Social work and multi-agency working*, Bristol: The Policy Press, pp 47–66.

Edwards, A., Daniels, H., Gallagher, T., Leadbetter, J. and Warmington, P. (2009) *Improving inter-professional collaborations: Multi-agency working for children's well being*, London: Routledge.

Ellis, K. and France, A. (2010) 'Being judged, being assessed: young people's perspective of assessment in youth justice and education', *Children and Society*, DOI:10.1111/j.1099-0860.2010.00328.x, accessed 17 September 2010.

Erikson, E. (1968) *Identity, youth and crisis*, New York: Norton.

Evans, K. and Jamieson, J. (2008) *Gender and crime: A reader*, Maidenhead: Open University Press.

Evans, T. and Hardy, M. (2010) *Evidence and knowledge for practice: Skills for contemporary social work*, Cambridge: Polity Press.

Evans, T. and Harris, J. (2004) 'Street-level bureaucracy, social work and the (exaggerated) death of discretion', *British Journal of Social Work*, vol 34, no 6, pp 871–95.

Ezell, L. and Cohen, M. (2005) *Desisting from crime: Continuity and change in long-term crime patterns of serious chronic offenders*, Oxford: Oxford University Press.

Falshaw, L. and Browne, K. (1997) 'Adverse childhood experiences and violent acts of young people in secure accommodation', *Journal of Mental Health*, vol 6, no 5, pp 443–55.

Farrall, S. (2004) 'Social capital and offender reintegration: making probation desistance focused', in S. Maruna and R. Immarigeon (eds) *After crime and punishment*, Cullompton: Willan, pp 57–82.

Farrall, S. and Maruna, S. (2004) 'Desistance-focused criminal justice policy research: introduction to a special issue on desistance from crime and public policy', *The Howard Journal*, vol 43, no 4, pp 358–67.

Farrington, D. (2002) 'Developmental Criminology and risk-focused prevention', in M. Maguire, R. Morgan and R. Reiner (eds) *The Oxford handbook of criminology* (3rd edn), Oxford: Oxford University Press, pp 657–701.

Farrington, D. (2007) 'Childhood risk factors and risk-focussed prevention', in M. Maguire, R. Morgan, and R. Reiner (eds) *The Oxford Handbook of Criminology* (4th edn), Oxford: Oxford University Press, pp 602–40.

Farrington, D., Coid, J., Harnett, J., Jolliffe, D., Soteriou, N., Turner, R. and West, D. (2006) *Criminal careers up to age 50 and life success up to age 48: New findings from the Cambridge Study in Delinquent Development* (2nd edn), Home Office Research Study 299, London: Home Office.

Farrow, K., Kelly, G. and Wilkinson, B. (2007) *Offenders in focus: Risk, responsivity and diversity*, Bristol: The Policy Press.

Farrow, K., Kelly, G. and Wilkinson, B. (2011) 'Risk management in the community: changing practice and priorities', in K. Doolin, J. Braine, J. Child and A. Beech (eds) *Whose criminal justice? Regulatory state or empowered communities?*, Hook: Waterside Press.

Field, S. (2007) 'Practice cultures and the "new" youth justice in (England and) Wales', *British Journal of Criminology*, vol 47, no 2, pp 311–30.

Field, S. and Nelken, D. (2010) 'Reading and writing youth justice in Italy and (England and) Wales', *Punishment and Society*, vol 12, no 3, pp 287–308.

Fielder, C., Hart, D. and Shaw, C. (2008) *The developing relationships between youth offending teams and children's trusts*, London: Youth Justice Board.

Fionda, J. (2005) *Devils and angels: Youth, policy and crime*, Oxford: Hart Publishing.

Fish, S. (2009) *What are the key questions for audit of child protection systems and decision-making?*, London: Centre for Excellence and Outcomes in Children and Young People's Services (C4EO).

Fleming, J. and Hudson, N. (2009) 'Young people and research participation', in J. Wood and J. Hine (eds) *Work with young people*, London: Sage, pp 114–26.

Forrester, D., Kershaw, S., Moss, H. and Hughes, L. (2008) 'Communication skills in child protection: how do social workers talk to parents?', *Child and Family Social Work*, vol 13, no 1, pp 41-51.

France, A. and Homel, R. (2006) 'Societal access routes and developmental pathways: putting social structure and young people's voices into the analysis of pathways into and out of crime', *The Australian and New Zealand Journal of Criminology*, vol 39, no 3, pp 295–309.

France, A., Freiberg, K. and Homel, R. (2010) 'Beyond risk factors: Towards a holistic prevention paradigm for children and young people', *British Journal of Social Work*, vol 40, no 4, pp 1192-1210.

Gano, D. (2008) *Apollo root cause analysis: A new way of thinking* (3rd edn), Yakima, WA: Apollonian Publications.

Garrett, P. (2003) 'Swimming with dolphins: the assessment framework, New Labour and new tools for social work with children and families', *British Journal of Social Work*, vol 33, no 4, pp 441–63.

Garrett, P. (2005) 'Social work's electronic turn: notes on the deployment of information and communication technologies in social work with children and families', *Critical Social Policy*, vol 25, no 4, pp 529–53.

Gelsthorpe, L. and Padfield, N. (2003) 'Introduction', in L. Gelsthorpe and N. Padfield (eds) *Exercising discretion: Decision-making in the criminal justice system and beyond*, Cullompton: Willan, pp 1–28.

Gelsthorpe, L., Raynor, P. and Robinson, G. (2010) 'Pre-sentence reports in England and Wales: changing discourses of need, risk and quality', in F. McNeill, P. Raynor and C. Trotter (eds) *Offender supervision: New directions in theory, research and practice*, Abingdon: Willan Publishing.

Gillingham, P. and Humphreys, C. (2009) 'Child protection practitioners and decision-making tools: observations and reflections from the front line', *British Journal of Social Work*, advance access doi:10.1093/bjsw/bcp 155, accessed 11 August 2010.

Glennie, S. (2007) 'Developing interprofessional relationships: tapping the potential of inter-agency training', *Child Abuse Review*, vol 16, no 3, pp 171–83.

Goldson, B. (ed) (2000) *The new youth justice*, Lyme Regis: Russell House Publishing.

Goldson, B. (2007) 'New Labour's new justice: a critical assessment of the first two terms', in G. McIvor and P. Raynor (eds) *Developments in social work with offenders*, London: Jessica Kingsley, pp 23–39.

Goldson, B. and Muncie, J. (2006) *Youth crime and justice*, London: Sage.

Goldstein, W. and Hogarth, R. (1997) 'Judgement and decision research: Some historical context', in W. Goldstein and R. Hogarth (eds) *Research on judgement and decision making: currents, connections and controversies*, Cambridge: Cambridge University Press.

Goldstein, A. (1999) *The Prepare curriculum: Teaching pro-social competences*, Champaign, IL: Research Press.

Gorman, K. (2006) 'Constructing a convincing narrative: the art of persuasive storytelling within the tight constraints of formal pre-sentence assessments for the criminal courts', in K. Gorman, M. Gregory, M. Hayles and N. Parton (eds) *Constructive work with offenders*, London: Jessica Kingsley, pp 105–22.

Gough, D. (2010) 'Multi-agency working in corrections: cooperation and competition in probation practice', in A. Pycroft and D. Gough (eds) *Multi-agency working in criminal justice*, Bristol: The Policy Press, pp 21–34.

Government Social Research Unit (2007) *The Magenta Book: Guidance notes for policy evaluation and analysis*, London: HM Treasury.

Graham, J. and Bowling, B. (1995) *Young people and crime*, Home Office Research Study 145, London: Home Office.

Graham, K. and Wells, S. (2003) '"Somebody's gonna get their head kicked in tonight!" Aggression among young males in bars – a question of values?', *British Journal of Criminology*, vol 43, no 3, pp 546–66.

Graham, P. (ed) (2004) *Cognitive behaviour therapy for children and families* (2nd edn), Cambridge: Cambridge University Press.

Griffin, H. and Beech, A. (2004) *Evaluation of the AIM framework for assessment of adolescents who display sexually harmful behaviour*, London: Youth Justice Board.

Grimshaw, R. with Malek, M., Oldfield, M. and Smith, R. (2008) *Young people who sexually abuse: Source document*, London: Youth Justice Board.

Gubrium, J., Buckholdt, D. and Lynott, R. (1989) 'The descriptive tyranny of forms', *Perspectives on Social Problems*, vol 1, pp 195–214.

Haas, H., Farrington, D., Killias, M. and Sattar, G. (2004) 'The impact of different family configurations on delinquency', *British Journal of Criminology*, vol 44, no 4, pp 520–32.

Hall, I. (2000) 'Young offenders with a learning disability', *Advances in Psychiatric Treatment*, vol 6, no 4, pp 278–85.

Hancock, D. (2007) 'Assessment', in R. Canton and D. Hancock (eds) *Dictionary of probation and offender management*, Cullompton: Willan, p 16.

Hannah-Moffat, K. (2006) 'Pandora's box: risk/need and gender-responsive corrections', *Criminology and Public Policy*, vol 5, no, 1, pp 183–92.

Hanson, R. and Harris, A. (2000) 'Where should we intervene? Dynamic predictors of sexual offense recidivism', *Criminal Justice and Behavior*, vol 27, no 1, pp 6–35.

Harden, J., Scott, S., Backett-Milburn, K. and Jackson, S. (2000) 'Can't talk, won't talk? Methodological issues in researching children', *Sociological Research Online*, vol 5, no 2, www.socresonline.org.uk/5/2/harden.html.

Hart, D. (2006) *Tell them not to forget about us*, London: NCB.

Hart, D. and Thompson, C. (2009) *Young people's participation in the youth justice system*, London: NCB.

Hart, R. (1997) *Children's participation*, London: Earthscan/UNICEF.

Hart, S., Michie, C. and Cooke, D. (2007) 'Precision of actuarial risk assessment instruments', *British Journal of Psychiatry*, vol 190, supplement 49, pp 60–5.

Hawkins, K. (1992) *The uses of discretion*, Oxford: Clarendon Press.

Hayles, M. (2006) 'Constructing safety: a collaborative approach to managing risk and building responsibility', in K. Gorman, M. Gregory, M. Hayles and N. Parton (eds) *Constructive work with offenders*, London: Jessica Kingsley, pp 67–86.

HMG (Her Majesty's Government) (2003) *Every child matters*, London: The Stationery Office.

HMG (2010) *Working together to safeguard children: A guide to interagency working to safeguard and promote the welfare of children*, London: The Stationery Office.

HMIP (Her Majesty's Inspectorate of Probation) (2005) *Inquiry into the supervision of Peter Williams by Nottingham City Youth Offending Team*, London: HMIP.

HMIP (2006) *Putting risk of harm in context*, Joint Thematic Inspection Report, London: HMIP.

HMIP (2008) *On the right road*, Risk of Harm Inquiry Report, London: HMIP.

HMIP (2009a) *End of programme report 2003–2009: Joint Inspection of Youth Offending Teams*, London: HMIP.

HMIP (2009b) *Public protection and safeguarding – an inspectorate perspective*, London: HMIP.

HMIP (2010) *Reports and court work: A thematic review*, London: HMIP.

HEA (Higher Education Academy), *Writing reports*, York: Higher Education Academy, www.heacademy.ac.uk/assets/hlst/documents/heinfe_exchange/Blended_Learning_PDP_Materials/5_reportwriting.pdf.

Hilder, S. (2010) 'Multi-agency working with black and minority ethnic offenders', in A. Pycroft and D. Gough (eds) *Multi-agency working in criminal justice*, Bristol: The Policy Press, pp 65–80.

Hill, A. (2010) *Working in statutory contexts*, Cambridge: Polity Press.

Hill, M., Lockyer, A. and Stone, F. (eds) (2007) *Youth justice and child protection*, London: Jessica Kingsley.

Hine, J. (2009) 'Young people's lives: taking a different view', in J. Wood and J. Hine (eds) *Work with young people*, London: Sage, pp 27–38.

Hobbs and Hook Consulting (2001) *Research into effective practice with young people in secure facilities*, London: Youth Justice Board.

Hoge, R. (2002) 'Standardized instruments for assessing risk and need in youthful offenders' *Criminal Justice and Behavior*, vol 29, no 4, pp 380–96.

Hoge, R. and Andrews, D. (1996) *Assessing the youthful offender*, New York: Plenum Press.

Hoge, R. and Andrews, D. (2002) *Youth level of service/case management inventory: User's manual*, North Tonawanda, NY: Multi-Health Systems.

Hoge, R. and Andrews, D. (2010) *Evaluation for risk of violence in juveniles*, Oxford: Oxford University Press.

Holland, S. (2004) 'Representing children in child protection assessments', *Childhood*, vol 8, no 3, pp 322–39.

Hollin, C., Browne, D. and Palmer, E. (2002) *Delinquency and young offenders*, Oxford: Wiley-Blackwell.

Hollows, A. (2008) 'Professional judgement and the risk assessment process', in M. Calder (ed) *Contemporary risk assessment in safeguarding children*, Lyme Regis: Russell House Publishing, pp 52–60.

Holt, P. (2000) *Case management: Context for supervision*, Leicester: De Montfort University.

Holt, P. (2002) 'Case Management evaluation: pathways to progress', *Vista*, vol 7, no 1, pp 16–25.

Home Office (1997) *No more excuses – a new approach to tackling youth crime in England and Wales*, London: The Stationery Office.

Home Office (1998) *The age–crime curve*, London: The Stationery Office.

Home Office and Ministry of Justice (2010) *National Support framework reducing reoffending, cutting crime, changing lives*, London: Home Office.

Hooper, C.-A., Gorin, S., Cabral, C. and Dyson, C. (2007) *Living with hardship 24/7: The diverse experiences of families in poverty in England*, London: The Frank Buttle Trust.

Hopkins-Burke, R. (2009) *An introduction to criminological theory*, Cullompton: Willan.

Horlick-Jones, T. (2005) 'On "risk work": professional discourse, accountability and everyday action', *Health, Risk and Society*, vol 7, no 3, pp 293–307.

Hörnqvist, M. (2007) *The organised nature of power: On productive and repressive interventions based on consideration of risk*, Stockholm: Stockholm University.

Howard, J. (2010) 'The beauty of reflection and the beast of multi-agency cooperation', in A. Pycroft and D. Gough (eds) *Multi-agency working in criminal justice*, Bristol: The Policy Press, pp 231–44.

Howard, P. (2009) *Improving the prediction of re-offending using the Offender Assessment System*, London: Ministry of Justice.

Howard, P., Francis, B., Soothill, K. and Humphreys, L. (2009) *OGRS3: The revised Offender Group Reconviction Scale*, London: Ministry of Justice.

Hudson, B. (2005) 'Grounds for optimism', *Community Care*, Sutton: Community Care, www.communitycare.co.uk/Articles/2005/12/01/51988/Grounds-for-optimism.htm.

Hudson, B. and Bramhall, G. (2005) 'Assessing the "other": constructions of "Asianness", in risk assessments by probation officers', *British Journal of Criminology*, vol 45, no 5, pp 721–40.

Hughes, L. and Owen, H. (2009) *Good practice in safeguarding children: Working effectively in child protection*, London: Jessica Kingsley.

Hutton, A. and Partridge, K. (2006) *'Say it your own way': Children's participation in assessment: a guide and resources*, London: Barnardo's/The Stationery Office.

Institute of Medicine (1999) *To err is human: Building a safer health system*, Washington DC: National Academic Press.

IYJS (Irish Youth Justice Service) (2009) *Designing effective local responses to youth crime*, Dublin: Department of Justice, Equality and Law Reform.

Johnstone, J. and Burman, M. (eds) (2010) *Youth justice*, Edinburgh: Dunedin Academic Press.

Joint Chief Inspectors (2008) *Safeguarding children: The Third Joint Chief Inspector's Report on Arrangements to Safeguard Children*, London: Department of Health.

Jones, D. (2003) *Communicating with vulnerable children: A guide for practitioners*, London: Gaskell.

Jones, M. (2004) 'Supervision, learning and transformative practices', in N. Gould and M. Baldwin (eds) *Social work, critical reflection and the learning organization*, Aldershot: Ashgate, pp 11–22.

Jones, S. and Baker, K. (2009) 'Setting the scene: risk, welfare and rights', in K. Baker and A. Sutherland (eds) *Multi Agency Public Protection Arrangements and youth justice*, Bristol: The Policy Press, pp 17–24.

Jones, S. and Roberts, C. (2006) 'Examining the "involvement" in community involvement: a case study of referral order volunteers in one youth offending team', in T. Brannan, P. John and G. Stoker (eds) *Re-energizing citizenship*, Basingstoke: Palgrave MacMillan, pp 41–62.

Joughin, C. and Morley, D. (2007) *Conduct disorder in older children and young people: Research messages for practice problems*, Dartington: Research in Practice.

Juhila, K. (2009) 'From care to fellowship and back: interpretive repertoires used by the social welfare workers when describing their relationship with homeless women', *British Journal of Social Work*, vol 39, no 1, pp 128–43.

Kadushin, A. and Kadushin, G. (1997) *The social work interview: A guide for human service professionals* (4th edn), New York: Columbia University Press.

Keith, Mr Justice (2006) *Inquiry into the death of Zahid Mubarak*, London: Home Office.

Kemshall, H. (1996) *Reviewing risk: A review of research on the assessment and management of risk and dangerousness, implications for policy and practice in the probation service*, Croydon: Home Office.

Kemshall, H. (1998a) *Risk in probation practice*, Aldershot: Ashgate.

Kemshall, H. (1998b) 'Defensible decisions for risk: or 'It's the doers wot get the blame', *Probation Journal*, vol 45, no 2, pp 67–72.

Kemshall, H. (2003) *Understanding risk in criminal justice*, Buckingham: Open University Press.

Kemshall, H. (2008a) *Understanding the community management of high risk offenders*, Maidenhead: Open University Press.

Kemshall, H. (2008b) 'Risks, rights and justice: understanding and responding to youth risk', *Youth Justice*, vol 8, no 1, pp 21–37.

Kemshall, H. (2009) 'Risk, social policy and young people', in J. Wood and J. Hine (eds) *Work with young people*, London: Sage, pp 154–62.

Kemshall, H. (2010) 'Risk rationalities in contemporary social work policy and practice', *British Journal of Social Work*, vol 40, no 4, pp 1247–62.

Kemshall, H., Parton, N., Walsh, M. and Waterson, J. (1997) 'Concepts of risk in relation to organizational structure and functioning within the personal social services and probation' *Social Policy & Administration*, vol 31, no 3, pp 213–32.

Kemshall, H., Mackenzie, G., Wood, J., Bailey, R. and Yates, J. (2005) *Strengthening Multi-Agency Public Protection Arrangements (MAPPAs)*, London: Home Office.

Kemshall, H., Marsland, L., Boeck, T. and Dunkerton, L. (2006) 'Young people, pathways and crime: beyond risk factors', *The Australian and New Zealand Journal of Criminology*, vol 39, no 3, pp 354–70.

Kemshall, H., Mackenzie, G., Miller, J. and Wilkinson, B. (2007) *Assessing and managing risk*, Paisley: Risk Management Authority.

Klein, G. (1999) *Sources of power: How people make decisions*, Cambridge, MA: MIT Press.

Koprowska, J. (2010) *Communication and interpersonal skills in social work*, Exeter: Learning Matters.

Lakoff, G. and Johnson, M. (1980) *Metaphors we live by*, Chicago: University of Chicago Press.

LaMendola, W., Ballantyne, N. and Daly, E. (2009) 'Practitioner networks: professional learning in the twenty-first century', *British Journal of Social Work*, vol 39, no 4, pp 710–24.

Lancaster, E. and Lumb, J. (2006) 'The assessment of risk in the National Probation Service of England and Wales', *Journal of Social Work*, vol 6, no 3, pp 275–91.

Leadbetter, J. (2008) 'Learning in and for interagency working: making links between practice development and structured reflection', *Learning in Health and Social Care*, vol 7, no 4, pp 198–208.

Lefevre, M. (2010) *Communication with young people and children: Making a difference*, Bristol: The Policy Press.

Leonard, M. (2010) 'What's recreational about "recreational rioting"? Children on the streets in Belfast', *Children and Society*, vol 24, no 1, pp 38–49.

Lösel, F. and Bender, D. (2007) 'Protective factors and resilience', in D. Farrington and J. Coid (eds) *Early prevention of adult antisocial behaviour*, Cambridge: Cambridge University Press, pp 130–204.

Lowenkamp, C. and Latessa, E. (eds) (2004) *Residential community corrections and the risk principle: Lessons learned in Ohio*, Cincinatti: University of Cincinatti.

Luckock, B., Lefevre, M., Orr, D., Jones, M., Marchant, M. and Tanner, K. (2006) *Teaching, learning and assessing communication skills with children and young people in social work education*, London: Social Care Institute for Excellence, www.scie.org.uk/publications/knowledgereviews/kr12.pdf.

Lyng, S. (ed) (2005) *The sociology of risk-taking*, New York: Routledge.

McGhee, J. and Waterhouse, L. (2007) 'Classification in youth justice and child welfare: in search of the "child"', *Youth Justice*, vol 7, no 2, pp 107–20.

McGuire, J. (2000) *An introduction to theory and research: Cognitive behavioural approaches*, London: Home Office.

McGuire. J. (2002) *Offender rehabilitation and treatment: Effective Programmes and policies to reduce re-offending*, Chichester: John Wiley & Sons.

McGuire, J. (2004) 'Commentary: promising answers and the next generation of questions', *Psychology Crime and Law*, vol 10, no 3, pp 335–45.

McIvor, G., Murray, C. and Jamieson, J. (2004) 'Desistance from crime: is it different for women and girls?', in S. Maruna, and R. Immarigeon, (eds) *After crime and punishment*, Cullompton: Willan, pp 181–99.

McKimm, J. and Phillips, K. (2009) *Leadership and management in integrated services*, Exeter: Learning Matters.

McLaughlin, E. and Newburn, T. (eds) (2010) *The SAGE handbook of criminological theory*, London: Sage.

McMurran, M. (2002) 'Alcohol, aggression and violence', in J. McGuire (ed) *Offender rehabilitation and treatment*, Chichester: Wiley, pp 221–42.

McNeill, F. (2004) 'Desistance, rehabilitation and correctionalism: developments and prospects in Scotland', *The Howard Journal*, vol 43, no 4, pp 420–36.

McNeill, F. (2006) 'A desistance paradigm for offender management', *Criminology & Criminal Justice*, vol 6, no 1, pp 39–62.

McNeill, F. (2009a) *Towards effective practice in offender supervision*, Glasgow: The Scottish Centre for Crime and Justice Research.

McNeill, F. (2009b) 'Young people, serious offending and managing risk: A Scottish perspective', in K. Baker and A. Sutherland (eds) *Multi-agency public protection arrangements and youth justice*, Bristol: The Policy Press, pp 75–92.

McNeill, F. (2009c) 'What works and what's just?', *European Journal of Probation*, vol 1, no 1, pp 21 – 40.

McNeill, F. and Batchelor, S. (2002) 'Chaos, containment and change', *Youth Justice*, vol 2, no 1, pp 27 – 43.

McNeill, F. and Weaver, B. (2010) *Changing lives? Desistance research and offender management*, Glasgow: The Scottish Centre for Crime and Justice Research.

McNeill, F., Batchelor, S., Burnett, R. and Knox, J. (2005) *21st century social work: Reducing re-offending: key practice skills*, Edinburgh: Scottish Executive.

McNeill, F., Burns, N., Halliday, S., Hutton, N. and Tata, C. (2009) 'Risk responsibility and reconfiguration: penal adaptation and misadaptation', *Punishment and Society*, vol 11, no 4, pp 419–42.

McVie, S. (2005) *Patterns of deviance underlying the age–crime curve: The long term evidence*, Edinburgh: University of Edinburgh Centre for Law and Society.

McWilliams, W. (1985) 'The mission transformed: professionalisation of probation between the wars', *The Howard Journal*, vol 24, no 4, pp 257–74.

McWilliams, W. (1986) 'The English probation system and the diagnostic ideal', *The Howard Journal*, vol 25, no 4, pp 241–60.

Mair, G., Burke, L. and Taylor, S. (2006) 'The worst tax form you've ever seen? Probation officers' views about OASys', *Probation Journal*, vol 53, no 1, pp 7–23.

Mair, G., Cross, N. and Taylor, S. (2007) *The use and impact of the Community Order and the Suspended Sentence Order*, London: Centre for Crime and Community Justice Studies.

Marcia, J. (1980) 'Identity in adolescence', in J. Adelson (ed) *Handbook of adolescent psychology*, New York: Wiley.

Margo, J. (2008) *Make me a criminal: Preventing youth crime*, London: IPPR.

Maruna, S. (2000) 'Desistance from crime and offender rehabilitation: a tale of two research literatures', Offender Programs Report, vol 4, no 1, pp 1–13.

Mason, P. and Prior, D. (2008) *Engaging young people who offend*, London: Youth Justice Board.

Melde, C., Taylor, T. and Esbensen, F.-A. (2009) '"I got your back": an examination of the protective function of gang membership in adolescence', *Criminology*, vol 47, no 2, pp 565–94.

Melrose, M. (2004) 'Fractured transitions: disadvantaged young people, drug-taking and risk', *Probation Journal*, vol 51, no 4, pp 327–41.

Merrington, S. (2004) 'Assessment tools in probation', in R. Burnett and C. Roberts (eds) *What works in probation and youth justice: Developing evidence-based practice*, Cullompton: Willan, pp 46–69.

Millard, B. and Flatley, J. (2010) *Experimental statistics on victimisation of children aged 10 to 15: Findings from the British Crime Survey for the year ending December 2009 (England and Wales)*, London: Home Office.

Miller, C., Freeman, M. and Ross, N. (2001) *Interprofessional practice in health and social care: Challenging the shared learning agenda*, London: Arnold.

Miller, W. and Rollnick, S. (2002) *Motivational interviewing: Preparing people for change*, New York: Guildford.

Milner, J. and O'Byrne, P. (2009) *Assessment in social work* (3rd edn), Basingstoke: Palgrave Macmillan.

Ministry of Justice (2009) *MAPPA guidance version 3.0*, London: Ministry of Justice.

Minkes, J., Hammersley, R. and Raynor, P. (2005) 'Partnership in working with young offenders with substance misuse problems', *The Howard Journal*, vol 44, no 3, pp 254–68.

Mitchell, T., Tanner, T. and Haynes, K. (2009) *Children as agents of change for disaster risk reduction*, London: Children in a Changing Climate.

Moore, R., Gray, E., Roberts, C., Merrington, S., Waters, I., Fernandez, R., et al (2004) *National evaluation of the Intensive Supervision and Surveillance Programme: Interim report to the Youth Justice Board*, London: Youth Justice Board.

Morgan, R. (2006) *About social workers: A children's views report*, Newcastle upon Tyne: Commission for Social Care Inspection, www.rights4me.org/content/beheardreports/3/about_social_workers_report.pdf.

Morgan, R. and Haines, K. (2007) 'Services before trial and sentence', in L. Gelsthorpe and R. Morgan (eds) *Handbook of probation*, Cullompton: Willan, pp 182–209.

Morgan, R. and Newburn, T. (2007) 'Youth justice', in M. Maguire, R. Morgan and R. Reiner (eds) *The Oxford handbook of criminology* (4th edn), Oxford: Oxford University Press, pp 1024–60.

Morris, K. (2008) *Social work and multi-agency working: Making a difference*, Bristol: The Policy Press.

Morris, L. and Mason, J. (1999) 'Improving understanding and recall of the probation service contract', *Probation Journal*, vol 46, no 4, pp 259–62.

Muncie, J. (2004) *Youth and crime* (2nd edn), London: Sage.

Munro, E. (2004) 'A simpler way to understand the results of risk assessment instruments', *Children and Youth Services Review*, vol 26, no 9, pp 873–83.

Munro, E. (2008a) *Effective child protection* (2nd edn), London: Sage.

Munro, E. (2008b) 'Lessons learnt, boxes ticked, families ignored', *The Independent*, 16 November, www.independent.co.uk/opinion/commentators, accessed 9 March 2010.

Munro, E. (2009) 'Managing societal and institutional risk in child protection', *Risk Analysis*, vol 29, no 7, pp 1015–23.

Munro, E. (2010) 'Learning to reduce risk in child protection', *British Journal of Social Work*, vol 40, no 4, pp 1135–51.

Murphy, M. (2004) *Developing collaborative relationships in interagency child protection work*, Lyme Regis: Russell House Publishing.

Murphy, M., Shardlow, S., Davis, C. and Race, D. (2006) 'Standards – a new baseline for interagency training and education to safeguard children?', *Child Abuse Review*, vol 15, no 2, pp 138–51.

Murray, C. (2009) 'Typologies of young resisters and desisters', *Youth Justice*, vol 9, no 2, pp 115–29.

NACRO (2003) *Pre-sentence reports for young people: A good practice guide* (2nd edn), London: NACRO.

NACRO (2007) *Youth Crime Briefing: Effective Practice with children and young people who offend – Part 2*, London: NACRO.

NACRO (2008) *Youth Crime Briefing: Children in custody: Local authority duties, responsibilities and powers*, London: NACRO.

NACRO Cymru (2003) *Pre-sentence reports for young people sentenced to custody: A Welsh review*, London: NACRO.

Nash, M. (2010) 'Singing from the same MAPPA hymn sheet – but can we hear all the voices?', in A. Pycroft and D. Gough (eds) *Multi-agency working in criminal justice*, Bristol: The Policy Press, pp 111–22.

NCH (2007) *Young people growing strong: the role of positive, structured activities*, London: NCH.

Nutley, S., Walter, I. and Davies, T. (2007) *Using evidence: How research can inform public services*, Bristol: The Policy Press.

O'Connell, S. (2006) 'From Toad of Toad Hall to the "death drivers" of Belfast', *British Journal of Criminology*, vol 46, no 3, pp 455–69.

O'Mahony, P. (2009) 'The risk factors prevention paradigm and the causes of youth crime: a deceptively useful analysis?', *Youth Justice*, vol 9, no 2, pp 99–114.

O'Rourke, L. (2010) *Recording in social work*, Bristol: The Policy Press.

Ofsted (2009) *Learning lessons from serious case reviews: year 2*, Manchester: Ofsted.

Osmond, J. and O'Connor, I. (2004) 'Formalizing the unformalized: practitioners' communication of knowledge in practice', *British Journal of Social Work*, vol 34, no 5, pp 677–92.

Parker, J. and Bradley, G. (2007) *Social work practice: Assessment, planning, intervention and review*, Exeter: Learning Matters.

Peay, J. (2003) *Decisions and dilemmas: Working with mental health law*, Oxford: Hart.

Perry, A., Gilbody, S., Akers, J. and Light, K. (2008) *Mental health: Source document*, London: Youth Justice Board.

Phoenix, J. (2009) 'Beyond risk assessment: the return of repressive welfarism?', in M. Barry and F. McNeill (eds) *Youth offending and youth justice*, London: Jessica Kingsley, pp 113–31.

Phoenix, J. (2010) 'Pre-sentence reports, magisterial discourse and agency in the Youth Courts in England and Wales', *Punishment and Society*, vol 12, no 3, pp 348–66.

Porporino, F. (2010) 'Bringing sense and sensitivity to corrections: from programmes to "fix" offenders to services to support desistance', in J. Brayford, F. Cowe and J. Deering (eds) *What else works? Creative work with offenders*, Cullompton: Willan, pp 61–85.

Power, C. (2003) 'Irish Travellers: ethnicity, racism and pre-sentence reports', *Probation Journal*, vol 50, no 3, pp 252–66.

Powis, B. (2002) *Offenders' risk of serious harm: A literature review*, Occasional Paper 81, London: Home Office.

Presser, L. (2009) 'The narratives of offenders', *Theoretical Criminology*, vol 13, no 2, pp 177–200.

Print, B., Morrison, T. and Henniker, J. (2001) 'An inter-agency assessment framework for young people who sexually abuse: principles, processes and practicalities', in M. Calder (ed) *Juveniles and children who sexually abuse: Frameworks for assessment*, Lyme Regis: Russell House Publishing.

Prochaska, J. and DiClemente, C. (1983) 'Stages and process of self-change of smoking: toward an integrative model of change', *Journal of Consulting and Clinical Psychology*, vol 51, no 3, pp 390–5.

Punch, S. (2002) 'Interviewing with young people: the "secret box", stimulus material and task-based activities', *Children & Society*, vol 16, no 1, pp 45 – 56.

Pycroft, A. (2010) 'Consensus, complexity and emergence: the mixed economy of service provision', in A. Pycroft and D. Gough (eds) *Multi-agency working in criminal justice*, Bristol: The Policy Press, pp 7–20.

Raynor, P. (2004) 'Rehabilitative and reintegrative approaches', in A. Bottoms, S. Rex, and G. Robinson (eds) *Alternatives to prison: Options for an insecure society*, Cullompton: Willan, pp 195–223.

Raynor, P. and Vanstone, M. (1996) 'Reasoning and rehabilitation in Britain: the results of the Straight Thinking On Probation (STOP) Programme', *International Journal of Offender Therapy and Comparative Criminology*, vol 40, no 4, 272–84.

Reder, P., Duncan, S. and Gray, M. (1993) *Beyond blame: Child abuse tragedies revisited*, London: Routledge.

Reder, P. and Duncan, S. (1999) *Lost innocents: A follow up study of fatal child abuse*, London: Routledge.

Reder, P. and Duncan, S. (2004a) 'From Colwell to Climbié: inquiring into fatal child abuse', in J. Manthorpe and N. Stanley (eds) *The age of the inquiry*, London: Routledge, pp 92–115.

Reder, P. and Duncan, S. (2004b) 'Making the most of the Victoria Climbié Inquiry Report', *Child Abuse Review*, vol 13, no 2, pp 95–114.

Rennie, C. and Dolan, M. (2010) 'The significance of protective factors in the assessment of risk', *Criminal Behaviour and Mental Health*, vol 20, no 1, pp 8–22.

Ripley, K. and Yuill, N. (2005) 'Patterns of language impairment and behaviour in boys excluded from school', *British Journal of Educational Psychology*, vol 75, no 1, pp 37–50.

RMA (Risk Management Authority) (2007a) *Risk Assessment Tools Evaluation Directory (RATED) Version 2*, Paisley: RMA.

RMA (2007b) *Standards and guidelines: Risk management of offenders subject to an order for lifelong restriction*, Paisley: RMA.

Roberts, C., Baker, K., Jones, S. and Merrington, S. (2001) *The validity and reliability of Asset: Interim report to the Youth Justice Board*, Oxford: Centre for Criminological Research.

Robinson, G. (2002) 'Exploring risk management in probation practice', *Punishment and Society*, vol 4, no 1, pp 5–25.

Robinson, G. (2003a) 'Technicality and indeterminacy in probation practice: a case study', *British Journal of Social Work*, vol 33, no 5, pp 593–610.

Robinson, G. (2003b) 'Implementing OASys: lessons from research into LSI-R and ACE', *Probation Journal*, vol 50, no 1, pp 30–40.

Robinson, L. (2001) 'A conceptual framework for social work practice with black children and adolescents in the United Kingdom', *Journal of Social Work*, vol 1, no 2, pp 165–85.

Rogers, C. (1959) 'A theory of therapy, personality and interpersonal relationships as developed in the client-centered framework', in S. Koch (ed) *Psychology: A study of a science. Vol 3: Formulations of the person and the social context*, New York: McGraw Hill.

Rumgay, J. (2000) *The addicted offender*, Basingstoke: Palgrave.

Rutter, M., Giller, H. and Hagell, A. (1998) *Antisocial behaviour by young people*, Cambridge: Cambridge University Press.

Sale, A. (2006) 'Paralysed around culture', *Community Care*, no 1614, pp 28–9.

Sampson, R. and Laub, J. (1993) *Crime in the making: Pathways and turning points through life*, Cambridge, MA: Harvard University Press.

Savolainen, J. (2009) 'Work, family and criminal desistance: adult social bonds in a Nordic welfare state', *British Journal of Criminology*, vol 49, no 3, pp 285–304.

Schön, D. (1987) *Educating the reflective practitioner*, San Francisco, CA: Jossey-Bass Inc.

Schwalbe, C. (2004) 'Re-visioning risk assessment for human service decision making', *Children and Youth Services Review*, vol 26, no 6, pp 561–76.

Schwalbe, C. (2007) 'Risk assessment for juvenile justice: a meta-analysis', *Law and Human Behavior*, vol 31, no 5, pp 449–62.

Schwalbe, C. (2008a) 'A meta-analysis of juvenile justice risk assessment instruments: predictive validity by gender', *Criminal Justice and Behavior*, vol 35, no 11, pp 1367–81.

Schwalbe, C. (2008b) 'Strengthening the integration of actuarial risk assessment with clinical judgement in an evidence based practice framework', *Children and Youth Services Review*, vol 30, no 12, pp 1458–64.

Scottish Executive (2004) *National objectives for social work services in the criminal justice system: Standards for social enquiry reports and associated court services*, Edinburgh: Scottish Executive.

Scottish Government (2008) *A guide to getting it right for every child*, Edinburgh: Scottish Government, www.scotland.gov.uk/Publications/2008/09/22091734/0, accessed 16 August 2010.

Senge, P. (2006) *The fifth discipline: The art and practice of the learning organisation*, London: Random House Business Books.

Sentencing Guidelines Council (2009) *Overarching principles: Sentencing youths*, London: Sentencing Guidelines Council.

Serin, R. and Lloyd, C. (2009) 'Examining the process of offender change: the transition to crime desistance', *Psychology, Crime and Law*, vol 15, no 4, pp 347–64.

Shader, M. (2003) *Risk factors for delinquency: An overview*, Washington, DC: Office of Juvenile Justice and Delinquency Prevention.

Sharpe, G. and Gelsthorpe, L. (2009) 'Engendering the agenda: girls, young women and youth justice', *Youth Justice*, vol 9, no 3, pp 195 – 208.

Sheldrick, C. (1999) 'Practitioner review: the assessment and management of risk in adolescents', *Journal of Child Psychology and Psychiatry*, vol 40, no 4, pp 507–18.

Sheppard, M., Newstead, S., Di Caccavo, A. and Ryan, K. (2000) 'Reflexivity and the development of process knowledge in social work: a classification and empirical study', *British Journal of Social Work*, vol 30, no 4, pp 465–88.

Sheppard, M., Newstead, S., Di Caccavo, A. and Ryan, K. (2001) 'Comparative hypothesis assessment and quasi triangulation as process knowledge assessment strategies in social work practice', *British Journal of Social Work*, vol 31, no 6, pp 863–85.

Skills for Justice (2008) *National occupational standards for youth justice/resettlement of offenders*, Sheffield: Skills for Justice.

Smale, G. and Tuson, G. with Biehal, N. and Marsh, P. (1993) *Empowerment, assessment, care management and the skilled worker*, London: The Stationery Office.

Smith, D. and Bradshaw, P. (2005) *Gang membership and teenage offending*, Edinburgh: Centre for Law and Society.

Smith, D., Ray, L. and Wastell, L. (2002) 'Racist violence and probation practice', *Probation Journal*, vol 49, no 1, pp 3–9.

Smith, M., McMahon, L. and Nursten, J. (2003) 'Social workers' experiences of fear', *British Journal of Social Work*, vol 33, no 5, pp 659–71.

Smith, R. (2006) 'Actuarialism and early intervention in contemporary youth justice', in B. Goldson and J. Muncie (eds) *Youth crime and justice: Critical issues*, London: Sage, pp 110–24.

Smith, R. (2007) *Youth justice: Ideas, policy, practice* (2nd edn), Cullompton: Willan.

Snow, P. and Powell, M. (2008) 'Oral language competence, social skills and high-risk boys: what are juvenile offenders trying to tell us?', *Children and Society*, vol 22, no 1, pp 16–28.

Solomon, E. and Garside, R. (2008) *Ten years of Labour's youth justice reforms: An independent audit*, London: Centre for Crime and Justice Studies.

Souhami, A. (2007) *Transforming youth justice: Occupational identity and cultural change*, Cullompton: Willan.

SPICe (Scottish Parliament Information Centre) (2002) *Youth participation*, Edinburgh: SPICe.

Stephenson, M., Giller, H. and Brown, S. (2007) *Effective practice in youth justice*, Cullompton: Willan.

Strachan, R. and Tallant, C. (1997) 'Improving judgement and appreciating biases within the risk assessment process', in H. Kemshall and J. Pritchard (eds) *Good practice in risk assessment and risk management, vol 2*, London: Jessica Kingsley, pp 15–26.

Sutherland, A. (2009a) 'The 'scaled approach', in youth justice: fools rush in ...', *Youth Justice*, vol 9, no 1, pp 44–60.

Sutherland, A. (2009b) 'Youth offending teams and MAPPA: past problems, current challenges and future prospects', in K. Baker and A. Sutherland (eds) *Multi Agency Public Protection Arrangements and youth justice*, Bristol: Policy Press, pp 43–58.

Sutherland, A. and Jones, S. (2008) *MAPPA and youth justice: An exploration of Youth Offending Team engagement with multi-agency public protection arrangements*, London: Youth Justice Board.

Swain, P. (2005) '"No expert should cavil at any questioning": reports and assessments for courts and tribunals', *Australian Social Work*, vol 58, no 1, pp 44–57.

Tata, C., Burns, N., Halliday, S., Hutton, N. and McNeill, F. (2008) 'Assisting and advising the sentencing decision process: the pursuit of "quality" in pre-sentence reports', *British Journal of Criminology*, vol 48, no 6, pp 835–55.

Taylor, B. (2006) 'Risk management paradigms in health and social services for professional decision making on the long-term care of older people', *British Journal of Social Work*, vol 36, no 8, pp 1411–29.

Taylor, C. and White, S. (2006) 'Knowledge and reasoning in social work: educating for humane judgment', *British Journal of Social Work*, vol 36, no 6, pp 937–54.

Taylor, I. (2004) 'Multi-agency teams and the learning organization', in N. Gould and M. Baldwin (eds) *Social work, critical reflection and the learning organization*, Aldershot: Ashgate, pp 75–86.

Teoh, A., Laffer, J., Parton, N. and Turnell, A. (2003) 'Trafficking in meaning: constructive social work in child protection practice', in C. Hall, K. Juhila, N. Parton and T. Pösö (eds) *Constructing clienthood in social work and human services*, London: Jessica Kingsley, pp 147–60.

Tetlock, P. (1997) 'An alternative metaphor in the study of judgment and choice: people as politicians', in W. Goldstein and R. Hogarth (eds) *Research on judgment and decision making: Currents, connections and controversies*, Cambridge: Cambridge University Press, pp 657-680.

Thom, B., Sales, R. and Pearce, J. (2007) *Growing up with risk*, Bristol: The Policy Press.

Thomas, J. (2004) 'Using "critical incident analysis" to promote critical reflection and holistic assessment', in N. Gould and M. Baldwin (eds) *Social work, critical reflection and the learning organization*, Aldershot: Ashgate, pp 101–16.

Thomas, J. and Holland, S. (2009) 'Representing children's identities in core assessments', *British Journal of Social Work*, doi:10.1093/bjsw/bcp 154, accessed 11 August 2010.

Thomas, L. (2009) *Research on fire-setting*, Llantrisant: South Wales Fire and Rescue Service, www.southwales-fire.gov.uk/English/yoursafety/sci/Pages/FiresetterResearch.aspx.

Titterton, M. (2011) 'Positive risk taking with people at risk of harm', in H. Kemshall and B. Wilkinson (eds) *Good practice in assessing risk: Current knowledge, issues and approaches*, London: Jessica Kingsley.

Tooth, D. (2000) 'Houston, we have a problem (Apollo root cause analysis)', *Training Journal*, July 2000, pp 24-28..

Topalli, V. (2005) 'Criminal expertise and offender decision-making: an experimental analysis of how offenders and non-offenders differentially perceive social stimuli', *British Journal of Criminology*, vol 45, no 3, pp 269–95.

Towl, G. (2005) 'Risk assessment', *Vista*, vol 10, no 3, pp 134–7.

Trevithick, P. (2000) *Social work skills: A practice handbook*, Buckingham: Open University.

Trotter, C. (2006) *Working with involuntary clients: A guide to practice*, London: Sage.

Trotter, C. and Evans, P. (2010) 'Supervision skills in juvenile justice', in F. McNeill, P. Raynor and C. Trotter (eds) *Offender supervision: New directions in theory, research and practice*, Abingdon: Willan Publishing.

Tuddenham, R. (2000) 'Beyond defensible decision making: towards a reflexive assessment of risk and dangerousness', *Probation Journal*, vol 47, no 3, pp 173–83.

Tuklo Orenda Associates (1999) *Making a difference: A positive and practical guide to working with black offenders*, London: Tuklo Orenda Associates.

Turney, D. (2009) *Analysis and critical thinking in assessment*, Dartington: Research in Practice.

University of Birmingham and Institute of Education (2005) *The national evaluation of the Children's Fund*, London: Department for Children, Schools and Families.

Utting, D. and Vennard, J. (2000) *What works with young offenders in the community*, Ilford: Barnado's.

van de Luitgaarden, G. (2009) 'Evidence-based practice in social work: lessons from judgement and decision making theory', *British Journal of Social Work*, vol 39, no 2, pp 243–60.

van Mastrigt, S. and Farrington, D. (2009) 'Co-offending, age, gender and crime type: implications for criminal justice policy', *British Journal of Criminology*, vol 49, no 4, pp 552 – 573.

Vrij, A. (2002) 'Deception in children: literature review and implications for children's testimony', in H. Westcott, G. Davies and R. Bull (eds) *Children's testimony: A handbook of psychological research and forensic practice*, Chichester: Wiley, pp 175–94.

Ward, J. with Bayley, M. (2007) 'Young people's perceptions of "risk"', in B. Thom, R. Sales and J. Pearce (eds) *Growing up with risk*, Bristol: The Policy Press, pp 37–56.

Ward, T. (2002) 'Good lives and the rehabilitation of offenders: Promises and problems', *Aggression and Violent Behaviour*, vol 7, no 5, pp 513–28.

Ward, T. and Brown, M. (2004) 'The Good Lives Model and conceptual issues in offender rehabilitation', *Psychology, Crime and Law*, vol 10, no 3, pp 243–57.

Ward, T. and Maruna, S. (2007) *Rehabilitation: Beyond the risk paradigm*, London: Routledge.

Ward, T. and Stewart, C. (2003) 'Criminogenic needs and human needs: A theoretical model', *Psychology, Crime and Law*, vol 9, no 2, pp 125-43.

Ward, V., House, A. and Hamer, S. (2009) 'Knowledge brokering: the missing link in the evidence to action chain?', *Evidence & Policy*, vol 5, no 3, pp 267–79.

Warner, J. (2003) 'An initial assessment of the extent to which risk factors, frequently identified in research, are taken into account when assessing risk in child protection cases', *Journal of Social Work*, vol 3, no 3, pp 339–63.

Webster, C., MacDonald, R. and Simpson, M. (2006) 'Predicting criminality? Risk factors, neighbourhood influence and desistance', *Youth Justice*, vol 6, no 1, pp 7–22.

Welsh Assembly Government (2009) *Getting it right 2009*, Cardiff: Welsh Assembly Government.

White, R. and Cunneen, C. (2006) 'Social class, youth crime and justice', in B. Goldson and J. Muncie (eds) *Youth crime and justice*, London: Sage, pp 17–29.

White, S., Hall, C. and Peckover, S. (2009) 'The descriptive tyranny of the common assessment framework: technologies of categorization and professional practice in child welfare', *British Journal of Social Work*, vol 39, no 7, pp 1197–217.

Whitehead, P. and Thompson, J. (2004) *Knowledge and the probation service*, Chichester: Wiley.

Whitty, N. (2009) 'MAPPA for kids: discourses of security, risk and children's rights', in K. Baker, and A. Sutherland (eds) *Multi Agency Public Protection Arrangements and youth justice*, Bristol: The Policy Press, pp 111–24.

Whyte, B. (2004) 'Responding to youth crime in Scotland', *The British Journal of Social Work*, vol 34, no 3, pp 395–411.

Whyte, B. (2009) *Youth justice in practice: Making a difference*, Bristol: The Policy Press.

Wikström. P.-O. (2007) 'In search of causes and explanations of crime', in R. King and E. Wincup (eds) *Doing research on crime and justice* (2nd edn), Oxford: Oxford University Press, pp 117–40.

Wikström, P.-O. (2010) 'Situational action theory', in F. Cullen, and P. Wilcox (eds) *Encyclopaedia of criminological theory*, London: Sage.

Wikström, P.-O. and Butterworth, D. (2006) *Adolescent crime: Individual differences and lifestyles*, Cullompton: Willan.

Wikström, P.-O. and Sampson, R.J. (eds) (2006) *The explanation of crime: Contexts, mechanisms and development*, Cambridge: Cambridge University Press.

Wikström, P.-O. and Treiber, K. (2008) *Offending behaviour programmes: Source document*, London: Youth Justice Board.

Wilkinson, B. and Baker, K. (2005) *Managing risk in the community*, London: Youth Justice Board.

Williams, I. (2009) 'Offender health and social care: a review of the evidence on inter-agency collaboration', *Health and Social Care in the Community*, vol 17, no 6, pp 573–80.

Williams, J. (2009) 'Real "bad" girls. A study of the origins and nature of offending by girls and young women involved with a County Youth Offending Team and systemic responses to them', executive summary of unpublished PhD thesis.

Wilson, S. (2009) 'Leading practice improvement in front line child protection', *British Journal of Social Work*, vol 39, no 1, pp 64–80.

Wood, J. and Hine, J. (2009) *Work with young people*, London: Sage.

Wood, J. and Kemshall, H., with Maguire, M., Hudson, K. and Mackenzie, G. (2007) *The operation and experience of Multi-Agency Public Protection Arrangements*, London: Home Office.

Wood, R. (2009) *An investigation into the beliefs, moral reasoning and recidivism risk of young people involved in gangs*, unpublished MSc thesis, London Metropolitan University.

Yates, S. (2009) 'Good practice in guidance: lessons from Connexions', in J. Wood and J. Hine (eds) *Work with young people*, London: Sage, pp 176–86.

YJB (Youth Justice Board) (2003) *Screening for mental disorder in the youth justice system*, London: YJB.

YJB (2004) *Assessment, planning interventions and supervision tutor pack*, London: YJB.

YJB (2005a) *Sharing personal and sensitive information on children and young people at risk of offending: A practical guide*, London: YJB.

YJB (2005b) *Risk and protective factors*, London: YJB.

YJB (2006) *Asset guidance*, London: YJB.

YJB (2007a) *Panel matters*, London: YJB.

YJB (2007b) *Serious incidents: Guidance on serious incident reporting procedures*, London: YJB.

YJB (2008a) *Assessment planning interventions and supervision: Source document*, London: YJB.

YJB (2008b) *A review of safeguarding in the secure estate*, London: YJB.

YJB (2009a) *Community Serious Incidents Annual Report (October 2007 – December 2008)*, London: YJB.

YJB (2009b) *Fine art or science? Sentencers deciding between community penalties and custody for young people*, London: YJB.

YJB (2010a) *The Youth Rehabilitation Order and other youth justice provisions of the Criminal Justice Act 2008: Practice guidance for Youth Offending Teams*, London: YJB.

YJB (2010b) *Youth justice: The scaled approach*, London: YJB.

YJB (2010c) *National standards for youth justice services*, London: YJB.

YJB (2010d) *Case management guidance*, London: YJB.

YJB (2010e) *Public protection sentences and 'dangerousness': Guidance for Youth Offending Teams*, London: YJB.

YJB (2010f) *Guidance on 'Release and recall provisions for young people serving long term custodial sentences'*, London: YJB.

YJB (2010g) *Youth justice performance improvement framework (England)*, London: YJB.

Young, T., Fitzgerald, M., Hallsworth, S. and Joseph, I. (2007) *Groups, gangs and weapons*, London: Youth Justice Board.

Zuboff, S. (1984) *In the age of the smart machine*, New York: Basic Books.

Index of persons

Page references for notes are followed by n

Index of subjects

Page references for notes are followed by n